The Theatrical Notebooks of Samuel Beckett

VOLUME II
Endgame

The series of
The Theatrical Notebooks of Samuel Beckett
has been prepared under the
General Editorship of James Knowlson,
Emeritus Professor of French at the University of Reading.
It consists of:

THE THEATRICAL NOTEBOOKS OF
SAMUEL BECKETT

GENERAL EDITOR: JAMES KNOWLSON

VOLUME II

Endgame

with a revised text

EDITED WITH AN INTRODUCTION

AND NOTES

BY S. E. GONTARSKI

faber and faber

First published in 1992
by Faber & Faber Limited
Bloomsbury House, 74–77 Great Russell Street
London WC1B 3DA
This paperback edition first published in 2019

Photoset by Wilmaset Ltd, Birkenhead, Wirral
Printed in England by CPI Group (UK) Ltd, Croydon, CRO 4YY

A CIP record for this book
is available from the British Library

ISBN 978-0-571-34871-8

The colour scans of the original notebooks are reproduced with the assistance
of the Beckett Digital Manuscript Project, with permission from the Beckett Estate
and the Beckett International Foundation / Special Collections, University of Reading.

2 4 6 8 10 9 7 5 3 1

For Marsha,
who shared the vagabond years

De la musique avant toute chose,

De la musique encore et toujours!
Que ton vers soit la chose envolée
Qu'on sent qui fuit d'une âme en allée
Vers d'autres cieux et d'autres amours

Que ton vers soit la bonne aventure
Éparse au vent crispé du matin
Qui va fleurant la menthe et le thym . . .
Et tout le reste est littérature.
                    Paul Verlaine, 'Art poétique'

. . . and all the arts in common aspiring towards the principle of music; music being the typical, or ideally consummate art, the object of the great *Anders-streben* of all art, of all that is artistic, or partakes of artistic qualities.

All art constantly aspires towards the condition of music.

. . . the arts may be represented as continually struggling after the law or principle of music, to a condition which music alone completely realizes; and one of the chief functions of aesthetic criticism, dealing with the products of art, new or old, is to estimate the degree in which each of those products approaches, in this sense, to musical law.

Walter Pater, 'The School of Giorgione', *The Renaissance*

GENERAL EDITOR'S NOTE

Nothing can ever truly be said to be definitive in the theatre. A play or a role is constantly open to reinterpretation. A different directorial approach, different actors and actresses, a different stage space and the end result must inevitably differ. And Samuel Beckett's own productions illustrated this just as clearly as do anyone else's. It is a misconception to think that he believed he or anyone else could 'fix' his plays. He stressed that other productions would have a different 'music' from his own and he accepted different configurations of the stage set. On the very few occasions when he objected to certain directorial proposals it was because he felt that fundamental changes were being made that radically altered his plays.

When Beckett came to direct his own plays for the stage, he introduced numerous changes to the printed texts that consisted of cuts and additions as well as revisions. This was usually because he regarded these changes as improvements that he had discovered either as he was preparing to stage the plays or in the course of rehearsals themselves. Again it is worth stressing that his directorial decisions were inevitably determined by variable circumstances – the kind of actor that he was working with, the limitations of the stage set and so on. As with anyone else, they may even have derived from changes of mind on his part.

There is, nonetheless, a remarkable consistency in Beckett's changes. For the revisions appear to represent a further dynamic stage in the writer's own encounter with his texts and are of considerable interest for that very reason. In fact, some of the stage directions or, in the case of *Waiting for Godot*, with Beckett as director or aide to the director, whole sections of the text have *never* been played as printed in the original editions. It may surprise readers to learn that some of the cuts in Beckett's 1975 Schiller-Theater production in German of *Waiting for Godot* had already been made, as an annotated script shows, over twenty years earlier for the French world première. It is simply that, in the past, Beckett's texts have not been revised to take account of these changes – partly because of a somewhat ambiguous attitude on the part of the author towards his originals. Our aim in printing (at last with Beckett's full agreement) revised texts that are based on his productions has been to set down the changes that were made there. The texts are now as close as possible to how Beckett wanted them to be. And in presenting his theatrical notebooks our aim has also been to record, put into context and try to explain some of his directorial decisions.

Beyond that it would only be too easy to misunderstand or misrepresent what this series is intended to do. We too are decidedly not attempting to 'fix' the plays by limiting directorial freedom. How each director uses the production notes of the author will be up to him or her. And, in establishing a revised text, again it will be a matter of individual judgement as to whether readers, directors or actors prefer the revision to the original. On all occasions we have printed in the textual notes exactly what Beckett deleted and indicated what was added or revised. My own judgement is that practical experience confirms the rightness of most of the author's decisions concerning his texts. It is indeed a rather curious experience now, after one has seen Beckett's own revised versions, to watch a production that includes all of the text and follows the stage directions of the originals.

It is often said that authors are not the best directors of their own work. All I can say is that, to take *Waiting for Godot* as my example, the Schiller Theater and San Quentin productions by Beckett were two of the most beautiful productions of that play that I have ever seen. Once again misunderstandings or myths have arisen concerning Beckett's productions, as memory fades. Some critics have written as if they were uniformly serious, even heavy, when – as any glance at a video recording of the Schiller production shows – they blended comic and serious elements very successfully. What Beckett also did was to see the work in terms of clear visual patterns with movements so carefully charted that the word 'choreography' can quite properly be applied to a meticulously planned direction.

Detailed moves varied, of course, from production to production. And one would not want it otherwise. There is after all nothing worse in the theatre than a dull imitation. We have then incorporated such moves into the text itself only when they override the original stage directions or when they have importance as part of a complex piece of revised stage business. Otherwise, when such information is of interest, it has been placed in the textual notes. And although these volumes are specifically intended as editions of *production* texts, we have not hesitated to include other explanatory material in our notes whenever it seemed worthwhile.

We have also chosen to include a large amount of our information in the notes to the text rather than in the notes to the theatrical notebooks because it allowed more naturally for variants, because the notebook entries themselves often appeared to be self-explanatory and because such a system of reference seemed more convenient to a reader. And if, as well as providing approved revised texts, we are also (as John Lahr suggested in the *Guardian* in anticipation of the publication of these editions) preserving 'Beckett's blocking in the aspic of scholarship', the specimens that are offered here are, I contend, not dead museum pieces at all but living creatures, that may be seen evolving during a final phase of the author's creative process.

James Knowlson, October 1991

CONTENTS

ACKNOWLEDGEMENTS

For research time free of teaching obligations, I am grateful to the Department of English at the Georgia Institute of Technology, and I am pleased to acknowledge financial support from the American Council of Learned Societies and the Georgia Tech Foundation, which helped fund extended research in Paris. I also appreciate the support of the Djerassi Foundation, at whose SMIP Ranch I spent the fall of 1986 as a Resident Artist and where, amid other projects, substantial work on this volume was completed.

Michael Bott of the Reading University Library's Beckett Archive, and Holly Hall and Timothy D. Murray of the University Libraries, Washington University, St Louis, have kindly provided copies of essential documents long-distance, post-haste. Walter Asmus, Marek Kedzierski and Alan Mandell have generously lent or copied for me documents in their private possession. Tom Bishop has been gracious in arranging viewings of the videotaped version of the Berlin *Endspiel* which, along with the photographic edition of that production published by Suhrkamp as *Samuel Beckett inszeniert das 'Endspiel'* (Frankfurt, Suhrkamp, 1967), has proved invaluable for checking the details of failing memories. The rehearsal diary that Beckett's assistant in Berlin, Michael Haerdter, kept and published as 'Über die Proben für die Berliner Aufführung' in the Suhrkamp photographic edition of *Endspiel* has been indispensable, and I quote liberally from the Dougald McMillan translation in *Beckett in the Theatre* (London, John Calder Ltd., 1988; pp. 204–38). I am also grateful for the very useful research assistance of Christiane Silverthorne and Fita Ferguson.

I should like, moreover, to extend very warm thanks to my General Editor, James Knowlson, who has worked tirelessly on this project; his patience, diligence, and unparalleled knowledge of Beckett's theatre have improved this study immeasurably.

Finally, as always, my thanks, now posthumous, to Samuel Beckett, not only for his consent to have these invaluable theatrical notebooks published in the first place, but also for the time he generously gave the project, rereading his own theatrical notes, deciphering apparent indecipherabilia, and reading through this manuscript in its entirety, making suggestions and corrections. His comments on and corrections of my annotations, translations and prefatory material proved a daunting if exhilarating experience. His final revisions for the *Endgame* text, made exclusively for this volume, have ensured that the Revised Text published here contains the only revisions which distinguish between changes made for a particular production – that is, those made to accommodate the weaknesses or strengths of particular actors in particular venues – and those designed for publication. Those errors remaining in this volume are, of course, wholly my responsibility.

S. E. G.

INTRODUCTION
'The No against the Nothingness'

No, there are no accidents in *Endgame*,
it is all built on analogies and repetitions.
   Berlin Diary

If they did it my way they would empty the theatre.
   Samuel Beckett to Alan Schneider, letter, 1956

One might have expected that a collaborative and public art form such as theatre would be anathema to an artist as intensely private and solitary as Samuel Beckett. Yet while he shunned theatre's more public trappings, absenting himself even from his own first nights, Beckett reconciled himself to the process of theatre and the flux of rehearsals. Instructing an actor quietly against the din of the stage crew, acknowledging a visitor with a nod, rejecting a prop offered by a stage manager, he seemed at least as comfortable in the theatre as on the streets of Paris. To Michael Haerdter, his assistant at the 1967 Schiller-Theater *Endspiel* (*Endgame*), Beckett has even argued that theatre was relaxing: 'Theatre for me is first of all recreation from work on fiction. We are dealing with a given space and with people in that space. That is relaxing.' From the writing of *En attendant Godot* (*Waiting for Godot*), working in 'a given space' grew to be a major, if not the principal, part of Beckett's creative life. Rarely did much time pass thereafter during which he did not have something on the boards or in preparation. And from the 1967 *Endspiel*, Beckett used directorial opportunities to continue the creative process, cutting, revising, tightening his original script. Once Beckett took full control, directing was not a process separate from the generation of a text but its continuation if not its culmination. Writing, translating and directing were of a piece, part of a continuous creative process. He may have thought of theatre in 1967 as recreation (as he did in 1948 when he turned to *Waiting for Godot* 'in search of respite from the wasteland of prose' he had been writing), but directing often meant re-creation.

Beckett began his theatrical career tentatively, advising director Roger Blin, grateful to have the much delayed *Godot* appear on the boards at all. Even then, however, the unproduced playwright was deeply involved in production and very firm about his text. In a letter of 9 January 1953, only four days after the opening of *Godot*, he admonished Blin for a production deviation and insisted that Estragon's trousers should fall completely to his ankles. Pierre Latour had balked at the prospect, his dignity ruffled, but Beckett held his ground, insisting on a comic spirit to the tragedy. In anticipation of Nell's epigram in *Endgame*, Beckett noted that 'nothing is more grotesque than the tragic':

Mon cher Roger,
Bravo à tous. Je suis si content de votre succès à tous.

Ne m'en veuillez pas de m'être barré, je n'en pouvais plus.

Il y a une chose qui me chiffonne, c'est le froc d'Estragon. J'ai naturellement demandé à Suzanne s'il tombe bien. Elle me dit qu'il le retient à mi-chemin. Il ne le faut absolument pas, c'est ça à ce moment-là, il ne se rend même pas compte au grand dam de ce touchant tableau final, il n'y a absolument rien à y objecter, ils seraient du même ordre que les précédents. L'esprit de la pièce, dans la mesure où elle en a, c'est que rien n'est plus grotesque que le tragique, et il faut l'exprimer jusqu'à la fin, et surtout à la fin. J'ai un tas d'autres raisons pour vouloir que ce jeu de scène ne soit pas escamoté mais je vous en fais grâce. Soyez seulement assez gentil de le rétablir comme c'est indiqué dans le texte, et comme nous l'avions toujours prévu au cours des répétitions, et que le pantalon tombe complètement, autour des chevilles. Ça doit vous sembler stupide mais pour moi c'est capital. Et je vous croyais tous les deux d'accord avec moi là-dessus, quand je vous ai vus samedi dernier après l'incident de la couturière et que j'emportais votre assurance que cette scène serait jouée comme je la vois.

Bonne continuation et une amicale poignée de main à tous.*

Beckett's involvement in even his first staged drama was obviously substantial, and that involvement increased with his second play, according to Roger Blin: 'With *Fin de partie*, he attended rehearsals much more frequently.'[1] Beckett and Blin, however, did not always agree on staging, as Beckett admitted to Alan Schneider in a letter of 16 April 1957: 'Perhaps I have the wrong idea as to how it [*Endgame*] should be done. Blin and Martin have done a very good job – in spite of me.'[2] It would take Beckett another ten years, until his 1967 direction of *Endspiel*, to test that idea fully.

* My dear Roger,
Bravo to all. I am so happy with your success.

Don't be angry with me for quitting, but I had enough.

There is one thing which annoys me, it is Estragon's trousers. I naturally asked Suzanne if they fell completely. She told me that they were held up halfway. They should not, absolutely not, that's how it is at that point, he is not even conscious of the great wound inflicted on this touching final tableau, there are absolutely no grounds for objections, they would be of the same order as the preceding ones. The spirit of the piece, to the degree that it has any, is that nothing is more grotesque than the tragic, and it must be expressed until the end, and especially at the end. I have a stack of other reasons for wanting this effect not to be ruined but I will spare you them. Be only kind enough to restore it as indicated in the text and as always allowed for in the course of rehearsals, and let the trousers fall completely around his ankles. That must seem stupid to you but for me it is capital. And I believed you both agreed with me on the above when I saw you last Saturday after the incident at the final rehearsal and that I carried away your assurance that this scene would be played as I saw it.

Cordial greetings and a friendly handshake to all.

Beckett's letter to Blin, moreover, underscores a fundamental dilemma that would plague Beckett until he undertook full direction of his work: a hesitance to intrude on a director's production, on the one hand, and a concurrent determination that the play should be staged as it was written.

The move to taking full charge of his own work, however, would come slowly, almost imperceptibly, as Beckett evolved during some fourteen years of apprenticeship from adviser to credited director. The evolution was so gradual, in fact, that Beckett's directorial début is difficult to document. In *Just Play*, Ruby Cohn identifies a production of *Va et Vient* (*Come and Go*) at the Odéon Théâtre in 1966 as Beckett's first full production,[3] and James Knowlson[4] and Alfred Simon[5] agree. Beckett, however, credited Jean-Marie Serreau with the direction. The first work to carry directorial credit for Beckett, however, was not a stage production but the 1966 Stuttgart telecast of *He, Joe* (*Eh Joe*) (broadcast by German television on Beckett's sixtieth birthday, 13 April 1966, by SDR). Shortly thereafter, in 1967, Beckett accepted an invitation from the Schiller-Theater to direct a play; he chose *Endspiel*, the 'favourite of my plays' (*Berlin Diary*). The Schiller *Endspiel* would be his first stage production acknowledged in a playbill, and, more important, the first production for which he carefully prepared a production notebook.

By then Beckett was doing so much 'advising' on productions that the step to full directorial responsibility seemed a formality, a matter of programme credit. Taking full charge of his own work would at least allow for accurate productions. Watching those of others or even reviewing production photographs often dismayed him. Attending performances of *Godot* several nights running in London with Alan Schneider, Beckett would occasionally whisper, 'They're doing it ahl whrang.'[6] When Michael Haerdter asked why he began to direct, Beckett responded: 'I saw photographs of the first Berlin production [of *Endspiel*]; everything is wrong in it. The ash bins are separated, you can see Hamm's feet, they're touching the ground . . .' (*Berlin Diary*). But directing his own work afforded Beckett possibilities beyond mere accuracy. He could not only limit the deviations of others, but he could introduce some of his own. It remained surprising to hear Beckett disparage the structure of his work, but even of such tautly structured works as *Godot*, he said on more than one occasion, 'I knew nothing about theatre when I wrote it.' Acting as his own director, Beckett could remedy what he saw as excesses or imprecisions in his original script.

To prepare for production, Beckett first memorized his entire text, punctuation and stage directions included, to avoid the disruption of constantly looking down at the page and up at the stage, then down at the page and up at the stage again. Before he arrived at rehearsal, Beckett had already memorized everyone's part. For such intense preparation Beckett reviewed (literally re-viewed) his text and prepared a detailed production notebook, for, like many writers, Beckett thought on paper. That notebook charts Beckett's rethinking of the work in more theatrical or visual terms, a visualization that always entailed substantive revision, that is, clarification through excision, a process of disencumbering the work's theatrical shape. As he began rehearsals for *Endspiel*, having already pruned his text, Beckett announced to his cast, 'We have to retrench everything even further, it's got to become simple, just a few small precise motions.' And he made changes throughout rehearsals, adding, 'I have progressively simplified situations and persons, *toujours plus simple*' (*Berlin Diary*). During rehearsals of the same play at Riverside Studios some twelve years later, Beckett still found the text in need of trimming. 'There's too much text,' he told his cast. Beckett may have found the writing of plays relaxing at one point; directing, on the other hand, he found was hard work.

That Beckett should have chosen *Endgame* rather than *Waiting for Godot* as his first major production may at first seem surprising. But while *En attendant Godot*, the French original of *Waiting for Godot*, seems to have been written quickly – a first draft between October 1948 and January 1949, albeit some of the way having been paved by work on the then rejected *Mercier et Camier* (1946) – *Fin de partie* (*Endgame*) emerged only after a turbulent creative process that may have begun as early as 1952, just after *Textes pour rien*, and was not completed until 1956.[7] The composition of *Fin de partie* presented Beckett with extraordinary problems, and the manuscripts for no other theatrical work testify to such groping for form and matter. Structuring the myriad fragments he was working with, Beckett first tried the solution that seems to have come so easily with *Godot*, more or less symmetrical halves. In a letter to Alan Schneider, dated 11 January 1956, for instance, he referred to a two-act version of *Endgame*. But that structure did not seem to fit this material, or perhaps Beckett thought that a second symmetrical, two-act play would be precisely the sort of formal solution to writing he so abominated. The artistic danger was not only in bookkeeping, as he cautioned in his essay on Joyce's 'Work in Progress', but in self-imitation, if not self-parody. (In fact, Beckett may have responded to the difficulties of composing *Fin de partie* by a return to his native language and by a change of medium, a turn to pure voice, at first in the radio play *All That Fall* (1956) and then as an adaptation of that voice to the stage in the taped stage monologue of *Krapp's Last Tape* (1958). The machines, radio and tape-recorder, offered Beckett a sense of distance from his material, a means of objectification, which in the French works had been provided in good part by the foreign language.)

In the composition of *Fin de partie* one doesn't find the ease of composition that characterized *Godot*, nor the sort of free flow of memory that marked many of Beckett's later monologues, *Krapp's Last Tape, Happy Days, Not I, That Time, Ohio*

Impromptu, etc. These later works are certainly not without creative problems for Beckett, but the problems were more often those of fragmentation rather than assimilation. Often huge portions of the earliest drafts remained intact throughout composition. One doesn't find in any of the versions of *Fin de partie* that sort of free flow of memory. *Fin de partie* seems always to have been scenes, bits of dialogue, fragments that Beckett arranged and rearranged over and over again, groping intuitively towards an honest, satisfying form, a form that allowed the combination of so many disparate elements, including memories of war, family deaths, disastrous sexuality, the failures of religion – all countered with burlesque comedy. *Waiting for Godot* may have been the favoured first child, but *Endgame* retained for Beckett that special affection reserved for the difficult birth.

The process of mounting *Endgame* was almost as difficult as its composition. Despite the success of *Godot*, Roger Blin found no French producer for this new work, and he eventually accepted the invitation of the Royal Court Theatre in London where he opened the play in French on 3 April 1957. Beckett's comment on the production in a letter to Alan Schneider (12 August 1957) was particularly pithy: 'rather grim, like playing to mahogany, or rather teak'. On 27 April, the production moved to the Studio des Champs-Elysées in Paris. The first English-language production was directed by Alan Schneider at New York's Cherry Lane Theater on 28 January 1958. And in England the play (with the world première of *Krapp's Last Tape*) returned to the Royal Court Theatre in English on 28 October 1958, under the direction of George Devine. Patrick Magee played Krapp (a part Beckett essentially wrote for him), and, in *Endgame*, Jack MacGowran played Clov to Devine's Hamm. In 1964 MacGowran reprised his role in two productions. The first, mounted by the English Theatre in Paris, opened at the Studio des Champs-Elysées on 20 February 1964. And, in July of that same year, the Royal Shakespeare Company produced *Endgame* with the two Irishmen in the principal roles, Magee as Hamm and MacGowran as Clov. 'The play ran for nine weeks in Paris,' according to MacGowran, 'then for two seasons at the Aldwych in London and was still playing to packed houses when we closed it.'[8]

Offered the choice, Beckett mounted *Endgame* first in Berlin in 1967, and then, at the request of Rick Cluchey some thirteen years later, remounted it in English. His revisions for both these productions (1967 and 1980) maintain a consistency – with minor variations to allow for strengths or weaknesses of particular actors – so that a 'corrected' (Beckett's word) acting text is not only possible but desirable, a reflection of the substantial amount of rethinking and theatrical testing the work had undergone since its publication. To one of his Polish translators who was preparing a new version for a production in Cracow, for example, Beckett wrote on 15 November 1981,

[xvii]

Herewith corrected copy of *Fin de partie*. The cuts and simplifications are the result of my work on the play as director and function of the players at my disposal. To another director they may not seem desirable. Three however I strongly recommend. 1) The inspection of the audience (p. 45). 2) The vision of the boy (pp. 103–105). 3) The song (p. 107).[9]

Beckett's 1981 letter is remarkable for its concessions to the aleatory and collaborative nature of theatre itself, and for his admission that text is at least to some degree a function of the director and the actors available at any given time, and so, at least by implication, neither text nor production are final or invariable, even with the publication of his carefully detailed theatre notebooks. Beckett made no claims of *finality* even for his own productions. Asked by Michael Haerdter if he had come to 'give Berlin the authentic version', Beckett replied, 'No, I don't claim my interpretation is the only correct one. It's possible to do the play quite differently, different music, movements, different rhythm, the kitchen can be differently located and so on . . .' (*Berlin Diary*).

What we find in Beckett's two theatre notebooks and annotated texts for *Endgame* is a set of revisions and simplifications that form the foundation for a revised text. No previous edition – English, French or German – includes the *complete* production-generated changes.[10] For *Endgame* those changes fall into two broad categories. First, extraneous matter is excised. This process had already begun in Beckett's translation of the French original into English, and, in that respect, many of the revisions of the *Endspiel* and *Fin de partie* texts for the 1967 Schiller production were designed to bring those texts closer to the already revised English text.[11] But Beckett's revisions went well beyond such uniformity. He further cut all allusions to the audience, all comments that imply a public, keeping the work more insular, more hermetic. He cut Clov's song from the French and German texts in 1967,[12] as he had in making the English translation of 1957, but for the English text of 1980 he went even further, cutting all reference to the song.

Second, the Hamm/Clov conflict was sharpened by Beckett's excisions and alterations. Instead of standing as written beside the chair, for example, Clov is now poised midway between Hamm and the doorway, midway between obligation and relief, the point called 'O' in the Schiller notebook and 'A' in the Riverside notebook. To Hamm's final entreaty, 'Clov', the servant now responds, winces, communicating the anguish of disobedience. In Berlin Hamm called Clov a second time to echo the play's other doubles: Nell, Nell; Father, Father. Clov's second wince was even stronger than the first, and so the possibility of Clov's remaining in the shelter increased. In both productions the opening mime, Clov's dumbshow, was simplified, as was his later inspection of the without. In fact, by not following Hamm's instructions to ascend the ladder, Clov defied or deceived Hamm blatantly yet again, and so the possibility of his lying about the child increased. In Berlin, Beckett explained Clov's deception thus: 'You're not looking outside any more; Clov already knows there's nothing there.' Moreover, after Hamm's first tour he asks to be put 'right in the centre' of the shelter. Instead of moving the chair 'slightly' as originally written, Clov now 'thumps' the chair haphazardly, in a gesture of aggression and disobedience. Such apparently minor changes singularly clarify and develop the lines of conflict and sharpen the play's ambiguities.

Beckett's attraction to working directly in theatre, however, finally went beyond correcting the errors of others and continuing the simplification and shaping of his text. He saw in theatre the opportunity to develop his text visually and thereby to explore a medium close to his heart. An accomplished (if amateur) musician, with a lifelong passion for Schubert *Lieder*, and a writer with more than a casual interest in the visual arts, Beckett discovered that theatre allowed him to paint (or sculpt), that is, to work directly with form, as a plastic, a visual artist. For theatre is not language. It is a spatial as well as a temporal genre. 'The medium of drama,' wrote Ezra Pound, 'is not words but persons moving about on stage using words.' Beckett may have refined the concept of 'persons moving about on stage' nearly out of existence, but the notion that theatre is not (wholly) a linguistic art is not lost on him. Theatre – not playwriting, but staging – offered Beckett the opportunity to deal with form – with shape, relation, balance, but only occasionally colour – in a way that language alone – even poetry – never could. To the music and poetry of words, he could add or rather juxtapose the arrangement of forms in a controlled, framed space (hence Beckett's abiding interest in the proscenium stage and in television, both of which are frame dominated).[13]

Beckett's conception of the relationship of language to action is, however, in many respects, unique among modern dramatists. While his position on the question of what Ruby Cohn has alliteratively called 'jumping . . . genres' altered to the point where he has even *encouraged* some 'theatricians' to adapt his prose works to the stage, as a director Beckett has remained something of a generic purist, treating the systems of theatrical communication separately, keeping, for instance, music and motion distinct. Theoretically, such separation reaffirms a nearly Cartesian duality in Beckett's theatre; it is Beckett's almost Manichaean reluctance to mingle opposites. Theatrically, such separation maintains balance on action and language, on the theatrical and the linguistic. Beckett admonished his actors time and again in Berlin, for example: 'Never let your changes of position and voice come together. First comes (a) the altered bodily stance; after it, following a slight pause, comes (b) the corresponding utterance' (*Berlin Diary*). Such phrasing as 'changes of position' itself suggests a series of still pictures or photographs more than continuous action or movement. In Berlin, when Beckett asked his actors to forgo a curtain call, he used similar language. When they agreed, he seemed relieved and confessed, 'It would have hurt me to break up the picture at the end.' The phrase Beckett used in the Riverside notebook is similar, 'frozen postures'. As Michael Haerdter says, 'Over and over, he has them [the actors] freeze for seconds at a time into a tableau which is to achieve its effect through repetition' (*Berlin Diary*). To Beckett's sensibility, the whole of *Endgame* had been driving to that final 'frozen posture', outside, beyond language, yet as tied to and dependent on it as Lucky to Pozzo, as light to dark, as music to rest, as being to nothing: Clov dressed to leave, yet hesitating; Hamm resigned to an inevitable end, yet resisting. Such an ending tableau, moreover, was also how Beckett visualized the resolution of *Godot*. Some fourteen years earlier in his letter to Roger Blin, he had called the ending, 'ce touchant tableau final'.

Such divorce of movement from language as a principle of direction foregrounds Beckett's abiding interest in the theatrical equivalent of silence, mime. The periods of silence, the long pauses, and finally the emphasis on mime in Beckett's theatre are the theatrical equivalent of the Beethoven rest. The importance of mime to Beckett's drama is difficult to overestimate – most critics, in fact, have done the opposite. We find in Beckett's dramatic *oeuvre* not only wholly mimetic works like the pair of *Acts Without Words*, the pair of mimes singularly linked as *Quad*, a pair of jettisoned mimes, 'Mime du rêveur, A' ('Dreamer's Mime, A') and 'J. M. Mime' (i.e., 'Jack MacGowran Mime'),[14] and the tele-mime based on the Schubert *Lied* of the same name, *Nacht und Träume*, but such major works as *Endgame* and *Krapp's Last Tape* themselves open with mimes (albeit truncated in Beckett's productions). Other works are built around characters who are wholly or principally mute, like O in *Film*, Joe in *Eh Joe*, the Listener's face in *That Time*, the ghostly May in the central panel of the triptych *Footfalls*, the Male Figure of *Ghost Trio*, the Listener of *Ohio Impromptu*, W of *Rockaby*, and the Protagonist, the catastrophe himself, in *Catastrophe*. The sheer number of such works in which silence is person-ified, em-bodied, character-ized underscores the dominance of the visual in Samuel Beckett's theatre, and often as an element isolated and separated from the flow of words. Such separation is a means both of internalizing action and of retaining an emphasis on the visual. Beckett's very conception of drama is fugal, a counterpoint of poetry and physical form, and that principle of aesthetics emerges clearly and is most fully developed in his direction of his own plays.

Pattern is as crucial to Beckett's eye as to his ear, and that patterning dominates his theatrical notes: motion is repeated to echo other motion, posture to echo other posture, gestures to echo other gestures, sounds to echo other sounds. The principle of analogy is fundamental. In the Riverside notebook Beckett says, 'analogy N's knocks on lid, H's on wall'; 'Analogy Clov–dog when trying to make it stand';

'Analogy voice and attitude [of Hamm during his narration] with N's tailor story'. The action is filled with circles, arcs and crosses, from Hamm's rounds to Clov's thinking walk. The linguistic analogue to such patterning is the revision of phrases to echo each other. Even when the phrasing is not parallel, Beckett may establish an echo, as on *Page 13* of the Schiller notebook where he suggests that 'Why this farce' should have the 'same quality as "Let's stop playing"'. Beckett's own direction of *Endgame* seems a fulfilment of the structure he originally outlined for Roger Blin's *Fin de partie* in 1957. 'He had ideas about the play,' Blin noted, 'that made it a little difficult to act. At first, he looked on his play as a kind of musical score. When a word occurred or was repeated, when Hamm called Clov, Clov should always come in the same way every time, like a musical phrase coming from the same instrument with the same volume.'[15] Ten years later Beckett realized this musical conception of the play. 'The play is full of echoes,' he told his German cast. 'They all answer each other.'

As a director, Beckett revealed yet another component to his aesthetics. His direction is marked by a surprising amount of realistic subtext.[16] As usual Beckett insisted in Berlin on not intellectualizing his text in rehearsals. He noted early on, 'I don't want to talk about my play, it has to be taken purely dramatically, to take shape on the stage . . . Here the only interest of the play is as dramatic material.' Beckett's admonition is not surprising. It is one that many a director has delivered to his actors early in rehearsals. In the theatre, one plays action not ideas. What is surprising is that Beckett also suggested a realistic presentation: 'The play is to be acted as though there were a fourth wall where the footlights are.' While, on occasion, Beckett would say, 'Here it oughtn't to be played logically', more often he would provide 'realistic' motivation. For 'Have you bled', he told Clov, 'You see something in his face, that's why you're asking.' Examining the parasite in his trousers provides Clov with the occasion for, 'What about that pee?' Hamm's 'Since it's calling you' should be choked out to trigger Clov's 'Is your throat sore?' And Clov's opening speech is motivated by some barely perceptible change that he perceives while inspecting his environment. In the Riverside notebook, Beckett writes: 'C perplexed. All seemingly in order, yet a change.'

The notebooks then offer a wealth of information about Beckett's vision of *Endgame* which should be of interest to scholars and theatre people, as well as to that portion of the general readership interested in understanding Beckett's theatre in depth. How the publication of the *Theatrical Notebooks* and a revised text will affect future performances is difficult to predict. They should at least be more informed. How the information will be translated into stagecraft may finally depend on the inventiveness and the imagination of particular actors and directors. Rather than restrict the creative imagination, the publication of Beckett's theatrical notes should liberate it, as we begin to understand yet more fully not only what Beckett heard in his *Endgame* but what he saw as well. That Samuel Beckett was among the century's foremost poets, with a fine musical ear, is evident from a reading of his texts. That he was also an extraordinary visual artist is confirmed by viewing any of his productions and now also in the *Theatrical Notebooks*.

S.E.G.
Djerassi Foundation
Woodside, CA

Notes to the Introduction

1 – 'Blin on Beckett: Interview by Tom Bishop', translated by James Knowlson, *On Beckett: Essays and Criticism*, edited by S. E. Gontarski (New York, Grove Press, 1986), p. 233.

2 – The letters to American director Alan Schneider cited throughout the *Introduction* were published in the *Village Voice*, 19 March 1958, pp. 8 and 15.

3 – Ruby Cohn, *Just Play: Beckett's Theater* (Princeton, Princeton University Press, 1980), p. 233.

4 – James Knowlson, *Happy Days: Samuel Beckett's Production Notebook* (London, Faber and Faber, 1985), p. 11.

5 – Alfred Simon, 'Chronologie des principales mises en scène en français, en anglais', *Revue d'esthétique* (numéro hors série, 1986), edited by Pierre Chabert (Paris, Editions Privat, 1986), p. 436.

6 – Alan Schneider, 'Working with Beckett', Gontarski (ed.), *On Beckett: Essays and Criticism*, p. 252.

7 – For fuller details of the composition of *Endgame* see S. E. Gontarski, *The Intent of Undoing in Samuel Beckett's Dramatic Texts* (Bloomington, Indiana University Press, 1985), pp. 25–54.

8 – MacGowran almost conflates these productions in his remarks, but the Paris and London productions were entirely separate. MacGowran also claimed that this production was actually directed by Beckett, although the director on record for the Paris production was Michael Blake. 'Actually, the best *Endgame* we ever played was directed by Beckett in Paris in 1964. I got Patrick Magee to play Hamm, and I played Clov . . . Beckett came over [that is, to London where the production was rehearsed] and spent six weeks directing it. He didn't go on the programme as director because there was a young director who let Beckett take over.' ('MacGowran on Beckett: Interview by Richard Toscan', Gontarski (ed.), *On Beckett: Essays and Criticism*, p. 218.) No director's notebook was kept by Beckett for this production.

9 – Letter to Marek Kedzierski, who attended rehearsals at Riverside Studios in preparation for his translation of the play. Beckett's page references are, of course, to the French edition by Les Editions de Minuit. These cuts were originally made for the French text in 1967 as Beckett revised the German text for the Schiller Theater production. (See *Cuts and Changes*, pp. 250, 264–7.)

10 – The text that incorporates many of Beckett's revisions from the Schiller production is the German photographic edition: *Samuel Beckett inszeniert das 'Endspiel'* (Frankfurt, Suhrkamp, 1967). This text, however, is imperfect. While it includes many of Beckett's revisions of dialogue, it includes almost none of the revised stage directions (see *Cuts and Changes* for details).

11 – Before Beckett began his translation of *Fin de partie*, however, he believed that the English text would be inferior. In a letter to Alan Schneider of 30 April 1957, Beckett suggested that *Endgame* 'will inevitably be a poor substitute for the original (the loss will be much greater than from the French to English *Godot*)'. On the contrary, by the 1967 *Endspiel*, the English text seems to have become the standard for the revision of French and German texts.

12 – According to Roger Blin, the song and the longer discussion of the child whom Clov apparently sees outside the shelter were eliminated from the first French production to follow Beckett's 1967 Schiller staging, the 1968 revival at the Théâtre Chaptal 347, 'Blin on Beckett', Gontarski (ed.), *On Beckett: Essays and Criticisms*, p. 234. See also note 9.

13 – In a letter to Alan Schneider of 15 October 1956, Beckett wrote, 'I don't in my ignorance agree with [theatre in] the round and feel *Godot* needs a very closed box.'

14 – Both mimes are published as appendices to my *The Intent of Undoing*, pp. 195–208.

15 – 'Blin on Beckett', Gontarski (ed.), *On Beckett: Essays and Criticisms*, p. 233.

16 – In *The Intent of Undoing* I explored in detail the function of realistic detail in the original composition of Samuel Beckett's theatrical works. Additional details appear in the *Textual Notes*.

ABBREVIATIONS

In the notes to this edition, the following abbreviations are used throughout:

Berlin Diary   Diary which Beckett's assistant, Michael Haerdter, kept for the Schiller-Theater Werkstatt production of *Endspiel* and published as 'Über die Proben für die Berliner Aufführung'.

F   Faber and Faber edition, London, 1958. References throughout are to this British edition.

Fac(B)   Annotated acting copy of the Faber and Faber edition of 1958, 1976 reprint, prepared by Beckett before rehearsals at the Riverside Studios, London, 1980. The front cover shows a scene from the 1976 production during London's *Samuel Beckett Season* with Patrick Magee and Stephen Rea. University of Reading MS 1974.

G   Grove Press edition, New York, 1958. References throughout are to this American edition.

Gac(A)   Acting copy of Grove text kept by Walter Asmus, Beckett's assistant at the Riverside Studios. Asmus then travelled with the group on tour.

Gac(M)   Acting copy of Grove text kept by Alan Mandell who played Nagg in the 1980 production. This is a volume from the *Collected Works* edition of 1970, the pagination for which corresponds to the standard Grove Press edition of 1958.

Photo   Photographic edition of the 1967 Schiller-Theater production, *Samuel Beckett inszeniert das 'Endspiel'* (Frankfurt, Suhrkamp, 1967).

Revised Text   Photocopy of *Fac(B)* which Beckett revised and annotated for this volume. This is the final text of *Endgame*.

Riverside Nb   Director's notebook Beckett prepared for the Riverside Studios rehearsals of *Endgame* May 1980, with the San Quentin Drama Workshop. Reproduced in this volume in facsimile and transcription. University of Reading MS 1975.

S   Suhrkamp trilingual edition, Frankfurt, 1981, in one volume, *Samuel Beckett Dramatische Dichtungen in drei Sprachen*. References throughout are to this most easily obtainable of the German editions.

Sac(B)   The annotated acting copy of the German trilingual text, Frankfurt, 1960, which Beckett prepared before arrival in Berlin and modified throughout rehearsals, dated in Beckett's hand, 'Berlin. Aug. Sept. 1967.' On deposit Washington University, St Louis.

Schiller Nb   Notebook Beckett prepared for the Schiller-Theater Werkstatt. production of *Endspiel* in 1967. Reproduced in this volume in facsimile and transcription. University of Reading MS 1396/4/5.

PRINCIPAL PRODUCTIONS

Royal Court Theatre, London, 3 April 1957
Transferred to Studio des Champs-Elysées, Paris, later that month

Director Roger Blin
HAMM Roger Blin
CLOV Jean Martin
NAGG Georges Adet
NELL Christine Tsingos

Cherry Lane Theater, New York, 28 January 1958

Director Alan Schneider
HAMM Lester Rawlins
CLOV Alvin Epstein (*and* Gerald Hiken)
NAGG P. J. Kelly
NELL Nydia Westman

Royal Court Theatre, London, 28 October 1958

Director George Devine
HAMM George Devine
CLOV Jack MacGowran
NAGG Richard Goolden
NELL Frances Cuka

English Theatre in Paris, Studio des Champs-Elysées, 17 February 1964

Director Michael Blake
HAMM Patrick Magee
CLOV Jack MacGowran
NAGG Sydney Bromley
NELL Elvi Hale

The Royal Shakespeare Company at the Aldwych, London, 9 July 1964

Director Donald McWhinnie
HAMM Patrick Magee
CLOV Jack MacGowran
NAGG Bryan Pringle
NELL Patsy Byrne

Schiller-Theater Werkstatt, Berlin, 26 September 1967

Director Samuel Beckett
HAMM Ernst Schröder
CLOV Horst Bollmann
NAGG Werner Stock
NELL Gudrun Genest

Royal Court Theatre, London, 6 May 1976

Director Donald McWhinnie
HAMM Patrick Magee
CLOV Stephen Rea
NAGG Leslie Sarony
NELL Rose Hill

Riverside Studios, Hammersmith, London, May 1980

Director Samuel Beckett
Assistant Director Walter Asmus
HAMM Rick Cluchey
CLOV Bud Thorpe
NAGG Alan Mandell
NELL Teresita Garcia Suro

Magic Theater, San Francisco, 17 January 1989
First production of Revised Text as published here

Director S. E. Gontarski
HAMM Tom Luce
CLOV R. G. Davis
NAGG Morgan Upton
NELL Susan Brecht

PART I

Endgame
Revised Text

TYPOGRAPHICAL NOTE

Text between square brackets [ ] has been added to the original English text.
Text between pointed brackets {} has been revised.
A pair of angle brackets <> indicates that a section of text has been cut from the original English text.
Line numbers indicate the presence of textual notes (see pages 43–72).
All changes indicated by the above brackets are explained in these notes.

PUBLISHER'S NOTE

The publisher has taken this opportunity to make a number of minor adjustments to the layout and typographical style adopted for earlier editions of *Endgame*.

Bare interior.
Grey light.
Left and right back, <> two small windows, curtains drawn.
Front right a door. <>
Front left, touching each other, covered with an old sheet, two ashbins.
Centre, in an armchair on castors, covered with an old sheet, Hamm.
Motionless {at A (a point midway between the door and the chair)}, his eyes fixed on
HAMM, CLOV. <>
Brief tableau.
{CLOV[,] bowed head. Then CLOV's eyes to HAMM, to bins (if necessary slight move
forward), to sea window [left] (if necessary slight move back)[,], to earth window [right].
Then a moment still with bowed head. Then suddenly off[.]} Stiff, staggering walk. Comes
back immediately with a small step-ladder, carries it over and sets it down under window
left, gets up on it, draws back curtain {,} <> looks out of window. Brief laugh. He gets
down, <> carries it over and sets it down under window right, gets up on it, {draws
back curtain,} looks out of window. Brief laugh. He gets down, <> goes to ashbins,
removes sheet covering them <>. He raises one lid, stoops and looks into bin. Brief laugh.
He closes lid. Same with other bin. He goes to HAMM, [trailing the sheet,] removes sheet
covering him <>. In a dressing-gown, a stiff toque on his head, a {dirty} handkerchief
over his face, a whistle hanging from his neck, a rug over his knees, thick socks on his feet,
HAMM *seems to be asleep.* CLOV <> *[lifts corner of handkerchief], {looks at his face}.*
Brief laugh. He goes to {A} [trailing the covers,] halts, turns towards auditorium.

CLOV: (*Fixed gaze<>.*) Finished, it's finished, nearly finished, it must be nearly
finished. (*Pause.*) Grain upon grain, one by one, and one day, suddenly,
there's a heap, a little heap, the impossible heap. (*Pause.*) I can't be punished
any more. (*Pause. [He moves towards door and back.]*) I'll go now to my kitchen,
ten feet by ten feet by ten feet, and wait for him to whistle me. (*Pause.*) Nice
dimensions, nice proportions, I'll lean on the table, and look at the wall, and
wait for him to whistle me.
(*He remains a moment motionless, then goes out. He comes back immediately, goes to*
window right, takes up the ladder and carries it out. Pause. HAMM *stirs. He yawns*
under the handkerchief. He removes the handkerchief from his face. <> Black
glasses.)

[3]

35 HAMM: Me – <> to play.

(*He holds the handkerchief spread out before him.*)

37 Old stancher!

38 (*He takes off his glasses, {wipes them,} puts them on again, folds the handkerchief*

39 [*four times*] *and puts it neatly in the breast pocket of his dressing gown. He clears his throat, joins the tips of his fingers.*)

41 Can there be misery – <> loftier than mine? No doubt. Formerly. But now? (*Pause.*) My father? (*Pause.*) My mother? (*Pause.*) My . . . dog? (*Pause.*) Oh I am willing to believe they suffer as much as such creatures can suffer. But does that mean their sufferings equal mine? No doubt. (*Pause.*) No, all is

44 a<> bsolute, (*proudly*) the bigger a man is the fuller he is. (*Pause. Gloomily*) And the emptier. (*He sniffs.*) Clov! (*Pause.*) No, alone. (*Pause.*) What dreams!

47 Those forests! (*Pause.*) Enough, it's time it ended, in the refuge too. (*Pause.*) And yet I hesitate, I hesitate to . . . to end. Yes, there it is, it's time it ended

49 and yet I hesitate to – <> to end. (*Yawns.*) God, I'm tired, I'd be better off in bed.

51 (*He whistles. Enter* CLOV *immediately. He halts {at A}.*)

You pollute the air! (*Pause.*) Get me ready, I'm going to bed.

CLOV: I've just got you up.

HAMM: And what of it?

CLOV: I can't be getting you up and putting you to bed every five minutes, I have things to do.

(*Pause.*)

HAMM: Did you ever see my eyes?

CLOV: No.

HAMM: Did you never have the curiosity, while I was sleeping, to take off my glasses and look at my eyes?

CLOV: Pulling back the lids? (*Pause.*) No.

HAMM: One of these days I'll show them to you. (*Pause.*) It seems they've gone all white. (*Pause.*) What time is it?

65 CLOV: <> Same as usual.

HAMM: (*Gesture towards window right.*) Have you looked?

CLOV: Yes.

HAMM: Well?

CLOV: Zero.

HAMM: It'd need to rain.

CLOV: It won't rain.

(*Pause.*)

[4]

HAMM: Apart from that, how do you feel?

CLOV: I don't complain.

HAMM: You feel normal?

CLOV: (*Irritably*) I tell you I don't complain!

HAMM: I feel a little {strange}. (*Pause.*) Clov!

77

CLOV: Yes.

HAMM: Have you not had enough?

CLOV: Yes! (*Pause.*) Of what?

HAMM: Of this . . . this . . . thing.

CLOV: I always had. (*Pause.*) Not you?

HAMM: (*Gloomily*) Then there's no reason for it to change.

CLOV: It may end. (*Pause.*) All life long the same questions, the same answers.

HAMM: Get me ready.

(CLOV *does not move.*)

Go and get the sheet.

(CLOV *does not move.*)

Clov!

CLOV: Yes.

HAMM: I'll give you nothing more to eat.

CLOV: Then we'll die.

HAMM: I'll give you just enough to keep you from dying. You'll be hungry all the time.

CLOV: Then we shan't die. (*Pause.*) I'll go and get the sheet.

(*He goes towards the door.*)

95

HAMM: No!

(CLOV *halts.*)

I'll give you one biscuit per day. (*Pause.*) One and a half. (*Pause.*) Why do you stay with me?

CLOV: Why do you keep me?

HAMM: There's no one else.

CLOV: There's nowhere else.

(*Pause.*)

HAMM: You're leaving me all the same.

CLOV: I'm trying.

HAMM: You don't love me.

CLOV: No.

HAMM: You loved me once.

CLOV: Once!

HAMM: I've made you suffer too much. (*Pause.*) Haven't I?

CLOV: It's not that.

HAMM: (*Shocked*) I haven't made you suffer too much?

CLOV: Yes!

HAMM: (*Relieved*) Ah you gave me a fright! (*Pause. Coldly*) Forgive me. (*Pause. Louder*) I said, Forgive me.

CLOV: I heard you. (*Pause.*) Have you bled?

118   HAMM: Less. (*Pause.*) Is it not time for my pain-killer?

CLOV: No.

     (*Pause.*)

HAMM: How are your eyes?

CLOV: Bad.

HAMM: How are your legs?

CLOV: Bad.

HAMM: But you can move.

CLOV: Yes.

HAMM: (*Violently*) Then move!

128   (CLOV {*marks time audibly*}.)

     Where are you?

130   CLOV: {There.}

HAMM: Come back!

132   (CLOV {*marks time audibly*}.)

     Where are you?

CLOV: Here.

HAMM: Why don't you kill me?

136   CLOV: I don't know the combination of the larder.

     (*Pause.*)

HAMM: Go and get two bicycle-wheels.

139   CLOV: There are no more bicycle-wheels.

HAMM: What have you done with your bicycle?

CLOV: I never had a bicycle.

HAMM: The thing is impossible.

CLOV: When there were still bicycles I wept to have one. I crawled at your feet.

144   You told me to get out to hell. Now there are none.

HAMM: And your rounds? When you inspected my paupers. Always on foot?

CLOV: Sometimes on horse.

     (*The lid of one of the bins lifts and the hands of* NAGG *appear, gripping the rim. Then his head emerges. Nightcap. Very white face.* NAGG *yawns, then listens.*)

[6]

I'll leave you, I have things to do.

149

HAMM: In your kitchen?

CLOV: Yes.

HAMM: Outside of here it's death. (*Pause.*) All right, be off.

    (*Exit* CLOV. *Pause.*)

    We're getting on.

NAGG: Me pap!

HAMM: Accursed progenitor!

NAGG: Me pap!

HAMM: The old folks at home! No decency left! Guzzle, guzzle, that's all they
    think of.

    (*He whistles. Enter* CLOV. *He halts* {*at A*}.)

160

    Well! I thought you were leaving me.

CLOV: Oh not just yet, not just yet.

NAGG: Me pap!

163

HAMM: Give him his pap.

CLOV: There's no more pap.

165

HAMM: (*To* NAGG) Do you hear that? There's no more pap. You'll never get any
    more pap.

NAGG: I want me pap!

HAMM: Give him a biscuit.

[CLOV: I'll go and get a biscuit.]

    (*Exit* CLOV.)

170

HAMM: Accursed fornicator! How are your stumps?

NAGG: Never mind me stumps.

    (*Enter* CLOV *with biscuit.*)

CLOV: I'm back again, with the biscuit.

    (*He gives the biscuit to* NAGG *who fingers it, sniffs it.*)

NAGG: (*Plaintively*) What is it?

CLOV: Spratt's {Bonio}.

178

NAGG: (*As before*) It's hard! I can't!

HAMM: Bottle him!

    (CLOV *pushes* NAGG *back into the bin, closes the lid.*)

CLOV: <> If age but knew!

182

[HAMM: Have you bottled him?]

183

[CLOV: Yes.]

184

HAMM: Sit on him!

CLOV: I can't sit.

HAMM: True. And I can't stand.

CLOV: So it is.

189 HAMM: Every man his speciality. (*Pause.*) No phone calls? (*Pause.*) Don't we laugh?

CLOV: (*After reflection*) I don't feel like it.

HAMM: (*After reflection*) Nor I.

193   (*Pause.* [CLOV *makes for door, stopped at A by* . . .])

    Clov!

CLOV: Yes.

HAMM: Nature has forgotten us.

CLOV: There's no more nature.

HAMM: No more nature! You exaggerate.

CLOV: In the vicinity.

HAMM: But we breathe, we change! We lose our hair, our teeth! Our bloom! Our ideals!

CLOV: Then she hasn't forgotten us.

HAMM: But you say there is none.

CLOV: (*Sadly*) No one that ever lived ever thought so crooked as we.

HAMM: We do what we can.

CLOV: We shouldn't.

    (*Pause.*)

HAMM: You're a bit of all right, aren't you?

CLOV: A smithereen.

    (*Pause.*)

HAMM: This is slow work. (*Pause.*) Is it not time for my pain-killer?

CLOV: No. (*Pause.*) I'll leave you, I have things to do.

213   [(CLOV *moves towards door.*)]

HAMM: In your kitchen?

215   [(CLOV *halts.*)]

CLOV: Yes.

HAMM: What, I'd like to know.

CLOV: I look at the wall.

219 HAMM: The wall! And what do you see on your wall? Mene, mene? Naked bodies?

CLOV: I see my light dying.

HAMM: Your light dying! Listen to that! Well, it can die just as well here, *your* light. Take a look at me and then come back and tell me what you think of *your* light.

[8]

(*Pause.*)

CLOV: You shouldn't speak to me like that.

(*Pause.*)

HAMM: (*Coldly*) Forgive me. (*Pause. Louder*) I said, Forgive me.

CLOV: I heard you.

(*The lid of* NAGG's *bin lifts. His hands appear, gripping the rim. Then his head emerges. In his mouth the biscuit. He listens.*) 230
231

HAMM: Did your seeds come up?

CLOV: No.

HAMM: Did you scratch round them to see if they had sprouted?

CLOV: They haven't sprouted.

HAMM: Perhaps it's still too early.

CLOV: If they were going to sprout they would have sprouted. (*Violently*) They'll never sprout.

(*Pause.* NAGG *takes biscuit in his* [right] *hand.*) 239

HAMM: This is not much fun. (*Pause.*) But that's always the way at the end of the day, isn't it, Clov?

CLOV: Always.

HAMM: It's the end of the day like any other day, isn't it, Clov?

CLOV: Looks like it.

(*Pause.*)

HAMM: (*Anguished*) What's happening, what's happening?

CLOV: Something is taking its course.

(*Pause.*)

HAMM: All right, be off.

(*He leans back in his chair, remains motionless.* CLOV *does not move, heaves a great groaning sigh.* HAMM *sits up.*)

I thought I told you to be off.

CLOV: I'm trying. (*He goes to door, halts.*) Ever since I was whelped.

(*Exit* CLOV.)

HAMM: We're getting on.

(*He leans back in his chair, remains motionless.* NAGG *knocks* [with biscuit] *on the lid of the other bin. Pause. He knocks harder. The lid lifts and the hands of* NELL *appear, gripping the rim. Then her head emerges. Lace cap. Very white face.*) 256

NELL: What is it, my pet? (*Pause.*) Time for love? 259

NAGG: Were you asleep?

NELL: Oh no!

NAGG: Kiss me.

[9]

NELL: We can't.

NAGG: Try.

265

(*Their heads strain towards each other, fail to meet, fall apart again.*)

NELL: Why this farce, day after day?

(*Pause.*)

NAGG: I've lost me tooth.

NELL: When?

NAGG: I had it yesterday.

NELL: (*Elegiac*) Ah yesterday!

(*They turn painfully towards each other.*)

NAGG: Can you see me?

NELL: Hardly. And you?

NAGG: What?

NELL: Can you see me?

NAGG: Hardly.

NELL: So much the better, so much the better.

NAGG: Don't say that. (*Pause.*) Our sight has failed.

NELL: Yes.

(*Pause. They turn away from each other.*)

NAGG: Can you hear me?

NELL: Yes. And you?

NAGG: Yes. (*Pause.*) Our hearing hasn't failed.

NELL: Our what?

286

NAGG: Our hearing.

NELL: No. (*Pause.*) Have you anything else to say to me?

NAGG: Do you remember —

NELL: No.

NAGG: When we crashed on our tandem and lost our shanks.

291

(*They laugh heartily.*)

NELL: It was in the Ardennes.

293

(*They laugh less heartily.*)

NAGG: On the road to Sedan.

295

(*They laugh still less heartily.*)

Are you cold?

NELL: Yes, perished. And you?

NAGG: I'm freezing. (*Pause.*) Do you want to go in?

NELL: Yes.

NAGG: Then go in.

(NELL *does not move.*)

Why don't you go in?

NELL: I don't know.

(*Pause.*)

NAGG: Has he changed your sawdust?

NELL: It isn't sawdust. (*Pause. Wearily*) Can you not be a little accurate, Nagg? 306

NAGG: Your sand then. {It is} not important. 307

NELL: It is important.

(*Pause.*)

NAGG: It was sawdust once.

NELL: Once!

NAGG: And now it's sand. (*Pause.*) From the shore. (*Pause. Impatiently*) Now it's 311 sand he fetches from the shore. 312

NELL: Now it's sand.

NAGG: Has he changed yours? 314

NELL: No.

NAGG: Nor mine. (*Pause.*) I won't have it! (*Pause. Holding up the biscuit*) Do you want a bit?

NELL: No. (*Pause.*) Of what?

NAGG: Biscuit. I've kept you half. (*He looks at the biscuit. Proudly*) Three-quarters. For you. Here. (*He proffers the biscuit.*) No? (*Pause.*) Do you not feel well?

HAMM: (*Wearily*) Quiet, quiet, you're keeping me awake. (*Pause.*) Talk softer. (*Pause.*) If I could sleep I might make love. I'd go into the woods. My eyes would see . . . the sky, the earth. I'd run, run, they wouldn't catch me. (*Pause.*) Nature! (*Pause.*) There's something dripping in my head. (*Pause.*) A heart, a heart in my head. (*Pause.*)

NAGG: (*Soft*) Do you hear him? A heart in his head! (*He chuckles cautiously.*)

NELL: One mustn't laugh at those things, Nagg. Why must you always laugh at them?

NAGG: Not so loud!

NELL: (*Without lowering her voice*) Nothing is funnier than unhappiness, I grant 333 you that. But –

NAGG: (*Shocked*) Oh!

NELL: Yes, yes, it's the most comical thing in the world. And we laugh, we laugh, with a will, in the beginning. But it's always the same thing. Yes, it's like the funny story we have heard too often, we still find it funny, but we don't laugh any more. (*Pause.*) Have you anything else to say to me?

NAGG: No.

NELL: Are you quite sure? (*Pause.*) Then I'll leave you.

NAGG: Do you not want your biscuit? (*Pause.*) I'll keep it for you. (*Pause.*) I thought you were going to leave me.

NELL: I am going to leave you.

NAGG: Could you give me a scratch before you go?

NELL: No. (*Pause.*) Where?

NAGG: In the back.

NELL: No. (*Pause.*) Rub yourself against the rim.

NAGG: It's lower down. In the hollow.

NELL: What hollow?

NAGG: The hollow! (*Pause.*) Could you not? (*Pause.*) Yesterday you scratched me there.

353 NELL: (*Elegiac*) Ah yesterday!

354 NAGG: Could you not? (*Pause.*) Would you like me to scratch you? (*Pause.*) Are you crying again?

NELL: I was trying.

  (*Pause.*)

HAMM: Perhaps it's a little vein.

  (*Pause.*)

NAGG: What was that he said?

NELL: Perhaps it's a little vein.

NAGG: What does that mean? (*Pause.*) That means nothing. (*Pause.*) Will I tell you the story of the tailor?

NELL: No. (*Pause.*) What for?

NAGG: To cheer you up.

NELL: It's not funny.

NAGG: It always made you laugh. (*Pause.*) The first time I thought you'd die.

NELL: It was on Lake Como. (*Pause.*) One April afternoon. (*Pause.*) Can you believe it?

NAGG: What?

NELL: That we once went out rowing on Lake Como. (*Pause.*) One April afternoon.

NAGG: We had got engaged the day before.

374 NELL: Engaged!

NAGG: You were in such fits that we capsized. By rights we should have been drowned.

NELL: It was because I felt happy.

NAGG: (*Indignant*) It was not, it was not, it was my story and nothing else. Happy! Don't you laugh at it still? Every time I tell it. Happy!

NELL: It was deep, deep. And you could see down to the bottom. So white. So clean.

NAGG: Let me tell it again. (*Raconteur's voice:*) An Englishman, needing a pair of striped trousers in a hurry for the New Year festivities, goes to his tailor who takes his measurements. (*Tailor's voice:*) 'That's the lot, come back in four days, I'll have it ready.' Good. Four days later. (*Tailor's voice:*) 'So sorry, come back in a week, I've made a mess of the seat.' Good, that's all right, a neat seat can be very ticklish. A week later. (*Tailor's voice:*) 'Frightfully sorry, come back in ten days, I've made a {botch} of the crotch.' Good, can't be helped, a snug crotch is always a teaser. Ten days later. (*Tailor's voice:*) 'Dreadfully sorry, come back in a fortnight, I've made a balls of the fly.' Good, at a pinch, a smart fly is a stiff proposition. (*Pause. Normal voice:*) I never told it worse. (*Pause. Gloomy*) I tell this story worse and worse. (*Pause. Raconteur's voice:*) Well, to make it short, the bluebells are blowing and he ballockses the buttonholes. (*Customer's voice:*) 'God damn you to hell, Sir, no, it's indecent, there are limits! In six days, do you hear me, six days, God made the world. Yes Sir, no less Sir, the WORLD! And you are not bloody well capable of making me a pair of trousers in three months!' (*Tailor's voice, scandalized:*) 'But my dear Sir, my dear Sir, look – (*disdainful gesture, disgustedly*) – at the world – (*pause*) – and look – (*loving gesture, proudly*) – at my TROUSERS!'

(*Pause. He looks at* NELL *who has remained impassive, her eyes unseeing, breaks into a high forced laugh, cuts it short, pokes his head towards* NELL, *launches his laugh again.*)

HAMM: Silence!

(NAGG *starts, cuts short his laugh.*)

NELL: You could see down to the bottom.

HAMM: (*Exasperated*) Have you not finished? Will you never finish? (*With sudden fury*) Will this never finish?

(NAGG *disappears into his bin, closes the lid behind him.* NELL *does not move.*)

(*Frenziedly*) My kingdom for a nightman!

(*He whistles. Enter* CLOV.)

Clear away this muck! Chuck it in the sea!

[13]

(CLOV *goes to bins, halts.*)

NELL: So white.

HAMM: What? What's she blathering about?

(CLOV *stoops, takes* NELL's *hand, feels her pulse.*)

417 NELL: (*To* CLOV) Desert!

418 (CLOV {*puts her hand down*}, *pushes her back in the bin, closes the lid.*)

419 CLOV: <> She has no [more] pulse.

HAMM: What was she drivelling about?

421 CLOV: She told me to go away, into the desert.

HAMM: Damn busybody! Is that all?

CLOV: No.

HAMM: What else?

CLOV: I didn't understand.

HAMM: Have you bottled her?

CLOV: Yes.

HAMM: Are they both bottled?

CLOV: Yes.

HAMM: Screw down the lids.

431 [CLOV: I'll go and get the driver.]

(CLOV *goes towards the door.*)

HAMM: Time enough.

434 (CLOV *halts* [*at A*].)

My anger subsides, I'd like to pee.

CLOV: (*With alacrity*) I'll go and get the catheter.

(*He goes towards the door.*)

HAMM: Time enough.

(CLOV *halts.*)

Give me my pain-killer.

CLOV: It's too soon. (*Pause.*) It's too soon on top of your tonic, it wouldn't act.

HAMM: In the morning they brace you up and in the evening they calm you down.
Unless it's the other way round. (*Pause.*) That old doctor, he's dead,
naturally?

CLOV: He wasn't old.

HAMM: But he's dead?

447 CLOV: Naturally. (*Pause.*) *You* ask *me* that?

(*Pause.*)

HAMM: Take me for a little turn.

450 (CLOV *goes behind the chair and* {*pulls*}.)

Not too fast!

(CLOV {*pulls*} *chair.*)   451

Right round the world!   452

(CLOV {*pulls*} *chair.*)

Hug the walls, then back to the centre again.

(CLOV {*pulls*} *chair.*)

I was right in the centre, wasn't I?

CLOV: ({*Pulling*}) Yes.

HAMM: We'd need a proper wheel-chair. With big wheels. Bicycle wheels!
  (*Pause.*) Are you hugging?

CLOV: ({*Pulling*}) Yes.

HAMM: (*Groping for wall*) It's a lie! Why do you lie to me?

CLOV: (*Bearing closer to wall*) There! <>   463

HAMM: Stop!

  (CLOV *stops chair close to back wall.* HAMM *lays his hand against wall.*)

Old wall! (*Pause.*) Beyond is the . . . other hell. (*Pause. Violently*) Closer!   466
Closer! Up against!

CLOV: <>
                                                                                                        468
  (HAMM *withdraws his hand.* CLOV *rams chair against wall.*)
There!

  (HAMM *leans towards wall, applies his ear to it.*)

HAMM: Do you hear? (*He strikes the wall with his knuckles.*) <> Hollow bricks! (*He*   472
strikes again.) All that's hollow! (*Pause. He straightens up. Violently*) <>   473
Enough. Back!

CLOV: We haven't done the round.

HAMM: Back to my place!

  (CLOV *pushes chair back to centre.*)

Is that my place?

CLOV: Yes, that's your place.

HAMM: Am I right in the centre?

CLOV: I'll measure it.

  [(*He moves.*)]
                                                                                                        482
HAMM: More or less! More or less!

CLOV: ({*Thumps chair.*}) There!
                                                                                                        484
HAMM: I'm more or less in the centre?

CLOV: I'd say so.

HAMM: You'd say so! Put me right in the centre!

CLOV: I'll go and get the tape.

489 [(*He moves.*)]

HAMM: Roughly! Roughly!

491 <>

Bang in the centre!

CLOV: There!

494 ([*Thump.*] *Pause.*)

HAMM: I feel a little too far to the left.

496 (CLOV {*thumps*} *chair* <>.)

Now I feel a little too far to the right.

498 (CLOV {*thumps*} *chair* <>.)

I feel a little too far forward.

500 (CLOV {*thumps*} *chair* <>.)

Now I feel a little too far back.

502 (CLOV {*thumps*} *chair* <>.)

Don't stay there (*i.e. behind the chair*), you give me the shivers.

504 (CLOV *returns to his place* {*at A*}.)

CLOV: If I could kill him I'd die happy.

(*Pause.*)

HAMM: What's the weather like?

508 CLOV: <> Same as usual.

HAMM: Look at the earth.

CLOV: I've looked.

HAMM: With the glass?

CLOV: No need of the glass.

HAMM: Look at it with the glass.

CLOV: I'll go and get the glass.

(*Exit* CLOV.)

HAMM: No need of the glass!

(*Enter* CLOV *with telescope.*)

CLOV: I'm back again, with the glass. (*He goes to window right, looks up at it.*) I need the steps.

HAMM: Why? Have you shrunk?

(*Exit* CLOV *with telescope.*)

522 <>

(*Enter* CLOV *with ladder, but without telescope.*)

CLOV: I'm back again, with the steps.

(*He sets down ladder under window right, gets up on it, realizes he has not the telescope, gets down.*)

[16]

I need the glass.

(*He goes towards the door.*)

HAMM: (*Violently*) But you have the glass!

CLOV: (*Halting, violently*) No I haven't the glass!

(*Exit* CLOV.)

HAMM: This is deadly.

(*Enter* CLOV *with telescope. He goes towards ladder.*)

CLOV: Things are livening up. <> (*He gets up on ladder, turns the telescope on the without.*) Let's see. (*He looks, moving the telescope.*) Zero . . . (*he looks*) . . . zero . . . (*he looks*) . . . and zero.   534

HAMM: Nothing stirs. All is –

CLOV: Zer–

HAMM: (*Violently*) Wait till you're spoken to! (*Normal voice:*) All is . . . all is . . . all is what? (*Violently*) All is what?   539

CLOV: What all is? In a word? Is that what you want to know? Just a moment. (*He turns the telescope on the without, looks, lowers the telescope, turns towards* HAMM.) Corpsed. (*Pause.*) Well? Content?

HAMM: Look at the sea.

CLOV: It's the same.

HAMM: Look at the ocean!

(CLOV *gets down,* <> *carries* {ladder} *over and sets it down under window left, gets up on it, turns the telescope on the without, looks at length. He starts, lowers the telescope, examines it, turns it again on the without.*)   547

CLOV: Never seen anything like that!

HAMM: (*Anxious*) What? A sail? A fin? Smoke?

CLOV: (*Looking*) The light is sunk.

HAMM: (*Relieved*) Pah! We all knew that.

CLOV: (*Looking*) There was a bit left.

HAMM: The base.

CLOV: (*Looking*) Yes.

HAMM: And now?   556

CLOV: (*Looking*) All gone.

HAMM: No gulls?   558

CLOV: (*Looking*) Gulls!

HAMM: And the horizon? Nothing on the horizon?   560

CLOV: (*Lowering the telescope, turning towards* HAMM, *exasperated*) What in God's name could there be on the horizon?

(*Pause.*)

HAMM: The waves, how are the waves?

566 CLOV: The waves? <> Lead.

567 HAMM: And the sun?

568 CLOV: <> Zero.

569 HAMM: But it should be sinking. Look again.

570 CLOV: <> Damn the sun.

HAMM: Is it night already then?

572 CLOV: <> No.

HAMM: Then what is it?

574 CLOV: <> Grey. ({*Pause.*} *Louder*) Grey. (*Pause. Still louder*) GRREY! (*Pause. He*
575   *gets down, approaches* HAMM *from behind, whispers in his ear.*)

HAMM: (*Starting*) Grey! Did I hear you say grey?

CLOV: Light black. From pole to pole.

HAMM: You exaggerate. (*Pause.*) Don't stay there, you give me the shivers.

579   (CLOV *returns to his place* {*at A*}.)

CLOV: Why this farce, day after day?

HAMM: Routine. One never knows. (*Pause.*) Last night I saw inside my breast.
    There was a big sore.

583 CLOV: Pah! You saw your heart.

HAMM: No, it was living. (*Pause. Anguished*) Clov!

CLOV: Yes.

HAMM: What's happening?

CLOV: Something is taking its course.

    (*Pause.*)

HAMM: Clov!

CLOV: (*Impatiently*) What is it?

HAMM: We're not beginning to . . . to . . . mean something?

CLOV: Mean something! You and I, mean something! (*Brief laugh.*) Ah that's a
    good one!

HAMM: I wonder. (*Pause.*) Imagine if a rational being came back to earth,
    wouldn't he be liable to get ideas into his head if he observed us long
596   enough. (*Voice of rational being:*) Ah, good, now I see what it is, yes, now I
    understand what they're at!
    (CLOV *starts, drops the telescope and begins to scratch his belly with both hands.*)
    (*Normal voice:*) And without going so far as that, we ourselves . . . (*with*
    emotion) . . . we ourselves . . . at certain moments . . . (*Vehemently*) To think
    perhaps it won't all have been for nothing!

CLOV: (*Anguished, scratching himself*) I have a flea!

HAMM: A flea! Are there still fleas?

CLOV: On me there's one. (*Scratching.*) Unless it's a crablouse.

HAMM: (*Very perturbed*) But humanity might start from there all over again! Catch   605
him, for the love of God!

CLOV: I'll go and get the powder.

(*Exit* CLOV.)

HAMM: A flea! This is awful! What a day!

(*Enter* CLOV *with a sprinkling-tin.*)

CLOV: I'm back again, with the insecticide.

HAMM: Let him have it!

(CLOV *loosens the top of his trousers, pulls it forward and shakes powder into the
aperture. He stoops, looks, waits, starts, frenziedly shakes more powder, stoops, looks,
waits.*)

CLOV: The bastard!

HAMM: Did you get him?

CLOV: Looks like it. (*He drops the tin and adjusts his trousers.*) Unless he's laying
doggo.

HAMM: Laying! Lying you mean. Unless he's *lying* doggo.

CLOV: Ah? One says lying? One doesn't say laying?

HAMM: Use your head, can't you. If he was laying we'd be bitched.

CLOV: Ah. (*Pause.*) What about that pee?

HAMM: I'm having it.

CLOV: Ah that's the spirit, that's the spirit!

(*Pause.*)

HAMM: (*With ardour*) Let's go from here, the two of us! South! You can make a   627
raft and the currents will carry us away, far away, to other . . . mammals!

CLOV: God forbid!

HAMM: Alone, I'll embark alone! Get working on that raft immediately.
Tomorrow I'll be gone for ever.

CLOV: (*Hastening towards door*) I'll start straight away.   632

HAMM: Wait!   633

(CLOV *halts.*)

Will there be sharks, do you think?

CLOV: Sharks? I don't know. If there are there will be.

(*He goes towards door.*)

HAMM: Wait!   638

(CLOV *halts.*)

Is it not <> time for my pain-killer?   640

CLOV: (*Violently*) No!

(*He goes towards door.*)

643 HAMM: Wait!

(CLOV *halts.*)

How are your eyes?

CLOV: Bad.

HAMM: But you can see.

CLOV: All I want.

HAMM: How are your legs?

CLOV: Bad.

651 HAMM: But you can {move}.

CLOV: I come . . . and go.

653 HAMM: In my house. (*Pause. With prophetic relish*) One day you'll be blind, like me. You'll be sitting there, a speck in the void, in the dark, for ever, like me.

655 (*Pause.*) One day you'll say to yourself, I'm tired, I'll sit down, and you'll go and sit down. Then you'll say, I'm hungry, I'll get up and get something to eat. But you won't get up. You'll say, I shouldn't have sat down, but since I have I'll sit on a little longer, then I'll get up and get something to eat. But you won't get up and you won't get anything to eat. (*Pause.*) You'll look at the wall a while, then you'll say, I'll close my eyes, perhaps have a little sleep, after that I'll feel better, and you'll close them. And when you open them again there'll be no wall any more. (*Pause.*) Infinite emptiness will be all around you, all the resurrected dead of all the ages wouldn't fill it, and there you'll be like a little bit of grit in the middle of the steppe. (*Pause.*) Yes, one day you'll know what it is, you'll be like me, except that you won't have anyone with you, because you won't have had pity on anyone and because there won't be anyone left to have pity on.

(*Pause.*)

CLOV: It's not certain. (*Pause.*) And there's one thing you forget.

HAMM: Ah?

CLOV: I can't sit down.

HAMM: (*Impatiently*) Well, you'll lie down then, what the hell! Or you'll come to a standstill, simply stop and stand still, the way you are now. One day you'll say, I'm tired, I'll stop. What does the attitude matter?

(*Pause.*)

CLOV: So you all want me to leave you.

HAMM: Naturally.

CLOV: Then I'll leave you.

HAMM: You can't leave us.

CLOV: Then I shan't leave you.

(Pause.)   680

HAMM: Why don't you finish us? *(Pause.)* I'll tell you the combination of the
  larder if you promise to finish me.   683

CLOV: I couldn't finish you.

HAMM: Then you shan't finish me.   685

(Pause.)

CLOV: I'll leave you, I have things to do.

  [(CLOV *moves towards door.*)]   688

HAMM: Do you remember when you came here?

  [(CLOV *halts.*)]   690

CLOV: No. Too small, you told me.

HAMM: Do you remember your father?

CLOV: *(Wearily)* Same answer. *(Pause.)* You've asked me these questions millions
  of times.

HAMM: I love the old questions. *(With fervour)* Ah the old questions, the old
  answers, there's nothing like them! *(Pause.)* It was I was a father to you.

CLOV: Yes. *(He looks at HAMM fixedly.)* You were that to me.

HAMM: My house a home for you.

CLOV: Yes. *(He looks about him.)* This was that for me.

HAMM: *(Proudly)* But for me *(gesture towards himself)* no father. But for Hamm
  (gesture towards surroundings) no home.

  (Pause.)

CLOV: I'll leave you.

  [(CLOV *moves towards door.*)]   704

HAMM: Did you ever think of one thing?

  [(CLOV *halts.*)]   706

CLOV: Never.

HAMM: That here we're down in a hole. *(Pause.)* But beyond the hills? Eh?   708
  Perhaps it's still green. Eh? *(Pause.)* Flora! Pomona! *(Ecstatically.)* Ceres!
  (Pause.) Perhaps you won't need to go very far.

CLOV: I can't go very far. *(Pause.)* I'll leave you.

  [(CLOV *moves towards door.*)]   712

HAMM: Is my dog ready?   713

  [(CLOV *halts.*)]   714

CLOV: He lacks a leg.

HAMM: Is he silky?

[21]

717   CLOV: He's a kind of Pomeranian.

HAMM: Go and get him.

CLOV: He lacks a leg.

HAMM: Go and get him!

(*Exit* CLOV.)

We're getting on.

723   (*Enter* CLOV *holding by one of its three legs a black toy dog.* [*He halts at A.*])

724   CLOV: Your dogs are here.

725   *He {throws} the dog to* HAMM *who feels it, fondles it.*

HAMM: He's white, isn't he?

CLOV: Nearly.

HAMM: What do you mean, nearly? Is he white or isn't he?

CLOV: He isn't.

(*Pause.*)

HAMM: You've forgotten the sex.

CLOV: (*Vexed*) But he isn't finished. The sex goes on at the end.

(*Pause.*)

HAMM: You haven't put on his ribbon.

CLOV: (*Angrily*) But he isn't finished, I tell you! First you finish your dog and then you put on his ribbon!

(*Pause.*)

HAMM: Can he stand?

CLOV: I don't know.

HAMM: Try.

741   (*He {throws} the dog to* CLOV *who {holds it by its ears and lets it dangle}.*)

Well?

CLOV: Wait!

744   (*He squats down and tries to get the dog to stand on its three legs, fails, lets it go. The dog falls on its side.*)

HAMM: (*Impatiently*) Well?

CLOV: He's standing.

HAMM: (*Groping for the dog*) Where? Where is he?

(CLOV *holds up the dog in a standing position.*)

CLOV: There.

(*He takes* HAMM's *hand and guides it towards the dog's {rear}.*)

751

752   HAMM: (*His hand on the dog's {rear}.*) Is he gazing at me?

CLOV: Yes.

HAMM: (*Proudly*) As if he were asking me to take him for a walk?

[22]

CLOV: If you like.

HAMM: (*As before*) Or as if he were begging me for a bone. (*He withdraws his hand.*) Leave him like that, standing there imploring me.

(CLOV *straightens up. The dog falls on its side.*)

CLOV: I'll leave you.

[(CLOV *moves towards door.*)]   760

HAMM: Have you had your visions?

[(CLOV *halts.*)]   762

CLOV: Less.

HAMM: Is Mother Pegg's light on?

CLOV: Light! How could anyone's light be on?

HAMM: Extinguished!

CLOV: Naturally it's extinguished. If it's not on it's extinguished.

HAMM: No, I mean Mother Pegg.

CLOV: But naturally she's extinguished! (*Pause.*) What's the matter with you today?

HAMM: I'm taking my course. (*Pause.*) Is she buried?

CLOV: Buried! Who would have buried her?

HAMM: You.

CLOV: Me! Haven't I enough to do without burying people?

HAMM: But you'll bury me.

CLOV: No I shan't bury you.

(*Pause.*)   776

HAMM: She was bonny once, like a flower of the field. (*With reminiscent leer*) And a great one for the men!

CLOV: We too were bonny – once. It's a rare thing not to have been bonny – once.

(*Pause.*)

HAMM: Go and get the gaff.

(CLOV *goes to door, halts.*)

CLOV: Do this, do that, and I do it. I never refuse. Why?

HAMM: You're not able to.

CLOV: Soon I won't do it any more.

HAMM: You won't be able to any more.

(*Exit* CLOV.)

Ah the creatures, the creatures, everything has to be explained to them.

(*Enter* CLOV *with gaff.*)

CLOV: Here's your gaff. Stick it up.

[23]

793   (*He gives the gaff to* HAMM [*and moves away*]. {HAMM}, *wielding it like a punt-pole, tries to move his chair.*)

HAMM: Did I move?

CLOV: No.

(HAMM *throws down the gaff.*)

HAMM: Go and get the oilcan.

CLOV: What for?

HAMM: To oil the castors.

CLOV: I oiled them yesterday.

HAMM: Yesterday! What does that mean? Yesterday!

CLOV: (*Violently*) That means that bloody awful day, long ago, before this bloody
804   awful day. I use the words you taught me. If they don't mean anything any
more, teach me others. Or let me be silent.

(*Pause.*)

807   HAMM: I once knew a madman who thought the end of the world had come. He
was a painter – and engraver. I had a great fondness for him. I used to go
and see him, in the asylum. I'd take him by the hand and drag him to the
window. Look! There! All that rising corn! And there! Look! The sails of the
herring fleet! All that loveliness! (*Pause.*) He'd snatch away his hand and go
812   back into his corner. Appalled. All he had seen was ashes. (*Pause.*) He alone
had been spared. (*Pause.*) Forgotten. (*Pause.*) It appears the case is . . . was
not so . . . so unusual.

CLOV: A madman? When was that?

HAMM: Oh way back, way back, you weren't in the land of the living.

CLOV: God be with the days!

(*Pause.* HAMM *raises his toque.*)

HAMM: I had a great fondness for him. (*Pause. He puts on his toque again.*) He was
a painter – and engraver.

CLOV: There are so many terrible things.

HAMM: No, no, there are not so many now. (*Pause.*) Clov!

CLOV: Yes.

HAMM: Do you not think this has gone on long enough?

CLOV: Yes! (*Pause.*) What?

HAMM: This . . . this . . . thing.

827   CLOV: {I always did.} (*Pause.*) {Not you?}

HAMM: (*Gloomily*) Then it's a day like any other day.

CLOV: As long as it lasts. (*Pause.*) All life long the same inanities.

(*Pause.*)

[24]

HAMM: I can't leave you.

CLOV: I know. And you can't follow me.

  (*Pause.*)

HAMM: If you leave me how shall I know?

CLOV: (*Briskly*) Well you simply whistle me and if I don't come running it means
  I've left you.

  (*Pause.*)

HAMM: You won't come and kiss me goodbye?

CLOV: Oh I shouldn't think so.

  (*Pause.*)

HAMM: But you might be merely dead in your kitchen.

CLOV: The result would be the same.

HAMM: Yes, but how would I know, if you were merely dead in your kitchen?

CLOV: Well . . . sooner or later I'd start to stink.

HAMM: You stink already. The whole place stinks of corpses.

CLOV: The whole universe.

HAMM: (*Angrily*) To hell with the universe! (*Pause.*) Think of something.

CLOV: What?

HAMM: An idea, have an idea. (*Angrily*) A bright idea!

CLOV: Ah good. (*He starts pacing to and fro, his eyes fixed on the ground, his hands
  behind his back. He halts.*) The pains in my legs! It's unbelievable! Soon I
  won't be able to think any more.

HAMM: You won't be able to leave me.

  (CLOV *resumes his pacing.*)

  What are you doing?

CLOV: Having an idea. (*He paces.*) Ah!

  (*He halts.*)

HAMM: What a brain! (*Pause.*) Well?

CLOV: Wait! (*He meditates. Not very convinced*) Yes . . . (*Pause. More convinced*) Yes!
  (*He raises his head.*) I have it! I set the alarm.

  (*Pause.*)

HAMM: This is perhaps not one of my bright days, but frankly –

CLOV: You whistle me. I don't come. The alarm rings. I'm gone. It doesn't ring.
  I'm dead.

  (*Pause.*)

HAMM: Is it working? (*Pause. Impatiently*) The alarm, is it working?

CLOV: Why wouldn't it be working?

HAMM: Because it's worked too much.

850

[25]

CLOV: But it's hardly worked at all.

HAMM: (*Angrily*) Then because it's worked too little!

CLOV: I'll go and see.

872   (*Exit* CLOV. <> *Enter* CLOV *with alarm-clock. He holds it against* HAMM's *ear and releases alarm. They listen to it ringing to the end. Pause.*) Fit to wake the dead! Did you hear it?

HAMM: Vaguely.

CLOV: The end is terrific!

HAMM: I prefer the middle. (*Pause.*) Is it not time for my pain-killer?

CLOV: No! <> I'll leave you.

878   [(CLOV *moves towards door.*)]

879 HAMM: It's time for my story. Do you want to listen to my story?

880   [(CLOV *halts at A.*)]

CLOV: No.

HAMM: Ask my father if he wants to listen to my story.

    (CLOV *goes to bins, raises the lid of* NAGG's, *stoops, looks into it. Pause. He straightens up.*)

CLOV: He's asleep.

HAMM: Wake him.

    (CLOV *stoops, wakes* NAGG *with the alarm. Unintelligible words.* CLOV *straightens up.*)

CLOV: He doesn't want to listen to your story.

891 HAMM: I'll give him a bon bon.

    (CLOV *stoops. As before.*)

CLOV: He wants a sugar-plum.

HAMM: He'll get a sugar-plum.

    (CLOV *stoops. As before.*)

CLOV: It's a deal.

897   ([CLOV *slams lid.*] *He goes towards door.* <> {*He*} *reaches door, turns.*) Do you believe in the life to come?

HAMM: Mine was always that.

900   (*Exit* CLOV. [NAGG's *hands appear, gripping the rim. Then the head emerges.*]) Got him that time!

NAGG: I'm listening.

HAMM: Scoundrel! Why did you engender me?

NAGG: I didn't know.

HAMM: What? What didn't you know?

906 NAGG: That {it would} be you. (*Pause.*) You'll give me a sugar-plum?

HAMM: After the audition.

NAGG: You swear?

HAMM: Yes.

NAGG: On what?

HAMM: My honour.

(Pause. They laugh heartily.)

NAGG: Two.

HAMM: One.

NAGG: One for me and one for –

HAMM: One! Silence! *(Pause.)* Where was I? *(Pause. Gloomily)* It's finished, we're   916
finished. *(Pause.)* Nearly finished. *(Pause.)* There'll be no more speech.
(Pause.) Something dripping in my head, ever since the fontanelles.
(Stifled hilarity of NAGG.)
Splash, splash, always on the same spot. *(Pause.)* Perhaps it's a little vein.
(Pause.) A little artery. *(Pause. More animated)* Enough of that, it's story time,   921
where was I? *(Pause. Narrative tone:)* The man came crawling towards me, on
his belly. Pale, wonderfully pale and thin, he seemed on the point of – *(Pause.
Normal tone:)* No, I've done that bit. *(Pause. Narrative tone:)* I calmly filled my
pipe – the meerschaum, lit it with . . . let us say a vesta, drew a few puffs.
Aah! *(Pause.)* Well, what is it *you* want? *(Pause.)* It was an extra-ordinarily   926
bitter day, I remember, zero by the thermometer. But considering it was
Christmas Eve there was nothing . . . extra-ordinary about that. Seasonable
weather, for once in a way. *(Pause.)* Well, what ill wind blows you my way?   929
He raised his face to me, black with mingled dirt and tears. *(Pause. Normal
tone:)* That should do it. *(Narrative tone:)* No, no, don't look at me, don't look
at me. He dropped his eyes and mumbled something, apologies I presume.
(Pause.) I'm a busy man, you know, the final touches, before the festivities,
you know what it is. *(Pause. Forcibly)* Come on now, what is the object of this   934
invasion? *(Pause.)* It was a glorious bright day, I remember, fifty by the
heliometer, but already the sun was sinking down into the . . . down among
the dead. *(Normal tone:)* Nicely put, that. *(Narrative tone:)* Come on now,
come on, present your petition and let me resume my labours. *(Pause. Normal
tone:)* There's English for you. Ah well . . . *(Narrative tone:)* It was then he
took the plunge. It's my little one, he said. Tsstss, a little one, that's bad. My
little boy, he said, as if the sex mattered. Where did he come from? He
named the hole. A good half-day, on horse. What are you insinuating? That
the place is still inhabited? No no, not a soul, except himself and the child –
assuming he existed. Good. I inquired about the situation at Kov, beyond the

gulf. Not a sinner. Good. And you expect me to believe you have left your little one back there, all alone, and alive into the bargain? Come now! (*Pause.*) It was a howling wild day, I remember, a hundred by the anemometer. The wind was tearing up the dead pines and sweeping them . . . away. (*Pause. Normal tone:*) A bit feeble, that. (*Narrative tone:*) Come on, man, speak up, what is it you want from me, I have to put up my holly. (*Pause.*) Well to make it short it finally transpired that what he wanted from me was . . . bread for his brat. Bread? But I have no bread, it doesn't agree with me. Good. Then perhaps a little corn? (*Pause. Normal tone:*) That should do it. (*Narrative tone:*) Corn, yes, I have corn, it's true, in my granaries. But use your head. I give you some corn, a pound, a pound and a half, you bring it back to your child and you make him – if he's still alive – a nice pot of porridge (NAGG *reacts.*), a nice pot and a half of porridge, full of nourishment. Good. The colours come back into his little cheeks – perhaps. And then? (*Pause.*) I lost patience. (*Violently*) Use your head, can't you, use your head, you're on earth, there's no cure for that! (*Pause.*) It was an exceedingly dry day, I remember, zero by the hygrometer. Ideal weather, for my lumbago. (*Pause. Violently*) But what in God's name do you imagine? That the earth will awake in spring? That the rivers and seas will run with fish again? That there's manna in heaven still for imbeciles like you? (*Pause.*) Gradually I cooled down, sufficiently at least to ask him how long he had taken on the way. Three whole days. Good. In what condition he had left the child. Deep in sleep. (*Forcibly*) But deep in what sleep, deep in what sleep already? (*Pause.*) Well to make it short I finally offered to take him into my service. He had touched a chord. And then I imagined already that I wasn't much longer for this world. (*He laughs. Pause.*) Well? (*Pause.*) Well? Here if you were careful you might die a nice natural death, in peace and comfort. (*Pause.*) Well? (*Pause.*) In the end he asked me would I consent to take in the child as well – if he were still alive. (*Pause.*) It was the moment I was waiting for. (*Pause.*) Would I consent to take in the child . . . (*Pause.*) I can see him still, down on his knees, his hands flat on the ground, glaring at me with his mad eyes, in defiance of my wishes. (*Pause. Normal tone:*) I'll soon have finished with this story. (*Pause.*) Unless I bring in other characters. (*Pause.*) But where would I find them? (*Pause.*) Where would I look for them?

(*Pause. He whistles. Enter* CLOV.)

Let us pray to God.

NAGG: Me sugar-plum!

CLOV: There's a rat in the kitchen!

HAMM: A rat! Are there still rats?

CLOV: In the kitchen there's one.

HAMM: And you haven't exterminated him?

CLOV: Half. You disturbed us.

HAMM: He can't get away?

CLOV: No.

HAMM: You'll finish him later. Let us pray to God.

CLOV: Again!

NAGG: Me sugar-plum!

HAMM: God first! (*Pause.*) Are you right?

CLOV: (*Resigned*) Off we go.

HAMM: (*To* NAGG) And you?

NAGG: (*Clasping his hands, closing his eyes, in a gabble*) Our Father which art –

HAMM: Silence! In silence! Where are your manners? (*Pause.*) Off we go.
(*Attitudes of prayer. Silence.*)
(*Abandoning his attitude, discouraged*) Well?   997

CLOV: (*Abandoning his attitude*) What a hope! And you?

HAMM: Sweet damn all! (*To* NAGG) And you?   999

NAGG: Wait! (*Pause. Abandoning his attitude*) Nothing doing!

HAMM: The bastard! He doesn't exist!

CLOV: Not [just] yet.   1003

NAGG: Me sugar-plum!

HAMM: There are no more sugar-plums! [You'll never get any more sugar-plums.]   1005
(*Pause.*)

NAGG: It's natural. After all I'm your father. It's true if it hadn't been me it would have been someone else. But that's no excuse. (*Pause.*) Turkish delight, for example, which no longer exists, we all know that, there is nothing in the world I love more. And one day I'll ask you for some, in return for a kindness, and you'll promise it to me. One must live with the times. (*Pause.*) Whom did you call when you were a tiny boy, and were frightened, in the dark? Your mother? No. Me. We let you cry. Then we moved you out of earshot, so that we might sleep in peace. (*Pause.*) I was asleep, as happy as a king, and you woke me up to have me listen to you. It wasn't indispensable, you didn't really need to have me listen to you. Besides I didn't listen to you.   1016
(*Pause.*) I hope the day will come when you'll really need to have me listen to you, and need to hear my voice, any voice. (*Pause.*) Yes, I hope I'll live till   1018
then, to hear you calling me like when you were a tiny boy, and were

frightened in the dark, and I was your only hope. (*Pause.* NAGG *knocks on lid of* NELL's *bin. Pause.*) Nell! (*Pause. He knocks louder. Pause. Louder.*) Nell! (*Pause.* NAGG *sinks back into his bin, closes the lid behind him. Pause.*)

1023 HAMM: Our revels now are ended. (*He gropes for the dog.*) The dog's gone.

CLOV: He's not a real dog, he can't go.

HAMM: (*Groping*) He's not there.

CLOV: He's lain down.

HAMM: Give him up to me.

(CLOV *picks up the dog and gives it to* HAMM. HAMM *holds it in his arms. Pause.*
1029 HAMM *throws away the dog.*)

Dirty brute!

(CLOV *begins to pick up the objects lying on the ground.*)

What are you doing?

1033 {(CLOV *straightens up.*)

1034 CLOV: (*Fervently*) Putting things in order.} I'm going to clear everything away!

(*He starts picking up again.*)

HAMM: Order!

1037 CLOV: (*Straightening up*) I love order. It's my dream. A world where all would be silent and still and each thing in its last place, under the last dust.

(*He starts picking up again.*)

HAMM: (*Exasperated*) What in God's name do you think you are doing?

CLOV: (*Straightening up*) I'm doing my best to create a little order.

HAMM: Drop it!

1043 (CLOV *drops the objects he has picked up.*)

CLOV: After all, there or elsewhere.

(*He goes towards door.*)

1046 HAMM: (*Irritably*) What's wrong with your feet?

CLOV: My feet?

HAMM: Tramp! Tramp!

CLOV: I must have put on my boots.

HAMM: Your slippers were hurting you?

(*Pause.*)

CLOV: I'll leave you.

1053 [(CLOV *moves.*)]

HAMM: No!

CLOV: What is there to keep me here?

HAMM: The dialogue. (*Pause.*) I've got on with my story. (*Pause.*) I've got on with it well. (*Pause. Irritably*) Ask me where I've got to.

CLOV: [(*Moving to* HAMM)] Oh, by the way, your story?   1058

HAMM: (*Surprised*) What story?

CLOV: The one you've been telling yourself all your . . . days.

HAMM: Ah you mean my chronicle?

CLOV: That's the one.

    (*Pause.*)

HAMM: (*Angrily*) Keep going, can't you, keep going!

CLOV: You've got on with it, I hope.   1065

HAMM: (*Modestly*) Oh not very far, not very far. (*He sighs.*) There are days like
    that, one isn't inspired. (*Pause.*) Nothing {one} can do about it, just wait for   1067
    it to come. (*Pause.*) No forcing, no forcing, it's fatal. (*Pause.*) I've got on with
    it a little all the same. (*Pause.*) Technique, you know. (*Pause. Irritably*) I say
    I've got on with it a little all the same.

CLOV: (*Admiringly*) Well I never! In spite of everything you were able to get on
    with it!

HAMM: (*Modestly*) Oh not very far, you know, not very far, but nevertheless, better
    than nothing.

CLOV: Better than nothing! Is it possible?

HAMM: I'll tell you how it goes. He comes crawling on his belly –   1076

CLOV: Who?

HAMM: What?

CLOV: Who do you mean, he?

HAMM: Who do I mean! Yet another.

CLOV: Ah him! I wasn't sure.

HAMM: Crawling on his belly, whining for bread for his brat. He's offered a job   1082
    as gardener. Before –

    (CLOV *bursts out laughing.*)

    What is there so funny about that?

CLOV: A job as gardener!

HAMM: Is that what tickles you?

CLOV: It must be that.

HAMM: It wouldn't be the bread?

CLOV: Or the brat.

    (*Pause.*)

HAMM: The whole thing is comical, I grant you that. What about having a good
    guffaw the two of us together?

CLOV: (*After reflection*) I couldn't guffaw again today.

HAMM: (*After reflection*) Nor I. (*Pause.*) I continue then. Before accepting with gratitude he asks if he may have his little boy with him.

CLOV: What age?

HAMM: Oh tiny.

CLOV: He would have climbed the trees.

HAMM: All the little odd jobs.

CLOV: And then he would have grown up.

HAMM: Very likely.

(*Pause.*)

CLOV: Keep going, can't you, keep going!

HAMM: That's all. I stopped there.

(*Pause.*)

1107   CLOV: {Don't} you see how it goes on.

HAMM: More or less.

CLOV: Will it not soon be the end?

HAMM: I'm afraid it will.

CLOV: Pah! You'll make up another.

HAMM: I don't know. (*Pause.*) I feel rather drained. (*Pause.*) The prolonged creative effort. (*Pause.*) If I could drag myself down to the sea! I'd make a pillow of sand for my head and the tide would come.

CLOV: There's no more tide.

(*Pause.*)

1117   HAMM: Go and see is she dead.

(CLOV *goes to bins, raises the lid of* NELL's, *stoops, looks into it. Pause.*)

CLOV: Looks like it.

(*He closes the lid, straightens up.* HAMM *raises his toque. Pause. He puts it on again.*)

HAMM: (*With his hand to his toque*) And Nagg?

1123   (CLOV *raises lid of* NAGG's *bin, stoops, {peeps} into it. Pause.*)

CLOV: Doesn't look like it.

(*He closes the lid, straightens up.*)

HAMM: (*Letting go his toque*) What's he doing?

(CLOV *raises lid of* NAGG's *bin, stoops, looks into it. Pause.*)

CLOV: He's crying.

(*He closes the lid, straightens up.*)

HAMM: Then he's living. (*Pause.*) Did you ever have an instant of happiness?

CLOV: Not to my knowledge.

(*Pause.*)

[32]

HAMM: Bring me under the window.

(CLOV *goes towards chair.*)

I want to feel the light on my face.

(CLOV *pushes chair.*)   1135

Do you remember, in the beginning, when you took me for a turn? You used to hold the chair too high. At every step you nearly tipped me out. (*With senile quaver*) Ah great fun, we had, the two of us, great fun! (*Gloomily*) And then we got into the way of it.

(CLOV *stops the chair under window right.*)

There already? (*Pause. He tilts back his head.*) Is it light?

CLOV: It isn't dark.

HAMM: (*Angrily*) I'm asking you is it light.

CLOV: Yes.

(*Pause.*)

HAMM: The curtain isn't closed?

CLOV: No.

HAMM: What window is it?   1149

CLOV: The earth.

HAMM: I knew it! (*Angrily*) But there's no light there! The other!

(CLOV *pushes chair towards window left.*)

The earth!

(CLOV *stops the chair under window left.* HAMM *tilts back his head.*)

That's what I call light! (*Pause.*) Feels like a ray of sunshine. (*Pause.*) No?

CLOV: No.

HAMM: It isn't a ray of sunshine I feel on my face?

CLOV: No.

(*Pause.*)

HAMM: Am I very white? (*Pause. Angrily*) I'm asking you am I very white!

CLOV: Not more so than usual.

(*Pause.*)

HAMM: Open the window.

CLOV: What for?

HAMM: I want to hear the sea.

CLOV: You wouldn't hear it.

HAMM: Even if you opened the window?

CLOV: No.

HAMM: Then it's not worth while opening it?

CLOV: No.

[33]

HAMM: (*Violently*) Then open it!

1172   (CLOV {*marks time audibly.*} *Pause.*)

Have you opened it?

CLOV: Yes.

    (*Pause.*)

HAMM: You swear you've opened it?

CLOV: Yes.

    (*Pause.*)

HAMM: Well . . . ! (*Pause.*) It must be very calm. (*Pause. Violently*) I'm asking you is it very calm?

CLOV: Yes.

1182   HAMM: It's because there are no more navigators. (*Pause.*) You haven't much conversation all of a sudden. Do you not feel well?

CLOV: I'm cold.

HAMM: What month are we? (*Pause.*) Close the window, we're going back.

1186   (CLOV <> [*marks time audibly,*] *pushes the chair back to its place, remains standing behind it, head bowed.*)

Don't stay there, you give me the shivers!

1189   (CLOV *returns to his place* {*at A*}.)

Father! (*Pause. Louder*) Father! (*Pause.*) Go and see did he hear me.

1191   (CLOV *goes to* NAGG's *bin, raises the lid, stoops.* {*No sounds from* NAGG.} CLOV *straightens up.*)

CLOV: Yes.

HAMM: Both times?

    (CLOV *stoops. As before.*)

CLOV: Once only.

HAMM: The first time or the second?

    (CLOV *stoops. As before.*)

CLOV: He doesn't know.

HAMM: It must have been the second.

CLOV: We'll never know.

    (*He closes lid.*)

HAMM: Is he still crying?

CLOV: No.

1205   HAMM: The dead go fast. (*Pause.*) What's he doing?

CLOV: Sucking his biscuit.

HAMM: Life goes on.

1208   (CLOV {*goes towards door, stopped at A by:*})

[34]

Give me a rug, I'm freezing.

CLOV: There are no more rugs.

(*Pause.*)

HAMM: Kiss me. (*Pause.*) Will you not kiss me?

CLOV: No.

HAMM: On the forehead.

CLOV: I won't kiss you anywhere.

(*Pause.*)

HAMM: (*Holding out his hand*) Give me your hand at least. (*Pause.*) Will you not give me your hand?

CLOV: I won't touch you.

(*Pause.*)

HAMM: Give me the dog.

(CLOV *looks round for the dog.*)

No!

CLOV: Do you not want your dog?

HAMM: No.

CLOV: Then I'll leave you.

HAMM: (*Head bowed, absently*) That's right.

(CLOV *goes to door, turns.*)

CLOV: If I don't kill that rat he'll die.

HAMM: (*As before*) That's right.

(*Exit* CLOV. *Pause.*)

Me to play. <> We're getting on. (*Pause.*) You weep, and weep, for nothing, so as not to laugh, and little by little . . . you begin to grieve. <> All those I might have helped. (*Pause.*) Helped! (*Pause.*) Saved. (*Pause.*) Saved! (*Pause.*) The place was crawling with them! (*Pause. Violently*) Use your head, can't you, use your head, you're on earth, there's no cure for that! (*Pause.*) Get out of here and love one another! Lick your neighbour as yourself! (*Pause. Calmer*) When it wasn't bread they wanted it was crumpets. (*Pause. Violently*) Out of my sight and back to your petting parties! (*Pause.*) All that, all that! (*Pause.*) Not even a real dog! (*Calmer*) The end is in the beginning and yet you go on. (*Pause.*) Perhaps I could go on with my story, end it and begin another. (*Pause.*) Perhaps I could throw myself out on the floor. (*He pushes himself painfully off his seat, falls back again.*) Dig my nails into the cracks and drag myself forward with my fingers. (*Pause.*) It will be the end and there I'll be, wondering what can have brought it on and wondering what can have . . . (*he hesitates*) . . . why it was so long coming. (*Pause.*) There I'll be, in the old

1232
1233
1234

1237

1239
1240

[35]

1247 refuge, alone against the silence and . . . (*he hesitates*) . . . the stillness. If I can hold my peace, and sit quiet, it will be all over with sound, and motion,

1249 all over and done with. (*Pause.*) I'll have called my father and I'll have called my . . . (*he hesitates*) . . . my son. And even twice, or three times, in case they shouldn't have heard me, the first time, or the second. (*Pause.*) I'll say to myself, He'll come back. (*Pause.*) And then? (*Pause.*) And then? (*Pause.*) He couldn't, he has gone too far. (*Pause.*) And then? (*Pause. Very agitated*) All kinds of fantasies! That I'm being watched! A rat! Steps! Breath held and

1255 then . . . (*He breathes out.*) Then babble, babble, words, like the solitary child who turns himself into children, two, three, so as to be together, and whisper together, in the dark. (*Pause.*) Moment upon moment, pattering down, like

1258 the millet grains of . . . (*he hesitates*) . . . that old Greek, and all life long you wait for that to mount up to a life. (*Pause. He opens his mouth to continue, renounces.*) Ah let's get it over!

1261 (*He whistles. Enter* CLOV *with alarm-clock. He halts {at A}*) What? Neither gone nor dead?

CLOV: In spirit only.

HAMM: Which?

CLOV: Both.

HAMM: Gone from me you'd be dead.

CLOV: And vice versa.

HAMM: Outside of here it's death! (*Pause.*) And the rat?

CLOV: He's got away.

HAMM: He can't go far. (*Pause. Anxious*) Eh?

1271 CLOV: He doesn't need to go far.
  (*Pause.*)

HAMM: Is it not time for my pain-killer?

CLOV: Yes.

HAMM: Ah! At last! Give it to me! Quick!
  (*Pause.*)

CLOV: There's no more pain-killer.
  (*Pause.*)

1279 HAMM: (*Appalled*) {God} . . . ! (*Pause.*) No more pain-killer!

CLOV: No more pain-killer. You'll never get any more pain-killer.
  (*Pause.*)

HAMM: But the little round box. It was full!

CLOV: Yes. But now it's empty.

(*Pause.* CLOV *starts to move about the room. He is looking for a place to put down the alarm-clock.*)

HAMM: (*Soft*) What'll I do? (*Pause. In a scream*) What'll I do?

({ CLOV *puts the clock first on* NAGG's *bin, then after thought on* NELL's. })   1287

What are you doing?

CLOV: Winding up.

[(CLOV *moves towards door, stopped at A by:*)]   1290

HAMM: Look at the earth.

CLOV: Again!

HAMM: Since it's calling to you.

CLOV: Is your throat sore?   1293

(*Pause.*)

Would you like a lozenge?

(*Pause.*)

No?

(*Pause.*)

Pity.

<>

<>   1301

(*Pause.*)   1302

What did I do with that steps? (*He looks round for ladder.*) You didn't see that steps? (*He sees it.*) Ah, about time. (*He goes towards window left.*) Sometimes I wonder if I'm in my right mind. Then it passes over and I'm as lucid as before. (*He gets up on ladder, looks out of window.*) Christ, she's under water! (*He looks.*) How can that be? (*He pokes forward his head, his hand above his eyes.*) It hasn't rained. (*He wipes the pane, looks. Pause.*) Ah what a mug I am! I'm on   1309 the wrong side! (*He gets down, takes a few steps towards window right.*) Under water! (*He goes back for ladder.*) What a mug I am! (*He carries ladder towards   1311 window right.*) Sometimes I wonder if I'm in my right senses. Then it passes off and I'm as intelligent as ever. (*He sets down ladder under window right, gets up on it, looks out of window. He turns towards* HAMM.)

Any particular sector you fancy? Or merely the whole thing?

HAMM: Whole thing.

CLOV: The general effect? Just a moment.

(*He looks out of window. Pause.*)

HAMM: Clov.

CLOV: (*Absorbed*) Mmm.

HAMM: Do you know what it is?

CLOV: (*As before*) Mmm.

HAMM: I was never there. (*Pause.*) Clov!

CLOV: (*Turning towards* HAMM, *exasperated*) What is it?

HAMM: I was never there.

CLOV: Lucky for you.
  (*He looks out of window.*)

HAMM: Absent, always. It all happened without me. I don't know what's happened. (*Pause.*) Do you know what's happened?
  (*Pause.*)
  Clov!

CLOV: (*Turning towards* HAMM, *exasperated*) Do you want me to look at this muckheap, yes or no?

HAMM: Answer me first.

CLOV: What?

HAMM: Do you know what's happened?

CLOV: When? Where?

HAMM: (*Violently*) When! What's happened! Use your head, can't you! What has happened?

CLOV: What for Christ's sake does it matter?
  (*He looks out of window.*)

HAMM: I don't know.
  (*Pause.* CLOV *turns towards* HAMM.)

CLOV: (*Harshly*) When old Mother Pegg asked you for oil for her lamp and you told her to get out to hell, you knew what was happening then, no?
  (*Pause.*)
1347 You know what she died of, Mother Pegg? Of darkness.

HAMM: (*Feebly*) I hadn't any.

CLOV: (*As before*) Yes, you had.
  (*Pause.*)

1351 HAMM: Have you the glass?

CLOV: No, it's clear enough as it is.

HAMM: Go and get it.
  (*Pause.* CLOV *casts up his eyes, brandishes his fists. He loses balance, clutches on to*
1355 *the ladder.* {*He gets down.*})

1356 CLOV: There's one thing I'll never understand. <> Why I always obey you. Can you explain that to me?

HAMM: No . . . Perhaps it's compassion. (*Pause.*) A kind of great compassion.
1359 (*Pause.*) Oh you won't find it easy, you won't find it easy.

[38]

(*Pause.* CLOV *begins to move about the room in search of the telescope.*)

CLOV: I'm tired of our goings on, very tired. (*He searches.*) <> You'd need a microscope to find this – (*He sees the telescope.*) Ah, about time.   1361

(*He picks up the telescope, gets up on the ladder, turns the telescope on the without.*)

HAMM: Give me the dog.

CLOV: (*Looking*) Quiet!

HAMM: (*Angrily*) Give me the dog!

(CLOV *drops the telescope, clasps his hands to his head. Pause. He gets down precipitately, looks for the dog, sees it, picks it up, hastens towards* HAMM *and strikes him* <> *violently with the dog.*)   1369

CLOV: There's your dog for you!

(*The dog falls to the ground. Pause.*)   1371

HAMM: He hit me!

CLOV: You drive me mad, I'm mad!

HAMM: If you must hit me, hit me with the axe. (*Pause.*) Or with the gaff, hit me with the gaff. Not with the dog. With the gaff. Or with the axe.

(CLOV *picks up the dog and gives it to* HAMM *who takes it in his arms.*)   1376

CLOV: (*Imploringly*) Let's stop playing!

HAMM: Never! (*Pause.*) Put me in my coffin.   1378

CLOV: There are no more coffins.

HAMM: Then let it end!

(CLOV *goes towards ladder.*)

With a bang!

(CLOV *gets up on ladder, gets down again, looks for telescope, sees it, picks it up, gets up ladder* <>.)   1384

Of darkness! And me? Did anyone ever have pity on me?

CLOV: (<> *Turning towards* HAMM) What?   1386

(*Pause.*)

Is it me you're referring to?

HAMM: (*Angrily*) An aside, ape! Did you never hear an aside before?

(*Pause.*)

I'm warming up for my last soliloquy.

CLOV: I warn you. I'm going to look at this filth since it's an order. But it's the last time. (*He turns the telescope on the without.*) Let's see. (*He moves the telescope.*) Nothing . . . nothing . . . good . . . good . . . nothing . . . goo– <>   1394
Bad luck to it!

HAMM: More complications! <> Not an underplot, I trust.   1396
<>   1397

[39]

CLOV: (*Dismayed*) Looks like a small boy!

1399 HAMM: (*Sarcastic*) A small . . . boy!

CLOV: I'll go and see.

(*He gets down, drops the telescope, goes towards door, turns.*)

I'll take the gaff.

(*He looks for the gaff, sees it, picks it up, hastens towards door.*)

HAMM: No!

(CLOV *halts.*)

CLOV: No? A potential procreator?

HAMM: If he exists he'll die there or he'll come here. And if he doesn't . . .

(*Pause.*)

CLOV: You don't believe me? You think I'm inventing?

(*Pause.*)

HAMM: It's the end, Clov, we've come to the end. I don't need you any more.

(*Pause.*)

CLOV: Lucky for you.

1414 (*He {starts} towards door.*)

HAMM: Leave me the gaff.

1416 (CLOV *gives him the gaff* <>.)

CLOV: I'll leave you.

(*He goes towards door.*)

HAMM: Before you go . . .

1420 (CLOV *halts {at A}*)

. . . say something.

CLOV: There is nothing to say.

HAMM: A few words . . . to ponder . . . in my heart.

CLOV: Your heart!

HAMM: Yes. (*Pause. Forcibly*) Yes! (*Pause.*) With the rest, in the end, the shadows, the murmurs, all the trouble, to end up with. (*Pause.*) Clov . . . He never spoke to me. Then, in the end, before he went, without my having asked him, he spoke to me. He said . . .

CLOV: (*Despairingly*) Ah . . . !

HAMM: Something . . . from your heart.

CLOV: My heart!

HAMM: A few words . . . from your heart.

(*Pause.*)

1434 CLOV: (*Fixed gaze, tonelessly, towards auditorium*) They said to me, That's love, yes
1435 yes, not a doubt, now you see how – <> easy it is. They said to me, That's

[40]

friendship, yes yes, no question, you've found it. They said to me, Here's the place, stop, raise your head and look at all that beauty. That order! They said to me, Come now, you're not a brute beast, think upon these things and you'll see how all becomes clear. And simple! They said to me, What skilled attention they get, all these dying of their wounds. <> ([*Moves towards door and back*] {*to A.*}) I say to myself – sometimes, Clov, you must learn to suffer better than that if you want them to weary of punishing you – one day. I say to myself – sometimes, Clov, you must be there better than that if you want them to let you go – one day. But I feel too old, and too far, to form new habits. Good, it'll never end, I'll never go. (*Pause.*) Then one day, suddenly, it ends, it changes, I don't understand, it dies, or it's me, I don't understand that either. I ask the words that remain – sleeping, waking, morning, evening. They have nothing to say. (*Pause.*) I open the door of the cell and go. I am so bowed I only see my feet, if I open my eyes, and between my legs a little trail of black dust. I say to myself that the earth is extinguished, though I never saw it lit. (*Pause.*) It's easy going. (*Pause.*) When I {drop} I'll weep for happiness.

(*Pause. He goes towards door.*)

HAMM: Clov!

(CLOV *halts, without turning.*)

Nothing.

(CLOV *moves on.*)

Clov!

(CLOV *halts, without turning.*)

CLOV: This is what we call making an exit.

HAMM: I'm obliged to you, Clov. For your services.

CLOV: (*Turning <>*) Ah pardon, it's I am obliged to you.

HAMM: It's we are obliged to each other.

(*Pause.* CLOV *goes towards door.*)

One thing more.

(CLOV *halts.*)

A last favour.

(*Exit* CLOV.)

Cover me with the sheet. (*Long pause.*) No? Good. (*Pause.*) Me to play. (*Pause. Wearily*) Old endgame lost of old, play and lose and have done with losing. (*Pause. More animated*) Let me see. (*Pause.*) Ah yes!

(*He tries to move the chair, using the gaff as before. Enter* CLOV, *dressed for the road. Panama hat, tweed coat, raincoat over his arm, umbrella, bag. He halts by the*

1440
1441

1448

1451

1462

1469

1473

[41]

door and stands there, impassive and motionless, his eyes fixed on HAMM, *till the end.* HAMM *gives up.*)

1476 [No?] Good. (*Pause.*) Discard. (*He throws away the gaff, makes to throw away the dog, thinks better of it.*) Take it easy. (*Pause.*) And now? (*Pause.*) Raise hat. (*He raises his toque.*) Peace to our . . . arses. (*Pause.*) And put on again. (*He puts on his toque.*) Deuce. (*Pause. He takes off his glasses.*) Wipe. ({*Wipes on*

1479
1480 *gown.*}) And put on again. (*He puts on his glasses <>.*) We're coming. A few

1481 more squirms like that and I'll call. (*Pause.*) A little poetry. (*Pause.*) You prayed – (*Pause. He corrects himself.*) You CRIED for night; it comes – (*Pause. He corrects himself:*) It FALLS: now cry in darkness. (*He repeats, chanting:*) You cried for night; it falls: now cry in darkness. (*Pause.*) Nicely put, that. (*Pause.*) And now? (*Pause.*) Moments for nothing, now as always, time was never and time is over, reckoning closed and story ended. (*Pause. Narrative tone:*) If he

1486 could have his child with him . . . (*Pause.*) It was the moment I was waiting

1488 for. (*Pause.*) You don't want to abandon him? You want him to bloom while you are withering? Be there to solace your last million last moments? (*Pause.*) He doesn't realize, all he knows is hunger, and cold, and death to crown it all. But you! You ought to know what the earth is like, nowadays. Oh, I put him before his responsibilities! (*Pause. Normal tone:*) Well, there we are, there I am, that's enough. (*He raises the whistle to his lips, hesitates, drops it. Pause.*) Yes, truly! (*He whistles. Pause. Louder. Pause.*) [No?] Good. (*Pause.*) Father!

1494 (*Pause. Louder*) Father! (*Pause.*) [No?] Good. (*Pause.*) We're coming. (*Pause.*)

1495 And to end up with? (*Pause.*) Discard. (*He throws away the dog. He tears the whistle from his neck.*) With my compliments. (*He throws whistle towards auditorium. Pause. He sniffs. Soft*) Clov!

1498

1499 ([CLOV *winces.*] *Long pause.*) No? Good.

1500 ([CLOV's *eyes back on* HAMM. HAMM] *takes out the handkerchief.*)
Since that's the way we're playing it . . . (*he unfolds handkerchief*) . . . let's play it that way . . . (*he unfolds*) . . . and speak no more about it . . . (*he finishes unfolding*) . . . speak no more. (*He holds the handkerchief spread out before him.*) Old stancher! (*Pause.*) You . . . remain.

1505 (*Pause. He covers his face with handkerchief, {drops} his arms to armrests, remains

1506 motionless. Brief tableau.*)

CURTAIN

[42]

1 – *Bare interior* (F11, G1). Although the physical details of the set were the same nondescript grey cell of the original printed text, in his working versions Beckett used a decidedly more realistic ambience in order to develop the play. A typescript called 'Avant *Fin de partie*' contains a wealth of realistic detail. Here the play was set specifically in the region of Picardy, 'et plus précisément dans le Boulonnais . . . alentours de Wissant' ('and more precisely in Boulonnais . . . near Wissant'). The Clov-like character F (Factotum) at this point, describes the living quarters: 'Votre habitation, édifiée sur la falaise, comporte un living room et un couloir transformé en cuisine' ('Your dwelling, erected on a cliff, is composed of a living room and a passageway transformed into a kitchen'). The protagonists are obviously survivors of a World War 1 battle: 'Détruite progressivement dans l'automne de 1914, le printemps de 1918 et l'automne suivant, dans des circonstances mystérieuses' ('Progressively destroyed in the autumn of 1914, the spring of 1918, and the following autumn, under mysterious circumstances'). These realistic details, necessary for the creative process, were progressively eliminated in revisions.

2 – *Grey light* (F11, G1). In the Berlin production, there were no lighting changes; the lights were further 'cooled' with blue gels. Beckett's lighting accents the door (although, in the Matias design, the entrance to the kitchen is doorless), the ashbins and the armchair. Lights were set up behind each window, the left one behind the sea window a bit closer than the right one behind the earth window.

3 – *High up* (F11, G1), cut. In *Riverside Nb*, Beckett writes, 'Windows not high – low steps – fixed – justifying – "Have you shrunk?" '

3 – *two small windows* (F11, G1). Audience left, the sea window; audience right, the earth window. Stage directions throughout are retained as originally written, from the audience perspective. In *Riverside Nb*, the windows are identified by the letters SW = sea window and EW = earth window.

4 – *Hanging near door, its face to wall, a picture* (F11, G1), cut in *Fac(B)*. While all references to the picture were cut in the Riverside production, it, along with the scene of Clov replacing the picture with the alarm-clock, was included in the Schiller production.

7 – *Motionless at A (a point midway between the door and the chair)* revised from *Motionless by the door* (F11, G1). Clov's spot midway between Hamm's chair

and kitchen entrance is called O in the *Schiller Nb*. See drawing early in *Riverside Nb*. In *Fac(B)*, the change from A to O can be seen clearly in a preliminary drawing on p.11.

8 – *Very red face* (F11, G1), cut. Although not deleted in Beckett's annotated text the first time it is mentioned, it is cut in line 35 of *Fac(B)*. Beckett eliminated the very red faces of Hamm and Clov and the very white faces of Nagg and Nell in the Schiller production in 1967 with the comment, 'C'était trop recherché.' (*Berlin Diary*.) In *Riverside Nb* he writes simply, 'Red faces: cut.' In an earlier version of the play, Hamm's complexion was to change from red to livid when he threw himself on the floor of the shelter. A trace of that scene remains in the final version only with Hamm's threat: 'Perhaps I could throw myself out on the floor' (F45, G69). Cutting the red face eliminates almost all traces of that rather melodramatic scene.

10 – *Clov*'s opening (F11, G1). In *Sac(B)* Beckett began simplifying the opening mime by having Clov look out immediately after drawing the curtains: 'Sea window, curtains, looks/Earth [window, curtains, looks.]' The *Schiller Nb*, however, contains an earlier, unsimplified version of the inspection which reverses the pattern as follows: 'Opening. Tableau. Clov bowed head. Then Clov's eyes to Hamm, to bins (if nec. [necessary] slight move forward), to sea window (if nec. [necessary] slight move back) to earth window. Then a moment still with bowed head. Then suddenly off. Ladder to earth window. Draws back curtain. Ladder to sea window. Draws back curtain. Ladder to earth window. Looks at earth. Laugh. Ladder to sea window, looks out. Laugh. Starts with ladder towards ashcans, sets it down, unveils cans. Laugh. To Hamm with can sheets, unveils Hamm. Laugh. With two sheets towards door, halts, turns and at O, meaning his place near chair, speaks. Exit. Comes back for ladder, exit with ladder, i.e., no forgetting of ladder between windows?' (*Schiller Nb*.) In production, however, the unveiling repeated the clockwise pattern of inspection as outlined in *Sac(B)*.

In the margin of *Fac(B)*, Beckett noted of Clov's opening mime, 'Simplify', but he did not make the actual cuts in that text. The revisions adopted here follow the pattern outlined in *Sac(B)*, used in the Schiller production and confirmed by Beckett for the Revised Text; this was, in fact, the original published pattern of unveiling. An acceptable alternative for Beckett was that outlined in both *Schiller Nb* and *Riverside Nb* and used in the Riverside production: the inspection is clockwise (Hamm, bins, sea window, earth window), but the unveiling is anti-clockwise (earth window, sea window, bins, Hamm).

A French text Beckett prepared after the Riverside production for the Polish scholar and translator Marek Kedzierski contains a substantial cut which provides the simplest and chronologically latest model for revising Clov's opening. After Clov returns with the ladder, mounts it at sea window (left) and draws back the curtains, Beckett made the following cut: 'He gets down, takes six steps (for example) towards window right, goes back for ladder, carries it over and sets it down under window right, gets up on it, draws back curtain. He gets down, takes three steps towards window left, goes back for ladder, carries it over and sets it down under window left, gets up on it.' This section may, however, be overcut since it eliminates Clov's drawing back the curtain to the right window. I have thus reinstated the drawing of the right curtain at its appropriate place, lines 15–16. See notes to lines 15, 16, 17 and 19 below for additional cuts.

12 – *Stiff, staggering walk* (F11, G1). In *Riverside Nb*, Beckett writes, 'moving painful [,] as economical as possible. When possible[,] none.'

14 – *Brief laugh* (F11, G1). Only the hint of a laugh, says Beckett, between tongue and teeth, not from the diaphragm. The objects in the shelter are brought into the action through Clov's looking at them here (*Berlin Diary*). In *Riverside Nb*, Beckett writes, 'Mirthless chuckle at each item unveiled.'

15 – *takes one step towards window right, goes back for ladder* (F11, G1), cut.

16, 17, 22 – *Brief laugh* (F11, G1), see note to line 14 above.

16 – *goes with ladder towards ashbins, halts, turns, carries back ladder and sets it down under window right* (F11, G1), cut.

17 – *removes sheet* (F11, G1). In *Schiller Nb* and *Riverside Nb*, Beckett calls this an unveiling.

17 – *folds it over his arm* (F11, G1), cut. Neither in the Berlin nor the Riverside productions did Clov fold the sheets but dragged them unfolded to the kitchen.

18 – *trailing the sheet*, added.

19 – *folds it over his arm (F12, G1)*, cut.

19 – *dirty* replaced *large blood-stained* (F12, G1). In Berlin, Beckett eliminated the blood-stained handkerchief. In a number of productions the stains resembled a human face or skull, which many critics associated with Veronica's veil, the cloth St Veronica used to wipe Jesus's face while he was carrying the cross to Calvary and which is said to have retained his image. Instead of the blood-stained handkerchief, which might also have suggested a haemorrhaging of Hamm, a grey rag was used in Berlin, and it appeared only twice, at the beginning and the end of the play. (See also cuts in lines 1479 and 1480.) When someone asked if the rag then represented the theatre curtain, Beckett responded with a simple 'Yes'. In London, the handkerchief contained 'faint trace of blood' (*Riverside Nb*).

21 – *lifts corner of handkerchief*, added. The line was revised so that Clov peeps under a corner of the handkerchief to look at Hamm's face. The *Brief laugh* that follows Clov's examination of Hamm's face is the 'laugh' Beckett cites after 'unveils Hamm' in the *Schiller Nb*.

21 – *looks at his face* replaced *looks him over* (F12, G1).

22 – *Brief laugh* (F12, G1), see note to line 14 above.

22 – *A* replaced *door* (F12, G1).

22 – *trailing the covers*, added.

24 – *tonelessly* (F12, G1), cut in all the acting copies for the Riverside production (*Gac(A), Gac(M)*).

24 – Finished (F12, G1). In Berlin, Beckett requested that this opening monologue be held down to the 'limits of audibility . . . As small as possible' (*Berlin Diary*). In *Gac(A)*, Walter Asmus notes that Clov's 'basic tone is sullen'. 'There are', however, 'occasional lyric lines' (*Gac (M)*).

Part of Beckett's formal innovation with this play is surely that it begins by announcing its ending, begins with its conclusion. 'The end is', after all, as Hamm tells us, 'in the beginning' (line 1240). Hamm's great fear, however, is that the beginning may also be in the end, that existence may indeed be cyclical. Such images of circularity have interested Beckett at least since his reading of the Italian philosopher Giordano Bruno. In his essay, 'Dante . . . Bruno. Vico . . Joyce', a defence of James Joyce's *Finnegans Wake*, Beckett summarized Bruno as follows: 'There is no difference, says Bruno[,] between the smallest possible chord and the smallest possible arc, no difference between the infinite circle and the straight line. The maxima and minima of particular contraries are one and indifferent. Minimal heat equals maximal cold. Consequently transmutations are circular. The principle (minimum) of one contrary takes its movement from the principle (maximum) of another. Therefore not only do the minima coincide with the minima, the maxima with the maxima, but the minima with the maxima in the succession of transmutations. Maximal speed is a state of rest.' (*Our Exagmination Round his Factification for Incamination of Work in Progress*, London, Faber and Faber, 1961, and New York, New Directions Books, 1962, p.6).

These opening lines, moreover, also echo Christ's final words on the cross: 'When Jesus therefore had received the vinegar, he said, It is finished: and he bowed his head, and gave up the ghost' (John, 19:30). That end, of course, represented for many a new beginning. In one of the play's many analogies, Hamm echoes these words (line 916).

25 – Grain upon grain (F12, G1). Most critics have taken this line and Hamm's subsequent reference to 'that old Greek' (F45, G70) as an allusion to the pre-Socratic Greek sophist, Zeno the Eleatic. And, in Berlin, Beckett spoke of 'Zeno's grains, a logical jest.' He explained Clov's 'impossible heap' as follows: 'What is a

[46]

heap? It can't possibly exist, since one grain isn't a heap, and two aren't either: one no-heap plus one no-heap can't produce any heap, and so on . . . Ergo: the grain must be a heap.' The paradox here is whether or not parts can ever add up to a whole. At what point do one separate grain and another separate grain make up a unit that we call a heap? Later in the play, Hamm states the paradox in more directly human terms. At what point do separate moments of existence make up a life: 'all life long you wait for that [the "moment upon moment"] to mount up to a life' (lines 1258–9)? With Hamm's repetition of the paradox, we further realize that Clov's opening may be his repetition of one of Hamm's set pieces. Clov repeats the words he has learned from Hamm: 'I use the words you taught me,' says Clov, 'If they don't mean anything any more, teach me others. Or let me be silent.' (lines 804–5).

Almost twenty years later, however, Beckett told Eoin O'Brien that the allusion was not to Zeno, but to a philosopher whom he no longer recalls. Another possible candidate might be Eubulides of Miletus, the dialectitian of the Megarian school who wrote a lampoon against Aristotle, hence the grains of millet alluded to by Hamm. Beckett later said, however, that the Miletus allusion was 'unintended'.

The identification of the exact philosopher, however, was less important to Beckett than the logical paradox itself, for Hamm, like Beckett, also forgets the name of the philosopher. What is important is Clov's opening perplexity. Both Riverside acting texts (*Gac(A)* and *Gac(M)*) contain the note, 'For opening discover Cl [Clov] in perplexed position – then he looks'; that is, he inspects the room, moving only his head, in the usual clockwise order: Hamm, Nagg and Nell, sea window, earth window. After inspection, 'Head bowed in perplexity before going for steps' (*Riverside Nb*). All *seems* to be in order, and yet Clov is uneasy, something has changed. As Beckett put it in his *Riverside Nb*: 'C perplexed. All seemingly in order, yet a change. Fatal grain added to form impossible heap. *Ratio ruentis acervi.*' The image of the impossible heap is alluded to again in the Latin quotation: Horace's argument in the Epistle to Augustus. Using the logical puzzle called *sorites* or 'heap' (*acervus*), he asks how many grains make up a heap. The analogy is to how many years it takes for a poet to be considered an 'ancient' and hence great. Horace is defending the value of modern writers. The fuller quotation would be '*dum cadat elusus ratione ruentis acervi*', or 'till after the fashion of the falling heap he is baffled and thrown down' (see Epistles of Horace II, 1, 47, Loeb translation). That is, in his inspection of the room, Clov senses the almost imperceptible change, the single extra grain 'needed to make the heap – the last straw', according to Beckett, and it is that sense of change which provides the impetus for Clov's speech. At another time, Beckett described the subtle change that takes place in this his second play 'in which nothing happens' as follows: 'Between the beginning and the end lies a small distinction which is that between "beginning" and "end"' (*Berlin Diary*). Such slight change, however, may constitute the whole of a human life, a view most succinctly summed up by Pozzo in *Waiting for Godot*: 'They give birth astride of a grave, the light gleams an instant, then it's night once more.'

27 – *He moves towards door and back*, added.

27 – I'll go now to my kitchen (F12, G2). 'Clov has only one wish, to get back into his kitchen – that must always be evident, just like Hamm's constant effort to stop him. This tension is an essential motif of the play' (*Berlin Diary*).

31 – *He remains a moment motionless* (F12, G2). As part of Beckett's principle of visual echoes, Clov's hunched, ape-like posture at the opening should correspond exactly with that of the last scene (*Berlin Diary, Photo*).

33 – *Very red face* (F12, G2), cut.

33 – *Black glasses* (F12, G2). White glasses, that is, white paper over ordinary glasses, were substituted in the 1964 production, according to Patrick Magee, apparently because dark glasses were not easily available, although such justification stretches credibility. But dark glasses were used in Berlin and London, and Beckett later said that he didn't much like the white glasses.

35 – HAMM (F12, G2). Critics have speculated on the character names of *Endgame* nearly as much as on those of *Waiting for Godot*. 'Hamm' certainly suggests a variety of possibilities, including the meat ham, which might be garnished with the complementary spice clove, or the ham actor, or the name may be a variant of 'Hamlet'. Furthermore, there is even a town in the Picardy region of France, where some of the early drafts of *Fin de partie* are specifically set, called Hamm. Another possible source for character names is the Bible. Ruby Cohn suggests, 'The names Nagg and Hamm pun on Noah and Ham of Genesis who are also survivors of a world catastrophe, safe in their shelter' (*Just Play*, p. 239). Ham is the youngest son of Noah and one of eight people to survive the flood. He became progenitor of the dark races, Egyptians, Ethiopians, Libyans and Canaanites (Genesis 10: 6–20). For his indelicacy while his father lay drunken, Ham brought a curse upon Canaan (Genesis 9: 20–7). Ham is also occasionally used as another name for Egypt (Psalms 78: 51; 105: 23; 106: 22). For additional analysis of the Noah imagery see the note to 'But humanity might start from there all over again' (line 605). Although the allusion to the Noah story is consistent with the anti-creation theme in *Endgame*, Beckett's acknowledged source for the character

[48]

names is the hammer and three nails: *Nagel*, *clou* and nail. (See also note to *He whistles* (line 51), for a fuller account of the sources for these names.)

35 – Me – to play (F12, G2). Hamm here introduces the chess motif. The line suggests the opening of a chess match, on the analogy of 'white to play'. Beckett said,

Hamm is king in this chess game lost from the start. He knows from the start that he is only making senseless moves. For instance, that he will not get anywhere at all with his gaff. Now at the last he's making a few more senseless moves, as only a poor player would; a good one would have given up long ago. He's only trying to postpone the inevitable end. Each of his motions is one of the last useless moves that delay the end. He is a poor player. (*Berlin Diary*)

Beckett's alteration of Shakespeare's line from *Richard III* also contains a subtle chess pun. (See also note to 'My kingdom for a nightman' (line 410).) But Beckett has also warned of the limits of such a chess image: 'Well, one can't carry the comparison too far' (*Berlin Diary*).

Endgame is not the first of Beckett's works to feature chess imagery. A game of chess figures prominently in the 1938 novel *Murphy*, but the image appears also in Beckett's first full-length play *Eleuthéria*, unpublished and unproduced, where a Spectator makes the following observation:

. . . si je suis toujours là, c'est qu'il y a dans cette histoire quelque chose qui me paralyse littéralement et me remplit de stupeur. Comment vous expliquer ça? Vous jouez aux échecs? Non. Ça ne fait rien. C'est comme lorsqu'on assiste à une partie d'échecs entre joueurs de dernière catégorie. Il y a trois quarts d'heure qu'ils n'ont pas touché à une pièce, ils sont là comme deux couillons à bayer sur l'échiquier, et vous aussi vous êtes là encore plus couillon qu'eux, cloué sur place, dégoûté, ennuyé, fatigué, émerveillé par tant de bêtise. Jusqu'au moment où vous n'y tenez plus. Alors vous leur dites, Mais faites ça, faites ça, qu'est-ce que vous attendez, faites ça et c'est fini, nous pourrons allez nous coucher. C'est inexcusable, c'est contraire au savoir-faire le plus élémentaire, vous ne les connaissez même pas, les types, mais c'est plus fort que vous, c'est ou ça ou une crise de nerfs. Voilà à peu près ce qui m'arrive.*

35 – (*yawns*) (F12, G2). Beckett cut the first four yawns from Hamm's speech: between 'Me' and 'to play'; between 'misery' and 'loftier'; between 'a' and 'bsolute'; and between 'to' and 'to end' (*Gac(A)*, *Gac(M)*).

---

*. . . if I am still here, it is because there is in this story something that literally paralyses me and fills me with stupefaction. How can I explain this to you? Do you play chess? No? It doesn't matter. It is like watching a chess game between very poor players. It's been three-quarters of an hour since they've touched a piece, they are like two morons yawning over the chess board, and here you are too, even more of a moron than they are, nailed to the spot, disgusted, bored, tired, awed by so much stupidity, up to the time when you can't stand it any longer. Then you say to them, 'But do this, do that, what are you waiting for? Do this and it's over, we can all go to bed.' It is inexcusable, it is contrary to the most elementary good breeding. You don't even know these people, but you can't help it. You do it or you will have a nervous breakdown. This is more or less what is happening to me.

37 – stancher (F12, G2), a variant of 'stauncher', has two meanings here: that which stops or checks the flow of blood and that which remains faithful.

38 – *wipes his eyes, his face, the glasses* (F12, G2), cut in acting texts *Gac(A)* and *Gac(M)*, but revised by Beckett for this volume to *wipes them*.

39 – *four times* was added to the fold of the handkerchief in acting texts *Gac(A)* and *Gac(M)*.

41 – misery – loftier. See note to line 35 above.

44 – 'absolute' (F12, G2) was originally divided by a yawn. 'With yawn cut,' noted Beckett, 'no reason for his pause. Print normal "absolute".'

47 – refuge (F12, G3). The American text prints 'shelter', which Beckett revised to the 'refuge' of the English text (*Gac(A)*, *Gac(M)*).

49 – (*he yawns*) (F12, G3), cut (*Gac(A)*, *Gac(M)*).

51 – *He whistles* (F13, G3). Beckett said, 'There must be maximum aggression between them from the first exchange of words onward. Their war is the nucleus of the play' (*Berlin Diary*). One image that Beckett used to express this war is the hammer (Hamm) driving his three nails: Clov (from the French *clou*), Nagg (from the German *Nagel*), and Nell (from the English nail). Asked directly in Berlin if *Endgame* is a play for a hammer and three nails, Beckett responded, 'If you like.' In the Riverside production, Beckett volunteered the information for his cast (*Gac(M)*). Mother Pegg, we might add, represents yet a fourth nail. The hammer and nails inevitably suggest the suffering of Christ, and in particular, the crucifixion. Throughout the play, then, all the banging, including Hamm's tapping on the wall, echoes this hammer-and-nail or crucifixion theme.

At another time, Beckett explained the Hamm–Clov relationship in terms of fire and ashes; one character is always disturbing the other, and from that stirring, the fire flares and their essentially internal natures become externalized in a violent outburst, a flame.

51 – Clov's movements (F13, G3) in and out of the kitchen, towards and away from Hamm, were carefully choreographed by Beckett. In Berlin, for example, he changed the number of steps taken by Clov from the kitchen entrance to the armchair from nine to eight. Naturally, such precision depends on one's offstage position and the foot chosen for the start, but such details are important to Beckett. 'It's almost like an exercise in dance,' he said in Berlin, 'equal number of paces, rhythm kept equal.' In the *Riverside Nb*, Beckett said, 'C's entrances identical – same number of steps to A, same half turn away.' Beckett strained to keep all of Clov's movements symmetrical. Clov's thinking walk, for instance, is choreographed into a 6 + 4 + 6 + 4 pattern. Such patterns, even if they go unnoticed consciously by the audience, are, Beckett believed, perceived on the subconscious level through repetition, like subliminal images in film. At one point in rehearsals, Beckett called such patterning 'Pythagorean'.

51 – *at A* replaced *beside the chair* (F13, G3), *Fac(B)*.

65 – The (F13, G4), cut (*Fac(B)*).

77 – 'strange' revised from 'queer' (F13, G4) in *Riverside Nb* and *Fac(B)*; 'strange' should be stretched out since it refers to *this* day (*Gac(M)*). This change was made originally at the request of Patrick Magee in 1964 because of the homosexual connotations of the word 'queer'.

95 – Then we shan't die (F13, G4). The American 'won't' revised to the British 'shan't' (*Gac(A), Gac(M)*).

118 – Is it not time for my pain-killer? (F14, G7). This is the first of seven mentions of a pain-killer. In both *Schiller Nb* and *Riverside Nb*, Beckett carefully tracked all seven mentions of an unspecified drug that would offer some hope or relief for Hamm. On the seventh mention, Clov delightedly announces, 'There's no more pain-killer' (Line 1277). (See also note to 'There are no more bicycle-wheels' (line 139).)

128 – *marks time audibly* is Beckett's rendering of his note, '*sur place,*' in *Fac(B)*. It replaced *goes to back wall, leans against it with his forehead and hands* (F14, G8). The first of many instances of disobedience as Clov takes four steps to deceive Hamm.

130 – 'There' replaced 'Here' (F14, G8). This is said as from a distance (*Berlin Diary*).

132 – *marks time audibly*, again Beckett's rendering of '*sur place*', which replaced *returns to his place beside the chair* (F15, G8) in *Fac(B)*. Again, Clov takes four steps on the spot.

136 – larder (F15, G8). The American 'cupboard' was changed to conform to the English 'larder', (*Gac(A), Gac(M)*).

139 – There are no more bicycle-wheels (F15, G8). In both director's notebooks (*Schiller Nb* and *Riverside Nb*), Beckett kept careful track of each mention of items that were no longer available: 1 bicycle-wheels, 2 pap, 3 nature, 4 sugar-plums, 5 tide, 6 navigators, 7 rugs, 8 pain-killer, and 9 coffins. Such emphasis on items no longer available develops the themes of deterioration, decay and entropy throughout the play. Hamm and Clov are part of a world running down. This decay is further developed by the mention of entities about which there is still some doubt. Are there still: 1 fleas, 2 sharks, and 3 rats? And apparently Turkish delight no longer exists.

144 – get out to hell. 'go to hell' (F15, G8) revised to 'get out to hell' (*Gac(A), Gac(M)*).

149 – I'll leave you (F15, G9). Another theme that Beckett tracked through

Schiller Nb and *Riverside Nb* was Clov's threatened departure, which Clov states ten times over the course of the play.

160 – *at A* replaced *beside the chair* (F15, G9).

163 – Me pap! (F15, G9). Alan Mandell's note to himself here is 'Nagg should be nervous energy, frail, senile' (*Gac(M)*).

165 – There's no more pap (F15, G9), see note to 'There are no more bicycle-wheels' (line 139).

170 – 'CLOV: I'll go and get a biscuit', added.

178 – Spratt's Bonio replaced Spratt's medium (F16, G10). The change, Beckett felt, suggested both the bone shape of the biscuit offered to the toothless Nagg and its hardness. 'Nagg knocks on lid,' Beckett notes, 'with bonehard biscuit.'

182 – (*Returning to his place beside the chair*) (F16, G10), cut.

183–4 – The exchange, 'HAMM: Have you bottled him? CLOV: Yes.', added.

189 – Every man his speciality (F16, G10). Beckett suggested to Patrick Magee and to Rick Cluchey that 'speciality' be pronounced with five syllables, i.e. spe-ci–a–li–ty (*Gac(A)*, *Gac(M)*); (Magee interview with McMillan/Fehsenfeld, and Cluchey observed in rehearsals by Gontarski).

193 – CLOV *makes for door, stopped at A by* . . . Beckett noted a problem with Clov's movement at this point. As Beckett stated it, 'Problem how to get Clov back to A. 2 possibilities: 1. After "speciality" C. *makes for door, stopped at A by* "No phone calls?" Or perhaps better after "nor I" and stopped by "Clov."'

213 – (CLOV *moves towards door.*), added for Revised Text.

215 – (CLOV *halts.*), added for Revised Text.

219 – Mene, mene? (F17, G12). Pronounced 'mee-nee, mee-nee'. Hamm is suggesting that Clov sees the handwriting on the kitchen wall, the warning to Belshazzar that his reign nears its end. The allusion is to the book of *Daniel*, 5:26: 'MENE; God hath numbered thy kingdom, and finished it.' In *Fac(B)*, Beckett noted 'Daniel V' in the margin. In *Riverside Nb*, however, he wrote out the transliterated Aramaic, 'mene, mene, tekel upharsin', and translated it, 'numbered, numbered, weighed, divided'. The exact source of the warning is still disputed by biblical scholars, but Daniel's interpretation was clear, that God had numbered the days of the kingdom; the King had been weighed in the balances and found wanting; his kingdom is divided and given to the Medes and the Persians. That very night Belshazzar was slain.

219 – Naked bodies? (F11, G12). Clov sees either a warning of the end of the kingdom or pornography written on his kitchen wall. 'Mene, mene?' should be said like a warning, threatening; 'Naked bodies?' light, amusing (*Gac(M)*).

230 – *The lid of* NAGG'*s bin lifts* (F17, G13). First the hands appear, a set distance apart, grasping the edges of the ashbins; then the head pushes up the lid. As soon as his shoulders are visible, he stops. Nell's emergence should be identical (*Berlin Diary*). Alan Mandell's note to himself is, 'lid on head, fingers on rim' (*Gac(M)*).

231 – *In his mouth the biscuit* (F17, G13), cut in actors' copies at Riverside Studios (*Gac(A)*, *Gac(M)*). However, Beckett restored the image for the Revised Text.

239 – *in his right hand* (F17, G13). For the Revised Text, Beckett specified Nagg's taking the biscuit in his right hand.

256 – NAGG *knocks with biscuit on the lid of the other bin* (F18, G14). He taps twice, same sound as Hamm's taps on the wall (*Gac(A)*, *Gac(M)*). *With biscuit* added for the Revised Text.

259 – What is it, my pet? (F18, G14). To be spoken, Beckett explained, 'without colour . . . Please hold back completely.' The only 'colour' in the Nagg–Nell dialogue is as follows: Our hearing (line 286); Can you not be a little accurate, Nagg? (line 306); Now it's sand (line 314); giggling together abruptly broken off discussing the tandem accident (lines 291, 293, 295); and Nagg's play within a play. A little later Beckett notes, 'Coloration is only for their memories': i.e. Once! (line 311); Ah yesterday! (line 353), and Engaged! (line 374) (*Berlin Diary*).

265 – *Their heads strain towards each other, fail to meet, fall apart again* (F18, G14). Almost no movement on the part of Nagg and Nell and they must not look at each other (*Berlin Diary*). The image of the unconsummated kiss also suggests the ending to John Keats's 'Ode to a Grecian Urn'. The allusion to Keats, Beckett noted, however, was unintended. And surely the three urned figures of *Play* have their roots in this legless, moribund couple reminiscing about their golden moment.

286 – Our hearing (F18, G14). See note to 'What is it, my pet?' (line 259).

291, 293, 295 – laughter (F19, G17). See note to 'What is it, my pet?' (line 259).

306 – Can you not be a little accurate, Nagg? (F19, G17). See note to 'What is it, my pet?' (line 259).

307 – It is not important (F19, G17). 'It isn't' replaced 'It's not' in the actors' texts (*Gac(A)*, *Gac(M)*) at Riverside Studios, but for the Revised Text Beckett preferred 'It is not'.

311 – Once! (F19, G17). See note to 'What is it, my pet?' (line 259).

312 – Now it's sand he fetches from the shore (F19, G17). This reference to Clov's activity outside the shelter was cut by Beckett in Berlin. With this cut, the only reference to Clov's external activity is eliminated, and, of course, the likelihood of Clov's actually leaving Hamm is diminished. The line, however, was retained in the London production and for the Revised Text.

314 – Now it's sand (F19, G17). See note to 'What is it, my pet?' (line 259).

333 – Nothing is funnier than unhappiness (F20, G18). 'That for me is the most important sentence in the play,' said Beckett (*Berlin Diary*). In a letter to the French director Roger Blin, dated 9 January 1953 and quoted in full in the *Introduction*, Beckett, speaking of *Waiting for Godot*, phrases a description of tragicomedy in slightly different but analogous terms: 'Nothing is more grotesque than the tragic.'

353 – Ah yesterday! (F20, G20). See note to 'What is it, my pet?' (line 259).

354 – Are you crying again? (F20, G20). 'Weeping takes place three times in the play,' Beckett said. 'To each his own tears' (*Berlin Diary*). In *Schiller Nb*, Beckett outlined the three instances: 1 Nell, 2 Nagg, and 3 Hamm's comment, 'You weep, and weep, for nothing' (F44, G68).

374 – Engaged! (F21, G22). See note to 'What is it, my pet?' (line 259).

382 – An Englishman needing a pair of striped trousers . . . (F21, G22). An analogy should be evident between Nagg's story and Hamm's narrative: 'Nagg, like Hamm in his narration, works with three voices which he must distinguish clearly.' Here, narrator plays against customer, as, in Hamm's narrative, the narrator, first-person voice and the beggar alternate. As with Hamm's narrative, a fixed look must make the change in roles clear: 'The customer stands, the tailor kneels . . . Gesture, please, towards the world and the trousers.' The gesture is simplified later in rehearsals to a glance towards the trousers and the world (*Berlin Diary*). In Riverside, Beckett said of the scene that the regret of the tailor is balanced with the impatience of the customer.

The image of the world (God's creation) contrasted with the trousers (man's creation) was also used by Beckett in his 1945 essay 'La Peinture des van Velde, ou, le monde et le pantalon', about an exhibition of paintings by Abraham and Geer van Velde which was held in Paris at the Galeries Mai et Maeght. The essay, Beckett's first publication in French, appeared in *Cahiers d'Art*, 20–1 (1945–6), 349–54, and is reprinted in *Disjecta: Miscellaneous Writings and a Dramatic Fragment by Samuel Beckett*, edited with a foreword by Ruby Cohn (London, John Calder, 1983), 118–32.

388 – 'a botch of the crotch' replaced 'a hash of the crotch' (F21, G22). In the Faber edition 'crotch' was originally printed as 'crutch', and Beckett made the correction in *Fac(B)*.

410 – My kingdom for a nightman! (F22, G23). Allusion to Shakespeare's *Richard III*, V. iv. 7, but, of course, Richard called for a horse. Hamm calls for the cleaner of cesspools to cart away his binned parents. The line also contains a subtle chess pun on the knight, as night-man (or knight) replaces or takes horse (or knight), i.e. (Kt × Kt). Beckett called the pun 'unintended', but both *Gac(A)* and *Gac(M)* note Beckett's comments on the pun.

417 – Desert! (F22, G23). Nell says, 'des*ert*'; Clov says, '*des*ert' (*Gac(A)*, *Gac(M)*).

418 – *puts her hand down* replaced *lets go her hand*. Pushing her down in the bin should happen very slowly, gently (*Gac(A)*, *Gac(M)*).

419 – *Returning to his place beside the chair* (F22, G23), cut. Clov simply straightens up in place, stage left of Nell's bin.

419 – 'no more pulse' replaced 'no pulse' (F22, G23).

421 – desert. See note to 'Desert!' (line 417).

431 – CLOV: I'll go and get the driver (F22, G24), added (*Fac(B)*).

434 – CLOV *halts at A* (F22, G24), location added for the Revised Text.

447 – *You ask* me *that?* (F23, G25). Beckett wanted the 'you' accented here because 'Clov holds Hamm responsible for everything concerned with death' (*Berlin Diary*).

450 *et seq. – pulls.* The *pushes* (F23, G25) in this section have been replaced with *pulls*.

451 – HAMM: Not too fast! (F23, G25), cut for Riverside Studios. Beckett, however, restored the line for the Revised Text.

452 – Beckett failed to revise *pushes* (F23, G25) to *pulls* in this line in *Fac(B)*, but the omission seems to have been an oversight. Both *Gac(A)* and *Gac(M)* have handwritten notes in the margins in which 'CLOV *pushes chair*' is revised to 'CLOV *pulls chair.*'

463 – There! (F23, G25). Second 'There!' cut.

466 – Old wall! (F23, G25), same tone as 'Old stancher' (line 37) (*Gac(A)*, *Gac(M)*).

468 – Take away your hand (F23, G26), cut.

472 – *He strikes the wall* (F23, G26). Same two raps as on bin (*Gac(A)*, *Gac(M)*), but not in *Fac(B)*. Beckett, then, clearly made this revision during rehearsals.

472 – Do you hear? (F23, G26). Second 'Do you hear?' cut in Riverside actors' texts (*Gac(A)*, *Gac(M)*).

473 – That's (F23, G26), cut.

482 – (*He moves.*), added.

484 – *Thumps chair* replaces *moving chair slightly* (F24, G26).

489 – (*He moves.*), added.

491 – (CLOV *moves chair slightly.*) (F24, G27), cut.

494 – *Thump*, added.

496, 498, 500, 502 – *thumps chair* replaced *moves chair slightly* (F24, G27). Clov moves the chair four times in this speech, each time with a thump, forming a crescendo of thumps (*Gac(A)*, *Gac(M)*). The thumping of Hamm's chair in a rhythmical and aggressive fashion, moreover, constitutes another direct disobedience on Clov's part.

504 – *at A* replaced *beside the chair* (F24, G27), revision made for the Revised Text.

508 – Same as usual (F24, G27). The American line reads, 'As usual', the English, 'The same as usual'. Beckett revised them both to 'Same as usual.'

522 – I don't like that. I don't like that (F24, G28). This line was not cut in *Fac(B)*, but it is emphatically cut in both *Gac(A)* and *Gac(M)*. In Walter Asmus's copy, in fact, the revision is also starred, but Beckett restored the excision for the Revised Text.

534 – Deleted passage (F25, G29). Beckett simplified the telescope scene considerably, cutting out all reference to the audience (*Gac(A)*, *Gac(M)*):

[CLOV:] (*He gets up on ladder, raises the telescope, lets it fall.*) I did it on purpose. (*He gets down, picks up the telescope, turns it on auditorium.*) I see . . . a multitude . . . in transports . . . of joy. (*Pause.*) That's what I call a magnifier. (*He lowers the telescope, turns towards* HAMM.) Well? Don't we laugh?

HAMM: (*After reflection*) I don't.

CLOV: (*After reflection*) Nor I.

539 – . . . all is . . . (F25, G29). In Riverside, Beckett cut '. . . all is . . . all is what?' with the comment, 'There's too much text' (*Gac(A)*, *Gac(M)*), but he restored the line for the Revised Text.

547 – CLOV *gets down* . . . (F25, G30). Beckett's note to this action in *Fac(B)* is 'Simplify', but no specific cuts were indicated. In *Gac(A)*, however, Clov's false start (*takes a few steps towards window left, goes back for ladder*) is cut. Beckett then revised *carries it* to *carries ladder* for the Revised Text.

556, 558, 560, 568, 570, 572, 574 – (*Looking*)/<(*Looking*)> (F26, G30–1). Beckett also simplified this part of Clov's inspection, cutting the stage direction (*Looking*) seven times, in *Sac(B)* and *Fac(B)*. In *Riverside Nb*, however, Beckett restored three of his original cuts, noting, 'After turn for "What in God's name . . ." no more looking.' In both *Gac(A)* and *Gac(M) Looking* is retained the first three times (lines 556, 558, 560), and Beckett restored those three instances of looking for the Revised Text.

566 – (*He turns the telescope on the waves*) (F26, G31), cut.

567–569 – And the sun . . . But it should be sinking. (F26, G31). Clov's 'Zero' would suggest that the sun has already sunk. Beckett told Patrick Magee, 'You see Hamm is the kind of man who likes things coming to an end but doesn't want them to end just yet' (Magee interview in Fehsenfeld/McMillan, *Beckett in the Theater*). Cf. 'Yes, there it is, it's time it ended and yet I hesitate to – to end' (lines 48–9).

In Berlin Beckett wanted special stress laid on the word 'sun'. Hamm already knows that there are no more gulls, horizon and waves, but 'With the sun,' Beckett added, 'he's not certain; he hopes that it is still there . . . Please give it with a "life voice",' by which Beckett meant something of a lyric quality (*Berlin Diary*).

574 – *Lowering the telescope, turning towards* HAMM cut and *Pause* substituted before *Louder* (F26, G31). *Lowering the telescope* cut in *Gac(A)*, but not in *Gac(M)*. This current revision was made for the Revised Text.

575 – *whispers in his ear* (F26, G31). In *Gac(A)* and *Gac(M)* the whisper in Hamm's ear was an audible 'Grey'.

579 – *at A* substituted for *beside the chair* (F26, G32).

583 – Pah! You saw your heart (F26, G32). Beckett suggested *Moves* here as an alternative to *at A* (line 579). In the margin of *Fac(B)*, Beckett wrote, 'Either'. But for the Revised Text, he settled on *at A*.

596 – Ah, good, now I see . . . (F27, G33). Right hand up, one finger (*Gac(A)*, *Gac(M)*).

605 – But humanity might start from there all over again (F27, G33). Another manifestation of Hamm's fear of a cyclical existence (see also note to 'Finished' (line 24)). Numerous critics have noted the anti-creation or anti-re-creation themes in *Endgame*; Ham, the cursed son of Noah (see notes to HAMM (line 35) and *He whistles* (line 51)), fears that the whole cycle of humanity might restart from the flea. Although Hamm fears the actual end, he fears more that the end may signal a new beginning. In an earlier version of the text, a two-act version on deposit at the University of Reading, the Clov-like B reads a portion of Genesis requested by the Hamm-like A. Clov reads Genesis 8 : 21–2 and 11 : 14–19, the story of Noah. Dissatisfied with the passage, A asks for another and B reads from the generations. All that emphasis on procreation excites the Hamm-like A sexually, and he calls for one Sophie so that he too might beget. But when B appears disguised as Sophie (a part of 'the game' that was eliminated in revision) eager for copulation, the Hamm-like A demurs for fear of procreation. Although such overt development of the anti-creation theme has been cut in revision, it remains at least implicit in this vaudeville flea scene. And Hamm's continuing desire for sexual gratification remains only as a trace: 'If I could sleep, I might make love' (line 323).

The threat of cyclical existence is also suggested by the play's chess imagery since even in the endgame of a chess match the possibility exists not only for a checkmate but for a stalemate as well.

627 – Let's go from here . . . (F28, G34). Hamm takes the hand of Clov (*Gac(A)*, *Gac(M)*).

632 – I'll start (F28, G34). Beckett considered replacing 'I'll start' with 'I'll get going' in *Fac(B)*, but finally decided against the change.

633, 638, 643 – Wait! (F28, G34). The three 'Wait!'s should build in volume (*Gac(A)*, *Gac(M)*).

640 – yet (F28, G35), cut.

651 – move (F28, G36). 'walk' revised to 'move'. The revision also suggests an echo of Hamm's 'But you can move . . . Then move!' (lines 125–7).

653 – In my house (F28, G36). Beckett noted that Hamm's prophecy here is an 'analogy with Nagg's malediction' (lines 1007–21).

655 – I'm tired, I'll sit down (F28, G36). Hamm uses Clov's voice here. That voice is 'inward, quiet, tired. Almost a whisper.' Beckett told his actors at the Riverside Studios that Clov reacts here as Hamm does when Nagg berates him. He winces and turns away (*Gac(A)*, *Gac(M)*).

680 – shan't (F29, G37). The English 'shan't' replaced the American 'won't' (*Gac(A)*, *Gac(M)*).

683 – larder (F29, G37). The English 'larder' replaced the American 'cupboard'.

685 – shan't (F29, G37). The English 'shan't' replaced the American 'won't' (*Gac(A)*, *Gac(M)*).

688 – (CLOV *moves towards door.*), added four times after 'I'll leave you' (F29, G37), on lines 687, 703, 711 and 759 in *Sac(B)*. In *Riverside Nb* Beckett notes, 'After each "I'll leave you" move towards door'; *towards door* added specifically by Beckett for Revised Text. Movement towards door then is presumably in three stages.

690 – (CLOV *halts.*) (F29, G37), added for Revised Text.

704 – (CLOV *moves towards door.*) See note to (CLOV *moves towards door.*) (line 688).

706 – (CLOV *halts.*), added for Revised Text.

708 – But beyond the hills? Eh? Perhaps it's still green? (F30, G39). Also in a 'life voice' (see note to *And the sun* . . . (line 567)). When actor Ernst Schröder asked Beckett if this section expressed hope, Beckett responded, 'Not hope, but the possibility of another situation than the present one' (*Berlin Diary*). The 'life voice' is also used for the visitor's comments to the madman, 'Look! There! All that rising corn!' (line 810).

709 – Flora! Pomona! . . . Ceres! (F30, G39). The Roman vegetation goddesses of flowers, fruit and crops, respectively, and an allusion to the Tiepolo frescos at the Bishop's Palace in Würzburg.

712 – (CLOV *moves towards door.*) See note to (CLOV *moves towards door.*) (line 688).

713 – Is my dog ready? (F30, G39). In an earlier draft of the play, the dog is called Zoulou, the name of the dog in *Molloy* that belongs to Moran's neighbours, the Elsner sisters, 'They had an aberdeen called Zulu.' The name of the dog evidently lies deep in Beckett's memory, for the Elsner sisters, Beckett's kindergarten teachers, actually owned a dog named Zulu, according to Eoin O'Brien in *The Beckett Country*, p. 18.

714 – (CLOV *halts.*), added for the Revised Text.

717 – He's a kind of Pomeranian (F30, G39). Changed to a poodle in Berlin in homage to Schopenhauer who favoured the breed, according to Beckett's German translator, Elmar Tophoven.

723 – *He halts at A*, added for the Revised Text.

724 – Your dogs are here (F30, G40). The plural, of course, includes Clov.

725, 741 – *throws* replaced *hands* (F30, G40), (*Gac(A)*, *Gac(M)*).

741 – *holds it by its ears and lets it dangle* replaced *places it on the ground* (F30, G40), (*Gac(A)*, *Gac(M)*).

744 – *He squats down* . . . (F30, G40). When Clov stoops to get the dog to stand, he ought to be poised like the dog so that the image is of two dogs in profile. In *Riverside Nb*, Beckett says, 'Analogy Clov-dog when trying to make it stand.'

751, 752 – *rear* (F31, G41). In one acting copy *rear* replaced *head* twice (*Gac(M)*). The change corresponds to *Riverside Nb* entry, 'C gives arse not head of dog into H's [Hamm's] hand.' Beckett confirmed this change for the Revised Text.

760 – (CLOV *moves towards door.*), added: *moves* for *Fac(B)*; *towards door* for Revised Text. See also note to (CLOV *moves towards door.*) (line 688).

762 – (CLOV *halts.*), added for Revised Text. Hamm's previous line, 'Have you had your visions?', is part of Hamm's conspiracy to keep Clov from his kitchen. 'Keep Clov from leaving' is the note in *Gac(A)*.

776 – shan't (F31, G42). The American 'won't' again revised to the English 'shan't' (*Gac(A)*, *Gac(M)*).

793 – *and moves away.* HAMM (F32, G42). *and moves away* added, and HAMM substituted for *who*, for the Revised Text. Beckett's original revision was for the addition of (*Moves away.*) after 'Stick it up' (*Fac(B)*).

804 – I use the words you taught me . . . (F32, G42). See note to *Grain upon grain* (line 25). Clov's words also call to mind Caliban's malediction in *The Tempest*: 'You taught me language; and my profit on't/ Is, I know how to curse:

The red plague rid you/ For learning me your language!' (I.ii.365–7).

807 – I once knew a madman . . . (F32, G44). The recollection was to be delivered with what Beckett called 'interiority'. 'All that rising corn!', gesture to earth window; 'The sails of the herring fleet!', gesture to sea window; 'All that loveliness!', both arms outstretched (*Berlin Diary*).

812 – All he had seen was ashes (F32, G44). 'Clov's interest is awakened at the word "ashes",' according to Beckett. Clov's response suggests that he takes this as a reference to himself, and hence his inquiry, 'When was that?' (*Berlin Diary*).

812 – He alone had been spared (F32, G44). A number of critics have associated the mad engraver of this recollection with the apocalyptic English poet, William Blake, and Dougald McMillan, for one, has suggested that this line alludes to Blake's etching of plate 4 of the Book of Job, 'I only am escaped to tell . . .'. Beckett, however, called this allusion 'unintended'.

827 – 'I always did' replaced 'I've always thought so' (F33, G45), (*Gac(A)*, *Gac(M)*).

827 – 'Not you?' transposed from 'You not?' (F33, G45), (*Fac(B)*).

850 – *He starts pacing to and fro . . .* (F33, G46). At Riverside, the walk was eight steps (*Gac(A)*, *Gac(M)*), although in *Riverside Nb*, Beckett evidently noted a five-step pattern of pacing.

872 – *Brief ring of alarm off* (F34, G48), cut (*Gac(A)*, *Gac(M)*).

872 – *Enter* CLOV *with alarm-clock* (F34, G48). Clov enters with alarm-clock, barefoot, shoes in hand, tiptoes to chair. Lets shoes gradually down. Rest of scene barefoot and exit leaving shoes on ground (*Schiller Nb*). 'On tip-toes, no sound,' is the note in *Gac(A)* and *Gac(M)*.

878 – (*He goes to the door, turns.*) (F34, G48), cut.

879 – (CLOV *moves towards door.*), added after 'I'll leave you' (F34, G48); *moves* added in *Fac(B)* and *towards door* added for the Revised Text.

880 – (CLOV *halts at A.*), added for Revised Text.

891 – bon bon (F34, G49). Hyphen removed.

897 – CLOV *slams lid*, added. *He* replaced CLOV.

900 – NAGG's *hands appear, gripping the rim. Then the head emerges* (F35, G49). Although in Berlin Beckett said, 'Nagg comes up just in time to be in position when Clov turns and says, "Do you believe . . ."', Beckett moved Nagg's entrance at Riverside to after Clov's exit 14. Of Clov's line, 'Do you believe in the life to come?', Beckett said in rehearsals that here Clov resurrects the life to come (*Gac(A)*, *Gac(M)*).

906 – 'That it would be you' substituted in the actors' texts for 'That it'd be you' (F35, G49), (*Gac(A)*, *Gac(M)*).

916 – It's finished (F35, G49). See note to 'Finished' (line 24).

921 – . . . it's story time . . . (F35, G50). In *Riverside Nb*, Beckett notes the analogy between Hamm's story and Nagg's: 'Tailor's story: analogy voice and attitude with H's [Hamm's].' Furthermore, Haerdter summarizes Beckett on this play within a play as follows: Four voices have to be connected with distinct attitudes. First Hamm carries on a monologue; second, he speaks to the beggar he is imagining lying at his feet; third, he lends the latter his own voice, and he uses the fourth to recite the epic, linking text of his own story. Each voice corresponds to a distinct attitude. Moreover, as Hamm changes his posture to address the beggar lying at his feet, for instance, movement and dialogue need always to be separated. First the change of posture, followed by an ordering pause, then the voice. Such movements on Hamm's part are also difficult and painful. 'Hamm is fenced in,' says Beckett, 'crippled; it is an effort for him to bend forward, to reach out his arm.' (See note to 'You don't want to abandon him?' (line 1488).)

The atmospheric reports amid Hamm's dialogue are to be spoken as though they were 'filler' while Hamm is inventing his story, thinking about how to continue it. The numerical readings also suggest a formal, circular structure to the tale, 0–50–100–0. The return to zero foretells the play's future progress (*Berlin Diary*).

At the Riverside Studios, Rick Cluchey, playing Hamm at the time, asked Beckett directly if the little boy in Hamm's story is actually the young Clov. 'Don't know if it's the story of the young Clov or not,' was Beckett's response. 'Simply don't know.'

926, 929, 934 – Well, what is it *you* want? (F35, G51). There should be an increasing intensification to Hamm's three questions: 'Well, what is it *you* want?'; 'Well, what ill wind blows you my way?'; and 'Come on now, what is the object of this invasion?'

950 – I have to put up my holly (F36, G52). Hamm's narrative is set on Christmas Eve and suggests another cycle, as the narrator, a thinly veiled version of Hamm himself, fails to show much mercy towards a traveller and his child. Cf. Hamm's later regret, 'All those I might have helped . . . Saved!' (line 1243).

956 – NAGG *reacts*. (F36, G52), i.e., makes sucking noises (*Gac(A), Gac(M)*).

979 – *Enter* CLOV (F37, G54). Clov heads directly for Hamm with news of having discovered a rat in the kitchen. The rat presents a potential threat to Hamm, who worries whether or not the rat can escape. See also note to 'He doesn't need to go far' (line 1271).

997 – *Attitudes of prayer* (F38, G55). Beckett's concern in his direction was with the symmetry of the three sets of praying hands. Each character was to come to the end of his prayer separately, one by one. The attitude of prayer was to be achieved quickly, hands together on Hamm's 'off we go', eyes closed, then successive reopening and ostentatious lowering of hands.

999 – What a hope! (F38, G55). Hamm, Clov and Nagg end prayer attitude with same sounds, Hamm's hands slapping chair, Clov's hands slapping thighs, Nagg's hands hitting rim of bin (*Gac(A), Gac(M)*). Clov's sound, however, was absent from the Schiller production.

1003 – 'just', added in Riverside (*Gac(A), Gac(M)*).

1005 – 'You'll never get any more sugar-plums', added in *Fac(B)*. Note in *Gac(A)* is 'to Nagg with relish'.

1016 – Besides I didn't listen to you (F38). The American text drops this line, which Beckett reinstated at Riverside Studios for those using American editions (*Gac(A), Gac(M)*).

1018 – Yes, I hope I'll live till then . . . (F38, G56). Hamm begins to shrink away from the mounting violence of Nagg's 'malediction' (Beckett's word, see also note to 'In my house' (line 653)). Clov meanwhile relishes Hamm's embarrassment (*Gac(A), Gac(M)*).

1023 – Our revels now are ended (F39, G56). The line, an allusion to *The Tempest*, IV. i. 148, opens the second half of *Endgame*. When it was still a two-act play, the first act ended with Nagg's realization of Nell's (apparent) death. Act II began with the allusion to *The Tempest*. In Berlin, Beckett emphasized the allusion to Shakespeare's play by substituting Schlegel's translation of the line from *The Tempest* for Tophoven's translation of Beckett's French. 'Das Fest is jest zu Ende' replaced 'Der Spass ist zu Ende.' In London, Beckett said that the pause that introduces this line should be the longest in the play.

1029 – HAMM *throws away the dog* (F39, G57). In London Beckett said, 'He doesn't like the feel of him . . . He hasn't any sex' (*Gac(M)*).

1033–4 – CLOV *straightens up* . . . in order (F39, G57). 'Putting things in order' was transposed with the stage direction (*Fac(B)*). To be delivered with the same tone as 'If age but knew' (line 182), very softly spoken (*Gac(A), Gac(M)*).

1037 – I love order (F39, G57). Like Bruno's vision, Clov's sense of order is itself circular and emphasizes the fundamental paradox to the second law of thermodynamics, entropy, according to which all systems, the universe included, are running down, moving towards greater and greater levels of disorder. The end result, however, is the perfectly equal distribution of energy, at which time motion stops and we have, 'A world where all would be silent and still and each thing in its last place.' That is, even according to the principles of contemporary physics, especially chaos theory, the points of maximum disorder and maximum order are identical. See also the discussion of Bruno in note to 'Finished' (line 24).

1043 – *drops* (F39, G57). *throws* replaced *drops* in *Gac(A)* and *Gac(M)* and Clov threw them *strongly* near Hamm. For the Revised Text, however, Beckett retained *drops*.

1046 – What's wrong with your feet? (F39, G58). Allan Mandell's note on this dialogue is 'feverish and urgent'. Just after this exchange Beckett noted to his cast at Riverside Studios, 'The danger throughout is slowness' (*Gac(A), Gac(M)*). In Walter Asmus's copy, he notes of the play in general, 'Keep it moving' (*Gac(A)*). See also note to 'You've got on with it, I hope' (line 1065).

1053 – (CLOV *moves.*), added after 'I'll leave you' (F39, G58).

1058 – (*Moving to* HAMM), added (*Fac(B)*).

1058 – Oh, by the way, your story? (F40, G58). For this entire exchange Clov's right shoulder is up against the left side of Hamm's chair (*Gac(A), Gac(M)*).

1065 – You've got on with it, I hope (F40, G59). Said with exaggerated interest as of a great author by an admiring journalist. Of this entire exchange, Beckett said, 'The livelier the exchange, the more value in the pause' (*Gac(M)*).

1067 – one (F40, G59). 'you' revised to 'one' (*Fac(B)*).

1076 – He comes crawling on his belly – (F40, G59). Clov looks where Hamm is pointing. The following exchange should also move quickly (*Gac(A), Gac(M)*).

1082 – whining for bread for his brat (F40, G60). In the 1976 Royal Court production, Beckett made the following comment at the final dress rehearsal: 'I've got an idea. If you don't think it will work don't do it. So it'll go like this: "It wouldn't be the bread, ha–ha, ha–ha, or the brat." They laugh a little louder.' Beckett retained these two laughs for the Riverside production.

1107 – 'Don't' replaced 'Do' (F41, G61), (*Gac(A), Gac(M)*).

1117 – Go and see is she dead (F41, G62). When German actress Gudrun Genest asked Beckett directly if Nell had died, he answered smilingly, 'So it seems, but no one knows' (although in the *Schiller Nb* Beckett clearly indicates that she is dead). When Clov checks to see if Nagg and Nell are dead, Hamm raises his cap and, after Clov closes the two ashbins, he puts it on as a third 'lid', a third note of the chord. Beckett also indicated that a 'new feeling' is arising at this point in Clov because the death of Nell suggests the possibility of change; 'a confusion, a lack of understanding', which then recurs in Clov's final monologue. That is, this is the point at which the play's ending is prepared for (*Berlin Diary*). In Riverside, Clov's announcement of Nell's death was delivered like 'good news'; the fact that Nagg still lived was delivered as 'bad news'. Throughout this section, Clov was 'very clean and formal with the bins', closing lids softly (*Gac(A), Gac(M)*).

1123 – *peeps* replaced *looks* (F41, G62), (*Gac(A)*, *Gac(M)*).

1135 – I want to feel the light on my face (F42, G62), see note for *Wipes on gown* (line 1479).

1149 – What window is it? (F42, G62). In Riverside, Hamm actually said, 'What window are we?' (*Gac(A)*, *Gac(M)*), but Beckett never made the change in his copy, *Fac(B)*.

1172 – *marks time audibly* replaced *gets up on the ladder, opens the window* (F43, G65) (see also notes to *marks time audibly* (lines 128 and 132)). In Riverside, Clov actually kicked the ladder rhythmically to feign ascent, and so the scene became another of Clov's deceptions. Clov kicked with his right foot, and the sound was to echo Clov's knocks on Hamm's chair, and Hamm's taps on the wall (*Gac(A)*, *Gac(M)*).

1182 – It's because there are no more navigators (F43, G65). Beckett said to Patrick Magee and Donald McWhinnie, 'It's not worth the waves' while being angry because there are no more navigators to drown' (Magee interview with McMillan/Fehsenfeld).

1186 – *closes the window, gets down* (F43, G65), cut. Descent is feigned again by Clov's rhythmically kicking the ladder.

1189 – *at A* replaced *beside the chair* (F43, G65), (*Gac(A)*, *Gac(M)*).

1191 – *No sounds from* NAGG replaced *Unintelligible words* (F43, G66), (*Gac(A)*, *Gac(M)*). One might expect that the *unintelligible words* of the original text might as well have come from Clov. All that seems to have been prohibited in Beckett's revised stage direction is sound from Nagg, so that potentially this scene contains another of Clov's deceptions.

1205 – The dead go fast (F44, G66). The French version, 'Pauvres morts!' is more clearly an allusion to Baudelaire: 'Les pauvres morts, les pauvres morts, ils ont de grandes douleurs.'

1208 – *goes towards door, stopped at A by* replaced *returns to his place beside the chair* (F44, G67) in *Fac(B)*, but Beckett revised the line again for the Revised Text.

1232 – (*He takes out his handkerchief, unfolds it, holds it spread out before him*) (F44, G68), cut. Both references to handkerchief are cut in Hamm's monologue, but in *Fac(B)*, there is a question mark in the margin beside each. The cuts, however, were clearly made in Riverside.

1233 – (*He folds the handkerchief, puts it back in his pocket, raises his head*) (F44, G68), cut.

1234 – Helped! . . . Saved! (F44, G68). 'A cosmic resentment with human beings,' Beckett said of these lines (*Gac(M)*).

1237 – Lick your neighbour as yourself! (F44, G68). Compare this ironic version to the original commandment in Matthew, 19:19.

1239 – Out of my sight . . . (F44, G69). 'Left hand gestures away the crawlers – a sweeping gesture' (*Gac(A)*, *Gac(M)*).

1240 – The end is in the beginning (F44, G69). See note to 'Finished' (line 24).

1247 – refuge (F45, G69). The American text prints 'shelter' which Beckett revised to the British 'refuge' (*Gac(A)*, *Gac(M)*).

1249 – I'll have called my father and I'll have called my . . . my son (F45, G69). 'Please, no pathos on "father" and "son",' warned Beckett. '"Son" can have an ironic touch instead. What is meant here is that which has served me as a son.' Beckett further noted, 'Pathos is the death of the play' (*Berlin Diary*).

1255 – like the solitary child who turns himself into children (F45, G70). This paradoxical image of creativity, unity in division, is used again in *That Time* where the protagonist of narrative A would hide as a child, 'making up talk breaking up two or more talking to himself being together that way' (*Collected Shorter Plays of Samuel Beckett* (London, Faber and Faber, 1984), p. 233).

1258 – that old Greek (F45, G70). Of Hamm's display of learning, Beckett said, 'Spinning his sophistries in the sand' (*Gac(A)*, *Gac(M)*).

1258 – all life long you wait for that to mount up to a life (F45, G70), see note to 'Grain upon grain' (line 25).

1261 – *at A* replaced *beside the chair* (F45, G70).

1271 – He doesn't need to go far (F45, G71). Clov takes great pleasure in announcing the escape of the rat. Hamm is helpless, seated, unable to move, and the half-dead rat will eventually get him. Of this report of the rat's escape and Clov's tormenting Hamm about the possibility of pain-killer only to announce 'There's no more pain-killer' (line 1277), Beckett said during Riverside rehearsals, 'One of the cruellest sections of the play' (*Gac(M)*).

1279 – 'God' replaced 'Good' (F46, G71), (*Gac(A)*, *Gac(M)*).

1287 – (*Puts clock first on* NAGG's *bin, then after thought on* NELL's.) replaced (CLOV *sees the picture, takes it down, stands it on the floor with its face to wall, hangs up the alarm-clock in its place.*) (F46, G72). That is, Clov realizes that Nagg may come up again but Nell won't, and so he moves the clock to Nell's bin.

1290 – (CLOV *moves towards door, stopped at A by*:), added.

1293 – Since it's calling to you (F46, G72). Hamm recognizes here Clov's interest in the without. The line should come out choked and so provide motivation for Clov's response, 'Would you like a lozenge?' Clov's proffered medication is, of course, a poor substitute for pain-killer.

1301 – Deleted passage (F46, G72–3). In *Riverside Nb* Beckett suggested to himself, 'Consider cutting song', and in *Fac(B)* Beckett noted of the following section, 'Cut?' In rehearsals, however, Beckett definitely decided yes. The following lines were cut to eliminate all reference to the song:

(CLOV *goes, humming, towards window right, halts before it, looks up at it.*)

HAMM: Don't sing.

CLOV: (*Turning towards Hamm.*) One hasn't the right to sing any more?

HAMM: No.

CLOV: Then how can it end?

HAMM: You want it to end?

CLOV: I want to sing.

HAMM: I can't prevent you.

Clov's response to Hamm's 'No', 'Then how can it end?', was doubtless an allusion to the French proverb *Tout se termine par des chansons* (Everything ends with song). See also the end of *Happy Days*.

1302 – *Clov turns towards window right* (F46, G73), cut.

1309, 1311 – mug (F47, G73). Beckett revised 'fool' of the American edition to the 'mug' of the English.

1347 – You know what she died of, Mother Pegg? Of darkness (F48, G75). At least one critic has identified this story of Mother Pegg with the Parable of the Foolish Virgins (Matthew 25 : 1–13), which is itself like the story of the two thieves crucified with Christ that so haunts Vladimir in *Waiting for Godot* and Hamm's own narrative, a tale of salvation and damnation (Kristin Morrison, 'Neglected Biblical Allusions in Beckett's Plays: 'Mother Pegg Once More', *Samuel Beckett: Humanistic Perspectives*, edited by Morris Beja, S. E. Gontarski and Pierre Astier (Ohio State University Press, Columbus, Ohio, 1983), 91–8):

Then shall the kingdom of heaven be likened unto ten virgins, which took their lamps, and went forth to meet the bridegroom.
And five of them were wise, and five were foolish.
They that were foolish took their lamps, and took no oil with them:
But the wise took oil in their vessels with their lamps.
While the bridegroom tarried, they all slumbered and slept. And at midnight there was a cry made, Behold, the bridegroom cometh; go ye out to meet him.
Then all those virgins arose, and trimmed their lamps.
And the foolish said unto the wise, Give us of your oil; for our lamps are gone out.
But the wise answered, saying, Not so; lest there be not enough for us and you: but go ye rather to them that sell, and buy for yourselves.
And while they went to buy, the bridegroom came; and they that were ready went in with him to the marriage: and the door was shut.

Afterward came also the other virgins, saying, Lord, Lord, open to us.
But he answered and said, Verily I say unto you, I know you not.
Watch therefore, for ye know neither the day nor the hour wherein the Son of man cometh.

The allusion seems to justify Hamm's refusal to share his commodities, his grain and oil. That is, he was not about to share his oil with the foolish virgin and miss the opportunity for his own salvation. Apparently, Hamm can even find biblical precedent for his selfishness. Of the direct allusion, however, Beckett said, 'unintended'.

1351 – Have you the glass? (F48, G75). Hamm is, of course, changing the subject.

1355 – *He gets down. He starts to get down, halts* (F48, G75) replaced by *He gets down* which is brought forward.

1356 – (*He gets down.*) (F48, G75) has been cut here as it has been brought forward to Line 1355.

1359 – Oh you won't find it easy . . . (F48, G76), i.e. when Hamm is dead (*Gac(A), Gac(M)*).

1361 – I'm tired of our goings on, very tired (F48, G76). The actors' notes at this point say, 'slow, weary' (*Gac(A), Gac(M)*).

1361 – Deleted passage (F48, G76). The following exchange was cut:

[CLOV:] You're not sitting on it?
> *He moves the chair, looks at the place where it stood, resumes his search.*
HAMM: (*Anguished.*) Don't leave me there! (*Angrily* CLOV *restores the chair to its place.*) Am I right in the centre?

1369 – *on the head* (F48, G76), cut.

1371 – (*The dog falls to the ground. Pause.*) (F49, G77), cut in *Gac(A)* and *Gac(M)*, but restored by Beckett for the Revised Text. In the Riverside production, however, Hamm retained the dog when Clov hit him with it.

1376 – (CLOV *picks up the dog and gives it to* HAMM *who takes it in his arms.*) (F49, G77), cut in *Gac(A)* and *Gac(M)*, but restored by Beckett following *Fac(B)* and the Schiller production so that Hamm has something to discard on line 1496.

1378 – Put me in my coffin (F49, G77). In a preliminary two-act version of *Endgame*, a coffin, the presence of which was denied by both characters, sat on the stage for the entire play. Near the end of the first act of this version, Hamm told his story of the man who has left his son behind and came to the shelter seeking food. Hamm stopped his story at this point to say that he was nearly finished unless he introduced new characters (as he does in lines 976 ff.), but where would he get them. At this point in the manuscript, the lid of the coffin opened, a head

[67]

emerged and looked straight ahead at the audience. The head re-emerged at the opening of the second act, and then again during yet another narrative when Hamm was praying to Thanatos. That overt emphasis on death and the surreal quality of the coffin were cut, but the image survives in this brief reference.

Moreover, the coffin existed before the introduction of the ashbins and may have been their anticipation.

1384 – *raises telescope* (F49, G77), cut (*Gac(A)*, *Gac(M)*).

1386 – *lowering the telescope* (F49, G77), cut (*Gac(A)*, *Gac(M)*)

1394 – (*He starts, lowers the telescope, examines it, turns it again on the without. Pause.*) (F49, G78). This and the following two stage directions were cut to simplify the telescope scene (*Fac(B)*).

1396 – (CLOV *gets down.*) (F49, G78), cut (*Fac(B)*).

1397 – CLOV *moves ladder nearer window, gets up on it, turns telescope on the without* (F49, G78), cut (*Fac(B)*).

1399 – A small . . . boy! (F49, G78). Clancy Sigal reports Beckett's saying, 'There should be nothing out there . . . He wants Clov to see what he's going out into, but if there is something out there alive, it is not as he supposed, and that would be terrible.' ('Is This the Person to Murder Me?' *The Sunday Times* Colour Magazine, 1 March 1964, pp. 17–22.)

1414 – *starts* replaced *goes* (F50, G79), (*Gac(A)*, *Gac(M)*).

1416 – *goes towards door* . . . (F50, G79), cut. Since both the picture and the nail on which it hung had been cut in Riverside, Beckett also cut the following in *Fac(B)*: *goes towards door, halts, looks at alarm-clock, takes it down, looks round for a better place to put it, goes to bins, puts it on lid of* NAGG's *bin. Pause.*

1420 – *at A* replaced *near door* (F50, G79).

1434 – They said to me, That's love . . . (F50, G80). Clov's monologue here is built around what Beckett called 'the five dispensers of life's consolations: 1. "That's love"; 2. "That's friendship"; 3. "that beauty. That order!" – that's nature; 4. "all becomes clear. And simple!" – that's science; and 5. "all these dying of their wounds," that's mercy' (*Berlin Diary*).

1435 – Articulate! (F50, G80). Beckett cut Hamm's interruption of this speech, 'Articulate!' and 'CLOV: (*as before*). How . . .', (*Fac(B)*).

1440 – Enough! (F51, G80). Again Hamm's interruption is cut, (*Fac(B)*), 'Enough!' and 'CLOV: (*as before*).'

1440 – *Moves towards door and back.* This time Hamm's interruption is replaced by Clov's false move towards kitchen. The action here then is a visual analogue to Clov's move towards door in his opening monologue, according to Beckett.

1441 – *To A*, added.

1441 – you must learn to suffer better than that (F51, G80). Beckett notes, 'The notion is that when one has given the tyrant his full account of suffering, he lets the victim go. Only when one has given life its full accounting can one leave it' (*Berlin Diary*).

1448 – I open the door of the cell and go (F51, G81). Beckett notes of Clov that 'the happiness starts' with this line (*Berlin Diary*).

1451 – 'drop' replaced 'fall' (F51, G81).

1462 – *sharply* (F51, G81), cut (*Gac(A)*, *Gac(M)*).

1469 – Me to play (F51, G82). The mood and tempo of Hamm's first and last monologues should be identical, since, as Beckett notes, 'The voice comes out of the silence and returns into silence' (*Berlin Diary*).

1473 – *Panama hat, tweed coat, raincoat over his arm, umbrella, bag* (F51, G82). With sun hat and raincoat, Clov seems prepared for all meteorological contingencies, except that he seems inappropriately dressed for a world in which there is no more nature. Beckett was precise in his arrangement of Clov's objects: bag in left hand with umbrella over it, coat in right hand. This final image of Clov poised ambiguously at the end was a late addition to the play's composition. Through most versions, B (Clov) appears dressed like the boy he purports to have seen outside the shelter. The following summary from the two-act University of Reading manuscript develops the theme of circularity considerably more explicitly. A, apparently convinced that B has departed, seems prepared to accept solitude. The curtain begins to fall. A seems very near his end, and the play itself appears finished. But the curtain halts midway and is raised again. B enters disguised as the boy (red hat, grey shirt, trousers rolled over thighs, sandals), assumes the child's voice, is obedient to A, says his name is Edward, age and place of origin unknown. A questions him about whether or not he has passed anyone on the way into the shelter, some kind of old scarecrow or a body lying on the kitchen floor. The boy has not, and A begins the process of accepting the boy into his service, offering him some milk chocolate.

For the New York première of 1958, the director, Alan Schneider, had added some embellishments to Clov's attire. Clov appeared wearing the raincoat, carried a pair of skis in his right hand, a suitcase with a canoe paddle tied to it in his left, a knapsack on his back, and a climbing rope over his left shoulder.

1476 – 'No?' added in Riverside (*Gac(A)*, *Gac(M)*), but not included in *Fac(B)*.

1479 – *Wipes on gown* replaced *He takes out his handkerchief and, without unfolding it, wipes his glasses* (F52, G83). In Berlin, the glasses were wiped on the dog with one hand, partly, no doubt, to avoid use of the handkerchief. In Riverside they were wiped on the front of Hamm's lapel. As at the opening, the gesture also contains a fundamental irony as the blind Hamm cleans his glasses. In the untitled two-act version of *Fin de partie* on deposit at the University of Reading, the Hamm-like A says, 'Allez, dépêche-toi, the night cometh etc.' (Come on, hurry up . . .) The English quotation in the midst of the French text is an allusion to John 9:4, the miracle of Jesus's curing the man born blind: 'I must work the works of him that sent me, while it is day: the night cometh, when no man can work.' The allusion resonates (perhaps too directly) throughout the play, as it suggests not only a cliché about work but also A's desire for a miracle to cure his blindness. A desires light; he asks to be brought to the window so that he can feel the light on his face. The line (1135) was spoken as if it were a fond memory (*Gac(A)*, *Gac(M)*).

Much of the light imagery in the play is associated with life and hope, and Hamm's continued interest in light suggests again his reluctance to abandon 'the game'. Hamm refuses to share his light with the dying Mother Pegg. Like Mother Pegg, A too is dying of darkness or obscurity. Like Hamm himself, this earlier character is a conflation of sufferers: Christ and the blind man. Suffering on earth, dying of lack of light, he can neither cure nor be cured, and in turn he is the denier of light or hope to others, among them Mother Pegg, who dies of darkness. The only trace of this allusion that remains in the final version of the play is Hamm's wiping his glasses. It is a bitter joke, but all the more bitter seen against this allusion to John, where Jesus cures the blind man by annointing his eyes with clay and then having him wash his eyes clean. In a world turned perpetually grey, Hamm is trying to wipe his own eyes clear.

1480 – *puts back the handkerchief in his pocket* (F52, G83), cut in *Gac(A)* but not in *Fac(B)*. Beckett did, however, make the cut for this Revised Text. *Gac(A)* and *Gac(M)* have contradictory notes on this scene. At first, apparently, Hamm was to take out the handkerchief, unfold it once, wipe the glasses on it, then leave the handkerchief on his lap. In rehearsals, however, the change was made to wipe the glasses on the gown, and these current revisions are consistent with that change.

1481 – *A little poetry* (F52, G83). This poignant little poem is Hamm's rendering of the opening quatrain of Baudelaire's sonnet, 'Recueillement' ('Recollection'), No. CLIX in *Les fleurs du mal*:

> Sois sage, ô ma Douleur, et tiens-toi plus tranquille.
> Tu réclamais le Soir; il descend; le voici:
> Une atmosphère obscure enveloppe la ville,
> Aux uns portant la paix, aux autres le souci.

In Riverside, Hamm's poem was introduced by 'and now' before 'A little poetry', but Beckett did not make the change part of the Revised Text.

1486 – and story ended (F52, G83). Again, however, Hamm is reluctant to end. Immediately after announcing the end of his narrative, Hamm resumes it, introducing an underplot: (*Pause. Narrative tone:*).

1488 – You don't want to abandon him? (F52, G83). These three questions should be spoken with a threefold intensification. Moreover, in the following narrative, the placement of father and son should be precise. When the 'son' is addressed (i.e., 'He doesn't realize . . .'), Hamm should look, again painfully, to his right. When the son's father is addressed (i.e., 'But you! You ought to know . . .'), Hamm should bend and point front left to the (imagined) man lying at his feet (*Berlin Diary*). (See also textual note to '. . . it's story time . . .' (line 921) and the *Introduction*, pp. xix–xx, for the separation of gesture and speech.)

1494, 1495 – 'No?' To Hamm's final speech, Beckett added 'No?' twice in *Fac(B)*, each time before a 'Good' (F52, G84). (See also textual note to 'No?' (line 1476).)

1498 – Clov! (F52, G84). As Ruby Cohn suggests, Clov is 'under visible strain, forcing himself not to participate in the ending action' (*Just Play*, p. 244). In Berlin, Beckett added to the tension and symmetry of this moment by having Hamm call Clov a second time. The German photographic edition, *Samuel Beckett inszeniert das 'Endspiel'*, prints this revision. The second 'Clov', however, was not added to the Riverside *Endgame*. Beckett later said of this scene, 'Think I prefer one only, but not sure.'

1499 – CLOV *winces*, added. The wince is Clov's response to Hamm's call. See also the brief discussion of this gesture in the *Introduction*.

1500 – CLOV's *eyes back on* HAMM. HAMM, added.

1500 – HAMM *takes out the handkerchief* (F52, G84). The handkerchief should be folded and unfolded to the rhythm of the four slowly spoken phrases. At the opening and closing of the play, these gestures should be identical (*Berlin Diary*).

1505 – *He covers his face with handkerchief* (F53, G84). Asked if Hamm covers his face in order to die, Beckett responded, 'No, only in order to be more silent' (*Berlin Diary*).

1505 – *drops* replaced *lowered* (F53, G84), (*Gac(A)*, *Gac(M)*).

1506 – *Brief tableau* (F53, G84). Asked by the actors about a curtain call, Beckett responded, 'That's repugnant to me.' He suggested instead that the lights come up several times as Hamm and Clov remain unmoving in their final positions. When the actors agreed, Beckett, relieved, added, 'It would have hurt me to break up the picture at the end' (*Berlin Diary*).

PART II

Samuel Beckett's Production Notebooks
for *Endgame*

Samuel Beckett's Production Notebook
for *Endspiel* (*Endgame*)
at the Schiller-Theater Werkstatt,
Berlin
September 1967

Inoffiel
Berlin aug. sept 1967
(sept. 26)

les pingouins  éditions Sopalin

FACSIMILE OF BECKETT'S PRODUCTION NOTEBOOK
WITH TRANSCRIPTION AND TRANSLATION

Note on the Manuscript

The manuscript of Samuel Beckett's production notes prepared for his own production of *Endspiel* (*Endgame*) at the Schiller-Theater Werkstatt in Berlin in September 1967 is reproduced here from a manuscript notebook donated by Beckett to Reading University Library; the notebook is now part of the Beckett International Foundation's Archive.

This notebook, catalogued as MS 1396/4/5, is a soft-covered exercise book in the 'ZOO éditions Sopalin' series. It measures 22 by 17 cms and contains 36 leaves. The front cover is bright yellow and carries a colour photograph of two King Penguins. The rear cover is white and carries information about the birds. The notebook is lettered on the front in Beckett's hand 'Endspiel Berlin Aug-Sept 1967 (Sept. 26)'. The handwritten foliation on the right-hand pages is by J. A. Edwards, the former Reading archivist, who has numbered the front cover 1 and the notebook leaves 2–37. There are many blank pages – 35 in all – but the book has notes throughout, extending from the first inside leaf to the final page. The facsimile that follows reproduces all pages of the notebook except for double-page blanks, i.e. where neither a verso nor its facing recto is written on.

On the inside front cover there are two numerical listings in which Beckett divides *Endgame* into 16 sections. The first list of 16 refers to the page numbers of the published text that he used for this production. The second lists the same 16 sections in terms of the key moment of that section. The opening page has a fuller version of this second listing. Beckett's own numbering 1–16 on the verso pages refers to these sections, or scenes. The notebook includes several diagrams which detail the stage movements of Clov but also head movements for the three immobile characters, Hamm, Nagg and Nell. The manuscript is written in German and English and is in blue ink.

Quotations in the transcript are not literal translations of the German, which might be misleading for the reader working with the English text. Instead, the corresponding phrase from the English text is used. Since those phrases are readily recognizable to anyone working closely with Beckett's text and since Beckett's notebooks progress methodically through the scenes he outlines, additional page references were deemed unnecessarily cumbersome for the notebook transcription.

Minor anomalies are generally omitted from the transcription. Substantive differences are cited in the notes beginning on page 172, which are keyed to the editorial pagination (in italics in square brackets at the head of each page). When a cancelled line is legible it is included between angle brackets, <>.

```
1   9-11          2
2  11-29         18        30
3  31-41         10                 58
4  41-49          8
5  49-55          6    72    28
6  55-59          4
7  59-69         10
8  69-83         14
9  83-89          6
10 89-93          4        26
11 93-101         8                 54
12 101-105        4    54
13 105-109        4
14 109-113        4
15 113-133       20        28
16 133-137        4

                126
```

```
1  ⌐           9-13
2  ⌐          13-15
                15
```

```
1 ⎤
2 ⎥  30
3 ⎦

4 ⎤
5 ⎥
6 ⎥  42
7 ⎥
8 ⎦

(9)   6

10 ⎤
11 ⎥  20
12 ⎥
13 ⎦

14 ⎤
15 ⎥  28
16 ⎦
```

Clov   1 - 1st Inspection
Hamm "   2
Nagg-Nell   3
1st Ruine   4
2nd Inspection 5
Flea   6
Dog   7
Pegg - Prentwork - madman-Clovin 8
Hamm   9
Naggs curse 10
order - Hamm's story - Nell dead 11
2nd Ruine 12
Rug - Clov's refusal to touch 13
Hamm 14
Rat escaped - no more painK. - 3rd Inspection
Hamm

1. ~~~~ opening · 1ˢᵗ inspection – Aufräumung

2. ~~ Ende ~~~~~ to es geht voran ~~~~~~~

3. ~~ Nagg-Nell scene from Was ist es, mein Dicker to Ruhe! ~~~~~~

4. ~~ man sah bis auf den Grund to Bleib nicht da stehen.. (1ˢᵗ little turn)

5. ~~ Wenn ich ihn töten könnte Könnte to Bleib nicht da stehen.. (2ⁿᵈ inspection)

6. ~~ Warum diese Komödie to Wären wir bedient (Flea)

7. ~~ Und kein pipi to ... mich aufstehen (Hamm's prophecy ~~~~~. Dog)

8. ~~ Ich verlasse dich to still jetzt (mother Pegg – Boathook – mad painter –
alarm clock)

9. ~~ Hamm's story Wo war ich stehen geblieben to Wo soll ich sie suchen

10. ~~ Lass uns zu God beten to .. einzige Hoffnung. / Nell!.. Nell! (Prayer – Nagg's curse)

~~10 Der Spass ist zu Ende ·· wenn ich diese Ratte nicht töte ~~~~~~

~~11 Hamm's monologue / Ich bin wieder dran to ah so weit sein ~~~~~~~~~~~~~~~~~~~~~~~~~~~~~~

~~12 ~~~~~~~~~~~~~~~~~~~~~~~

11. ~~10 Der Spass ist zu Ende ... nicht, dass ich wüsste (Clov's dream of order –
~~~~~~~~~~~~~~~~~~ news of Hamm's story – Nell dead)

12. ~~11 Fahr mich unter's Fenster to bleib nicht da stehen (second turn)

13. ~~12 Vater! to wenn ich diese Ratte nicht töte ·· ja ja (Ring – Clov's
refusal to touch Hamm)

14. ~~13 Hamm's self prophetic monologue Ich bin wieder dran to Ah so
weit sein

15. ~~14 Sieh mal an! to Wir entlasten einander (Rat escaped –
no more painkiller – 3ʳᵈ inspection – mutual dismissal)

16. ~~15 Hamm's last monologue (Noch etwas to Dich behalte ich)

1¹	9– 11	2
2	11– 29	18
3	31– 41	10
4	41– 49	8
5	49– 55	6
6	55– 59	4
7	59– 69	10
8	69– 83	14
9	83– 89	6
10	89– 93	4
11	93–101	8
12	101–105	4
13	105–109	4
14	109–113	4
15	113–133	20
16	133–137	4

126

30   58

72   28

[erasure]

26   54

54   28

1		[erasure] Clov 1 – 1st inspection
2	30	Hamm ” 2
3		Nagg–Nell 3
4		1st Runde [round] 4
5	42	2nd inspection 5
6		Flea 6
7		Dog 7
8		Pegg – Boat hook – Madman – Alarm 8
⑨	6	Hamm 9
10		Nagg[’]s curse 10
11	20	Order – Hamm's story – Nell dead 11
12		2nd Runde [round] 12
13		Rug – Clov's refusal to touch 13
14		Hamm 14
15	28	Rat escaped – no more pain k. [killer] – 3rd inspection
16		Hamm

1. [*erasure*] Opening. 1st inspection – unveiling

2. [*erasure*] <u>Ende</u> [Finished] [*erasure*] to <u>[E]s geht voran</u> [We're getting on] [*erasure*]

3. [*erasure*] Nagg–Nell scene from <u>Was ist es, mein Dicker</u>[1] [What is it, my pet?] to <u>Ruhe!</u> [Silence!] [*erasure*]

4. [*erasure*] <u>Man sah bis auf den Grund</u> [You could see down to the bottom] to <u>Bleib nicht da stehen . .</u> [!][2] [Don't stay there . . . !] (1st little turn)

5. [*erasure*] <u>Wenn ich ihn töten Könnte</u> [I could kill him] <u>Könnte</u> to <u>Bleib nicht da stehen . .</u>[3] [Don't stay there . . .] (2nd inspection)

6. [*erasure*] <u>Warum diese Komödie</u> [Why this farce] to <u>Wären wir bedient</u>[4] [We'd be bitched] (flea)

7. [*erasure*] <u>Und dein Pipi</u> [What about that pee?] to . . . <u>mich anflehen</u>[5] [. . . imploring me] (Hamm's [*erasure*] prophecy. Dog)

8. [*erasure*] <u>Ich verlasse dich</u>[6] [I'll leave you] to <u>Still jetzt</u> [Silence!] (Mother Pegg – Boathook – mad painter – alarm clock)

9. [*erasure*] Hamm's story <u>Wo war ich stehengeblieben</u> [Where was I?] to <u>Wo soll ich sie suchen</u> [Where would I look for them?]

10. [*erasure*] <u>Lass uns zu Gott beten</u>[7] [Let us pray to God] to <u>. . einzige Hoffnung. Nell! . . . Nell!</u> [. . . your only hope. Nell! . . . Nell!] (Prayer – Nagg's curse)
    [*erasure*]
    [*erasure*]
    [*erasure*]

11. [*erasure*] <u>Der Spass ist zu Ende</u>[8] [Our revels now are ended] . . . <u>Nicht, dass ich wüsste</u> [Not to my knowledge] (Clov's dream of order – [*erasure*] news of Hamm[']s story – Nell dead)

12. [*erasure*] <u>Fahre mich unters Fenster</u> [Bring me under the window] to <u>bleib nicht da stehen</u> [Don't stay there] (second turn)

13. [*erasure*] <u>Vater!</u> [Father!] to <u>Wenn ich diese Ratte nicht töte . . Ja, ja</u> [If I don't kill that rat he'll die . . . That's right] (Rug – Clov's refusal to touch Hamm)

14. [*erasure*] Hamm's self-prophetic monologue <u>Ich bin wieder dran</u> [Me to play] to <u>Ah so weit sein</u> [Ah, let's get it over!]

15. [*erasure*] <u>Sieh mal an!</u> [What?] to <u>Wir entlassen einander</u>[9] [It's we are obliged to each other] (Rat escaped – no more painkiller – 3rd inspection – mutual dismissal)

16. [*erasure*] Hamm's last monologue (<u>Noch etwas</u>) [One thing more] to <u>Dich behalte ich</u> [You . . . remain]

I

~~Clor exit 1~~
~~" exit~~
~~1st mention of grains~~
~~menge~~

Clor exit 1 (for ladder)
Clor entrance 1
Clor exit 2 (with sheets)
"   entrance 2
"   exit 3 (with ladder

1st mention of ~~the~~ grains

Opening. Tableau. Clov bowed head. Then Clov's eyes to Hamm, to bins (if nec. slight move forward), to sea window (if nec. slight move back) to earth window. Then a moment still with bowed head. Then suddenly off.

Ladder to earth window. Draws back curtain. Ladder to sea window. Draws back curtain. Ladder to earth window. Looks at earth. Laugh. Ladder to sea window, looks out. Laugh. Starts with ladder towards ashcans, sets it down, unveils cans. Laugh. To Hamm with cane sheet, unveils Hamm. Laugh. [...] two sheets towards door, halts, turns and (speaks). Exit comes back for ladder, exit with ladder.

i.e. forgetting of ladder between windows? at O, ondoning his place near chair.

1¹ <Clov exit 1>

  <   ”   exit>

  <1st mention of grains>

  [*erasure*]

  Clov exit 1 (for ladder)

  Clov entrance 1

  Clov exit 2 (with sheets)

    ”   entrance 2

    ”   exit 3 (with ladder)

  1st mention of [*erasure*] grains

[*erasure*] Opening. Tableau. Clov bowed head. Then [*erasure*] Clov[']s eyes
to Hamm, to bins (if nec. [necessary] slight move forward), to sea window
(if nec. [necessary] slight move back) to earth window. Then a moment
still with bowed head. Then suddenly off.

    Ladder to earth window. Draws back curtain. Ladder to sea
window. Draws back curtain. Ladder to earth window, looks at
earth. Laugh. Ladder to sea window, looks out. Laugh.
Starts with ladder towards ashcans, sets it down, unveils cans.
Laugh. To Hamm with can sheets, unveils Hamm. Laugh.
With two sheets towards door, halts, turns and speaks. Exit[.]
[*erasure*] Comes back for ladder, exit with ladder.

    i.e. no forgetting of ladder between windows?[1]
    at O, meaning his place near chair.

früher 1

2

Clov entrance ~~♦~~ 3
once (früher) **2**
pardon 1
painkiller 1
Clov's eyes & legs 1
no more 1 (bicycle wheels)
I'll leave you 1
Clov exit **4**
Nagg entrance 1
Clov entrance **4**
no more 2 (pap)
Clov exit **5**
Es geht voran 1

Clov entrance ♦   ← I'm back again 1 (biscuit)
5
Clov can't sit 1
no more 3 (nature)
painkiller 2
I'll leave you 2
pardon 2
g rains 2
evening like any other 1
Something taking its course 1
Clov exit **6**
Es geht voran 2

Clov's first move towards door (ich hol das Tuch) very small.

" second " (also, lauf!) ~~perhaps quite~~ small, ~~perhaps~~ ~~smaller~~

Does Clov notice emergence of Nagg (manchmal zu Ross)? Does Hamm? ~~Both Hamm no~~, Hamm no, Clov yes to bring attention on Nagg. Change his time to Ich verlasse euch ??

Clov entrance 4: stops at his place near chair.

　　　　　　　　5: direct to Nagg behind / before

Hamm saying 1st back again on his way

After has kleine Tugend at bins and starts back towards door. Stopped ~~the~~ 1 by setz dich herauf ~~and on~~ + still hat jeder seine Spezialität. Then on first stopped again by kein Auftrag and still füll mir auch nicht. Then on still stopped by Clov at O.

on ich verlasse dich 2 more towards door stopped by In seiner Küche.

on ich verlasse dich 1 " " " " "

by Draussen ist der Tod and resumed after Gut geh hin

Clov towards Hamm or (away) back on Nein Hast du geblubet ←

2   früher[1] [formerly] 1

·Clov entrance [*erasure*] 3

once (früher) 2

pardon[2] 1

pain killer 1

Clov's eyes and legs 1

no more 1 (bicycle wheels)

I'll leave you 1

Clov exit 4

Nagg entrance 1

Clov entrance 4

no more 2 (pap)

Clov exit 5

Es geht voran[3] [We're getting on] 1

Clov entrance [*erasure*] ←————————

5   I'm back again 1 (biscuit)

Clov can't sit 1

no more 3 (nature)

pain killer 2

I'll leave you 2

pardon 2

grains 2

evening like any other 1

something taking its course 1

Clov exit 6

es geht voran [We're getting on] 2

Clov's first move towards door (<u>Ich hol[e] das Tuch</u> [I'll go and get the sheet])
very small.

" second " (<u>Also, lauf!</u> [Then move!]) \<perhaps quite\> very small [*erasure*]
[*erasure*]

Does Clov notice emergence of Nagg (<u>Manchmal zu Ross</u> [Sometimes on horse])?
Does Hamm?

[*erasure*]: Hamm no, Clov yes[,] to bring attention
on Nagg. Change his line to <u>Ich verlasse euch</u> [I'll leave you] ??[1]

Clov entrance 4: stops at his place near chair.

" " 5: direct to Nagg behind/before
Hamm[,] saying 1st <u>back again</u> on his way
<u>Alter hat keine Tugend</u> [If age but knew] at bins and starts back
towards door. Stopped [*erasure*] 1 by <u>Setz dich drauf</u> [sit on him!]
[*erasure*] & still till <u>Jedem seine Spezialität</u> [Every man his speciality]
Then on till stopped again by <u>Kein Anruf</u> [No phone calls?] and
still till <u>Mir auch nicht</u> [Nor I] Then on till stopped by <u>Clov</u> at 0.[2]
On <u>Ich verlasse dich</u> [I'll leave you] 2 move towards door stopped
by <u>In deiner Küche</u> [In your kitchen]
On <u>Ich verlasse dich</u> 1 [I'll leave you 1] 1 [move towards door stopped]
by <u>Draussen ist der Tod</u> (Outside here it's death] and resumed after <u>Gut[,] geh
nur</u> [All right, be off]
Clov towards Hamm at <u>Hast du geblutet</u> [Have you bled] &
back away on <u>Nein</u> [No]

3   once 3 (gestern)
    cold 1 (Nagg & Nell)
    once 4 (früher)
    once 5 (gestern)
    tears 1 (Nell)
    Warum diese Komödie 1
    Hamm's headheart 1 (es tröpft ..)
       "   "   2 (Äderchen)

3 once 3 (gestern [yesterday])

   cold[1] 1 (Nagg & Nell)

   once 4 (früher [once])

   once 5 (gestern [yesterday])

   tears[2] 1 (Nell)

   Warum diese Komödie [Why this farce] 1

   Hamm's headheart 1 (Es tropft . . [There's something dripping])

     ,,   ,,   2 (Äderchen [vein])

4   Clov entrance #6
    painkiller 3
    bleib nicht da stehen 1

Entrance 6. Does clor receive order ~~stop~~
at 0 or on his way clwc?

Nell raises hand to resist closing of lid
and say ~~sogleich~~ hau doch ab. Clor
takes pulse of this hand and closes lid
before saying Sie hat keinen Puls mehr and
following exchange under Wir werden die
Decke verwischen on which he hastens towards
door & is stopped on a little short of 0 by
1ᵗᵉ es litt nicht and at 0 by 2ᵘᵈ.

Clor, first (single) move towards Hamm
to say Es ist zu früh etc and back away on Er ist natürlich etc

1ᵗᵉ Runde

1. Nicht zu schnell
2. Scharf an der Wand etc.
3 Ich stand doch genau etc
4. Wir müssten etc.
5. Scharf an der Wand etc
6. Es ist ~~nicht~~ ~~wieder~~ etc
7. Stopp!

Du fragst mich das .: — same quality as Was hast du
eigentlich heute (8)

    4 Clov entrance <4> 6
      pain killer 3
      bleib nicht da stehen [Don't stay there] 1

on [erasure] <u>Hau doch ab</u> [Desert]

Entrance 6.[1] Does Clov receive order [erasure]
at o or on his way there?
Nell raises hand to resist closing of lid
and say[s] [erasure] <u>Hau doch ab</u> [Desert]. Clov
takes pulse of this hand and closes lid
before saying <u>Sie hat keinen Puls mehr</u> [She has no pulse] and
following exchange until <u>Wir werden die</u>
<u>Deckel vernieten</u> [Screw down the lids] on which he hastens towards
door & is stopped [erasure] a little short of o by
1st <u>Es eilt nicht</u> [Time enough] and at o by 2nd.
    Clov's first (slight) move towards Hamm
to say <u>Es ist zu früh</u> [It's too soon] etc. and back away on <u>Er ist natürlich</u> [He's
dead naturally] etc.

<u>1st Runde</u> [round]   1. Nicht zu schnell [Not too fast][2]
                 2. Scharf an der Wand [Hug the walls] etc.
                 3. Ich stand doch genau [I was right in the centre] etc.
    [sketch]   4. Wir müssten [We'd need] etc.
                 5. Scharf an der Wand [Are you hugging] etc.
                 6. Es <ist nicht wahr> stimmt nicht [It's a lie] etc.
                 7. Stop!

    [sketch]

<u>Du</u> fragst <u>mich</u> das [You ask me that]: same quality as <u>Was hast du</u>
<u>eigentlich heute</u> [What's the matter with you today] (8) [i.e., section 8]

5 Clov exit 4 (for glass)
" entrance 5 7
I'm back again 2 (glass)
Clov exit 8 (for ladder)
" entrance 8
I'm back again 3 (ladder)
Clov exit 9 (for glass)
" entrance 9
bleib nicht da stehen 2

(without stopping)

Entrance 7 . Slight deviation towards Hamm to say *Ich bin wieder 2* , then straight to window and stop looking up. Then slight deviation towards Hamm to say without stopping *Ich brauche die Leiter* and out without meaning to Hamm's *warum etc* . Then slight deviation towards to say without stopping *Ich bin wieder 3* , then straight to window + up ladder. Then down a slight deviation towards Hamm to say without stopping *Ich brauche das Fernglas*. Then stopped mean over by *Du hast Zeit etc* + turn to for reply, then out . Then slight deviation towards Hamm to say without stopping *es wird wieder Zeit* + straight to window + up .

Indicate forgetting of ladder when going to the window

From sea window : ~~looking + Hat see subject + and der Schiff glass ~~ looks , starts , checks glass , looks + says. Looking *hat man je etc* . Continued looking a moment after Hamm's *Was etc* then turns to say *Der Leuchtturm etc* and no more looking.

Only 2 grau from ladder

~~Deputy Chair's dropping telescope + scratch knife one ~~
~~offen Nicht Wenn Vielleicht ~~

~~2nd movement towards Hamm with desp. ~~
~~High light you want to Bück Nichten ~~

5 Clov exit 7 (for glass)
  ,, entrance <5> 7
I'm back again 2 (glass)
Clov exit 8 (for ladder)
  ,, entrance 8
I'm back again 3 (ladder)
Clov exit 9 (for glass)
  ,, entrance 9
bleib nicht da stehen [Don't stay there] 2

Entrance 7. Slight deviation towards Hamm to say without stopping
Ich bin wieder [I'm back again] <u>2</u>, then straight to window and stop
looking up. Then slight deviation towards Hamm to
say without stopping <u>Ich brauche die Leiter</u> [I need the steps] and out
without reacting to Hamm's <u>Warum</u> [Why?] <u>etc.</u> Then
slight deviation towards [Hamm] to say without stopping <u>Ich bin wieder</u>[1] [I'm back
again] <u>3</u>, then straight to window & up ladder. Then
down a [*recte* and] slight deviation towards Hamm to say without
stopping <u>Ich brauche das Fernglas</u> [I need the glass]. Then stopped near
door by <u>Du hast doch</u> [But you have] etc. & turns [*erasure*] for reply, then out.
Then slight deviation towards Hamm to say without
stopping <u>[E]s wird wieder heiter</u> [Things are livening up] & straight to window
& up.

Indicate forgetting of ladder when going to sea window.

From sea window: [*erasure*]
[*erasure*] looks, starts, checks glass,
looks & says looking <u>Hat man je</u> [Never seen anything] <u>etc.</u> Continues looking a moment after Hamm's <u>Was</u> [What] <u>etc.</u>
then turns to say <u>Der Leuchtturm</u> [The light is sunk] <u>etc.</u> and
<u>no more looking</u>[2].

Only 2 <u>Grau</u> [Grey] from ladder.
[*erasure*]
[*erasure*]

6   Warum diese Komödie 2
    something taking its course 2
    Clov exit 10 (for powder)
    "   entrance ● 10
    I'm back again 4 (insecticide)
    are there still 1 (fleas)
    ~~I'm back again (all) 3~~
    ~~"   "   " 4~~
    ~~"   "   " 5~~
    ~~"   "   " 6~~

Warum _ _ Köardte _ same quality as _ lass ans
aufhören, zu spielen 15

Did Chor's _ dropping telescope and scratching till
after Wenn man bedenkt etc.

sonorous elastic ?

6 Warum diese Komödie 2 [Why this farce 2]
  Something taking its course 2
  Clov exit 10 (for powder)
      ” entrance <8> 10
  I'm back again 4 (insecticide)
  Are there still 1 (fleas)[1]
  <I'll leave you (all) 3>[2]
  < ”   ”   ”   4>
  < ”   ”   ”   5>
  < ”   ”   ”   6>

Warum diese Komödie [Why this farce] same quality as <u>Lass uns</u>
<u>aufhören zu spielen</u> [Let's stop playing] 15 [i.e., section 15]
Delay Clov's dropping telescope and scratching till
after <u>Wenn man bedenkt</u> [To think perhaps] etc.

    Sonorous elastic?[1]

7   are there still 2 (sharks)
    painkiller 4
    don't eyes 2 legs 2
    I'll leave you all (3)
        "   "   " 4
        "   "   " 5
        "   "   " 6

    don exit ⬛|| (for dog) → es geht voran 3
      " entrance ⬛ ||
    ~~dead leave yours~~

Clov's slow movement towards Hamm on
and his Pipi and back away on Säugetieren

Three moves to go checked immediately by Hamm's 3
Warte mal so that Clov practically still at 0 for
Hamm's prophesy. How justify Hamm's 2ⁿᵈ & 3ʳᵈ
Warte mal? (with 2 extra ich verlasse dich?)

indicate more ~~move~~ to go on ich verlasse dich 4, 5, 6.
No more on 3.

Deine Hunde sind da still at 0 and only gives dog
on gesture from Hamm. So moves in and beside
chair till ich verlasse dich 7

Clov's pose when trying to make dog stand. Parallel
backs.

7 are there still 2 (sharks)
    pain killer 4
    Clov's eyes & legs 2
    I'll leave you all (3)
      „   „   „   4
      „   „   „   5
      „   „   „   6
    Clov exit <9> 11 (for dog)
    ⟶ Es geht voran [We're getting on] 3
      „   entrance <9> 11
    <I'll leave you 7>[1]

Clov's second movement towards Hamm on
Und dein Pipi [What about that pee] and back away on Säugetieren [mammals!]
Three moves to go checked immediately by Hamm's 3
Warte mal [Wait] so that Clov practically still at 0 for
Hamm's prophecy. How justify Hamm's 2nd and 3rd
Warte mal [Wait]? (with 2 extra ich verlasse dich [I'll leave you]?)[1]
    Indicate move [*erasure*] to go on ich verlasse dich [I'll leave you] 4, 5, 6.
No move on 3.
    Deine Hunde sind da [Your dogs are here] still at 0 and only gives dog
on gesture from Hamm. So moves in and beside
chair till ich verlasse dich [I'll leave you] 7
    Clov's pose when trying to make dog stand. Parallel
backs.

8   I'll leave you 7
(Hamm) taking his course 3
   once (further) ~~5~~ 6, 7, 8
Clov exit 12 (boothook)
" entrance 12
once (gestern) 9, 10
a day like any other 2 → Clov exit 13 (alarm)
   painkiller 5   " entrance 13
   Clov's legs 3
   Clov exit #14

Was hast du eigentlich heute? Same quality as
Du zeigst mir das (4), i.e. towards Hamm,
away from Tisch. Back away on ich gehe etc

Hol mir den Bootshaken. Clov stops on way to
door to turn + say zu dies zu das. Moves on
after Du kannst es nicht and stops again to turn
and say bald merke ich sie and exit on ...nicht
mehr können.

Gives bootshaken and comes back to O.
Answer to Hamm's efforts to move chair.
Turns away angrily on kann nicht hinzugehen
but interest aroused by Zurücksetzen
and gradually zoomes for story.

Clov's thinking walk!

H 2 1 →3 D

1 meine Beine ...
verlassen können

2 Was machst du ...
Ich plane

3 Ah!

H 2 3 D

3 Hands to head for concentration. Straightens up on
Ich habe es. Turns to Hamm for ich ziehe den Wecker auf

Clov entrance 13 with alarm, barefoot, shoes
in hand, goes to chair + sets shoes gently
down. Kneels to relace bare feet and
exit leaving shoes on ground. Scene
10 Clov with shoes laces through act
needed till 11.

8 I'll leave you 7
   (Hamm) taking his course 3
   once (früher) <5> 6, 7, 8
   Clov exit 12 [*erasure*] (boothook) [*i.e.*, boathook]
     „ entrance [*erasure*] 12
   once (gestern) 9, 10
   a day like any other 2
   ─────────────────────⟶ Clov exit 13 (alarm)
                            „ entrance 13

   pain killer 5
   Clov's legs 3
   Clov exit [*erasure*] 14

Was hast du eigentlich heute [What's the matter with you today?] same quality as
Du fragst *mich* das ["*You* ask *me* that"] (4) [i.e., section 4], i.e. towards Hamm,
un peu désolé. Back away on Ich gehe [I'm taking (my course)] etc.
Hol mir den Bootshaken [Go and get the gaff]. Clov stops on way to
door to <say> turn & say Tu dies[,] tu das [Do this, do that]. Moves on
after Du kannst es nicht [You're not able to] and stops again to turn
and say Bald werde ich [Soon I won't do it any more] etc. and exit on . . nicht
mehr können [You won't be able to any more],
Gives boathook and moves back to o.
Amused by Hamm's efforts to move chair.
Turns away angrily on lass mich schweigen [let me be silent]
but interest aroused by Verrückten [madman]
and gradually round for story.

    Clov's thinking walk!
        [sketch]   1 'Meine Beine [my legs] . . .
                      <to> verlassen können [leave me]
                2 Was machst du[?] [What are you doing?] . .
                Ich plane [Having an idea]
        [sketch]   3 Ah!
3 Hands to head for concentration. Straightens up on
Ich habe es[1] [I have it]. Turns to Hamm for Ich ziehe den Wecker auf [I set the
alarm].
Clov entrance 13 with alarm, barefoot, shoes
in hand, tiptoes to chair. Sets shoes gently
down. Rest of scene barefoot and
exit leaving shoes on ground. Scene
10 Clov with heavy boots though not
needed till 11.

straighten

Clov at Nagg's bin ~ turns to H ... Er will nicht

1. Opens, stoops, closes ~ straightens up, turns to Hamm: Er will nicht. ~ ~~~~~ starts to move, stops on ...: Ich werde ihm einen B. geben & returns to bin.

2. Opens, stoops, ~~~~ turns to Hamm holding lid a little open & without stooping: Er will

3. Turns back to bin, stoops, closes ~ straightens up, turns to Hamm: Er macht ... and starts for door.

Nagg raises up just in time to be in position when Clov turns & says: Glaubst du ...

[*erasure*]

[*erasure*]

Clov at Nagg's bin:

1. Opens, stoops, closes & straightens up, turns to
Hamm: Er will nicht . .[1] [He doesn't want to listen . .] [*erasure*] starts to move
stops on H's [Hamm's] Ich werde ihm einen B [Bonbon] geben [I'll give him a
bonbon]
and returns to bin.

2. Opens, stoops, [*erasure*] turns to Hamm holding
lid a little open & without stooping: Er will [eine Praline] [He wants (a sugar-
plum)]

3. Turns back to bin, stoops, closes & straightens up,
turns to Hamm: Er macht's [mit][2] [It's a deal] and starts
for door.

Nagg comes up just in time to be in
position when Clov turns and says:

Glaubst du . . [Do you believe . .]

9 | Hamm's headheart 3 (es klopft + Äderchen)

9 Hamm's headheart 3 (Es klopt [*recte* tropft][1] [Something dripping] & Äderchen [vein])

10

Clon entrance ~~1~~ / ~~2~~4
are there still 3 (rats)
~~xxxxxxxxxxxxx~~
no more 4 (sugarplums)

entrance 14 .: as through a flash from
rest . [...] once on way to [...] to look
behind and [...] Hamm's kitchen
when Hamm says Last words on

Prayer scene
Hamm's hands clasped for 1st Last words
unclasped on ça ne sert à rien ..
Reclasped on .. arrêtigen for 2nd Last words
Clov's hands clasped on wie in nirgen
Nagg's " " " Geid ihr kennt
Hamm " unclasped on .. Na?
Clov " " " .. Dankerte
Nagg " " " Kino Ihr

Clov during Hamm's curse:
one long look forward Kitchen from Wer riefst Du
                                    to schlafen zu können
" " " at Nagg from ich hoffe te
                                    Hoffnung war
after second Nul and exit Nagg, look at Hamm

Telescope [...] Krikler, boathook, shoes

4
    H 3   2
           5-1

D 1 boathook
   2 telescope
   3 shoes
5 Spraukler
4 dog

10 Clov entrance [*erasure*] 14
Are there still 3 (rats)
[*erasure*]
no more 4 (sugarplums)

Entrance 14: As though in flight from
rat. Stops once on way to o to look
behind and looking towards kitchen
when Hamm says <u>Lasset uns</u> etc. [beten][1] [Let us etc. (pray)]
<u>Prayer scene</u>
Hamm's hands clasped for 1st <u>Lasset uns</u> [Let us]
Unclasped on <u>Es ist eine Ratte</u> . . [There's a rat . .]
Reclasped on . . <u>erledigen</u> [. . finish him] for 2nd <u>Lasset uns</u> [Let us]
Clov's hands clasped on <u>Meinetwegen</u> [Off we go]
Nagg's 　　　" 　　　" 　　　" <u>Seid ihr soweit</u> [Are you right]
Hamm's " 　　unclasped on: <u>Na?</u> [Well?]
Clov's 　　" 　　　" 　　　" <u>Denkste</u>[2] [What a hope]
Nagg's 　　" 　　　" 　　　" <u>Keine Spur</u> [Nothing doing]
Clov during Hamm's curse:[3] <one look towards K>
one long look towards kitchen from <u>Wen riefst du</u> [Whom did you call]
　　　　　　　　　　　　to <u>schlafen zu können</u> [we might sleep in peace]
" 　　　　" 　　　" at Nagg from <u>ich hoffe</u> [I hope] to
　　　　　　　　　　　<u>Hoffnung war</u> [only hope].
After second <u>Nell</u> and exit Nagg, [Clov] looks at Hamm.
<Contrive for all objects on ground to be
kitchen side of Hamm, except [*illegible*] ladder
still [under?] sea window & perhaps boathook:
telescope, powder, sprinkler, boathook, shoes>

[*erasure*]		<1 boathook
		2 telescope
	D	3 shoes
		5 (4) sprinkler
		4 (5) dog>

<Having given dog Having given dog Clov picks up shoes,
[*illegible*] then goes after dog when H. throws it to 4
and is stooping to pick up 2 when: 'Was machst du?'
Straightens up: 'Ordnung etc.' Stoops again when
Ordnung! Straightens up again: 'Ich liebe die Ordnung etc.'
Picks up 2 [*illegible*], goes to 1, picks up 1 and
stoops for 5 when 'Lass das', [*illegible*]>

[*erasure*]
[*erasure*]

I'd leave you 8.
~~no relax it~~
no move 5- (tide)
tears 2 (Tragg)

was schafft du.
ich vermisse dir
Lass das

straighten to say
- drops on

Corridor for all objects on ground, except ladder, on the Kitchen side of Haman

3 shoes
4₉ dog
2₉ telescope
1 ~~the~~ crowbar
3 sprinkler

Having given dog Clov picks up 3, goes after dog.
When H. throws it to 4, ~~and is stooping to pick it~~
~~up when one makes it~~ picks it up, goes to 2
and is stooping to pick it up when : ~~the~~ Was
reacht he? Straightens up: Ordnung eh
and stoops again to pick up 2 when Ordnung!
Straightens: Du liebe eh, picks up 2, goes
to 1, picks it up and is stooping to pick up 5
when ~~he to he~~. Drops dear after wanders,
goes to A where stopped by Was ist das? Keines finds
for it. Ich verlasse dich at A. Then right up
& Hamm on Ou do ich vergesse and then I'll
schau nach ob die Tat ist. away on och dann wirst du
eben

Clov on things

1. inspects Hall, closes, straightens, turns :
   Es hat sich verändern

2. inspects Nagg, closes, straightens, turns :
   Es hat sich verändern nicht

3. Er went without disinspection.

4. Nicht du sich würste from same place.

11   I'll leave you 8
                  [*erasure*]
                  no more 5 (tide)
                  tears 2 (Nagg)

Was schaffst du [eigentlich] [What in God's name do you think you are doing].
Straighten to say
Ich versuche etc. [I'm doing my best (to create a little order)] & drops on
    Lass das [Drop it]

Contrive for all objects on ground, except ladder, 23
to be kitchen side of Hamm
3 shoes
4 dog   [sketch]
2 telescope
1 [*erasure*] boathook
5 sprinkler
Having given dog Clov picks up 3, goes after dog
when H. [Hamm] throws it to 4 [*erasure*]
[*erasure*] picks it up, goes to 2
and is stooping to pick it up when: [*erasure*] Was
machst du [da]? [What are you doing?]. Straightens up: Ordnung [in order] etc.
and stoops again to pick up 2 when Ordnung! [Order!]
Straightens: Ich liebe [I love] etc., picks up 2, goes
to 1, picks it up and is stooping to pick up 5
when <Lass das (Drop it)>. Drops there after woanders [elsewhere]
goes to A where stopped by Was ist [denn] mit deinen Füssen
los? [What's wrong with your feet] etc. Ich verlasse dich [I'll leave you] at A. Then
right up
to Hamm on Oh, ehe ich vergesse¹ [oh, by the way . . .] and there till
Schau nach, ob sie tot ist [Go and see is she dead]. Away on Och dann wirst du
eben² [Pah! You'll make up another].
Clov at bins
1. Inspects Nell, closes, straightens, turns:
   Es hat den Anschein [Looks like it]
2. Inspects Nagg, closes, straightens, turns:
   Es hat den Anschein nicht³ [Doesn't look like it]
3. Er weint [He's crying] without reinspection.
4. Nicht dass ich wüsste [Not to my knowledge] from same place.
   [*erasure*]

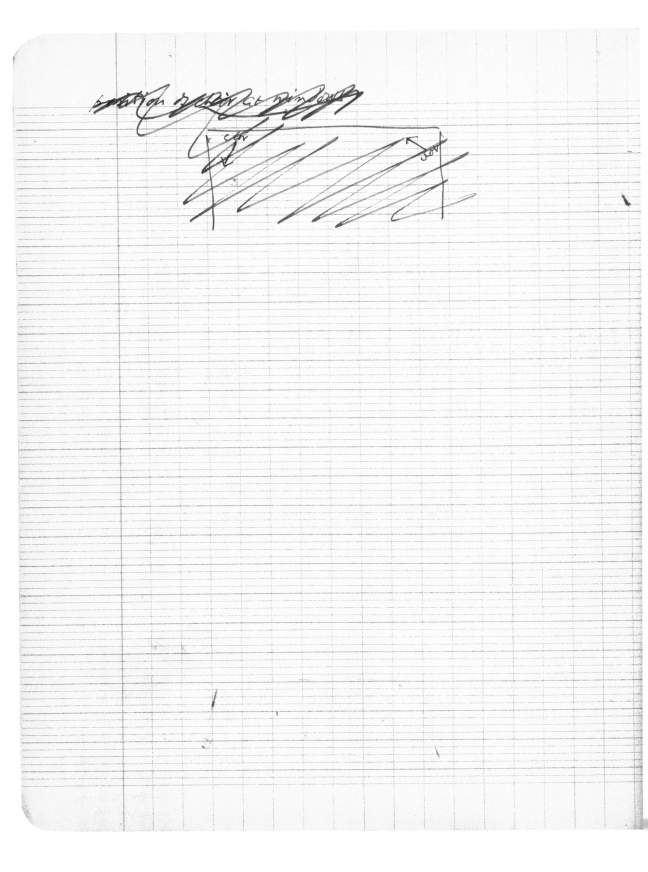

[*Page 28*]

<position of chair at windows>
[*erasure*]

12

no more 6 (navigators)
cold 2 (clov)
bleib nicht da stehen 3

9ᵉ Rueck

1. From *Weisst du noch* to *schon da?*

2. *Die Erde!* (perhaps more wedes i.a. *Vor da.. again a Die Erde!* again

3. *Silence?*

ce

cl.

chai at windows

12
 no more 6 (navigators)[1]
 cold 2 (Clov)
 bleib nicht da stehen [Don't stay there] 3

2nd Runde[1] [round]   25

                                       1. From Weisst du noch [Do you remember]
                                           to Schon da? [There already?]

[sketch]   2. Die Erde! [The Earth!] (perhaps more
                                         needed[2] e.g. Von da . . . [But there's . . .]
                                         again & Die Erde! [The Earth!] again.
                                      3. Silence?

[sketch]   Chair at windows[3]

B

no more 7 (rugs)
cold 3 (Hamm)
~~illegible~~
i'll leave you 9
don't exit ~~illegible~~ 15

Clov at Nagg's bin and foot.

1. Opens, stoops, straightens, turns his head and slightly open: Ja

2. " " " " " " " " noch einmal

3. " " " " " " " " " schreie es nicht

4. Ja es wird wohl das Zweite gewesen sein. Clov aus .:
   man kann es nicht wissen.

Silence. Clov starts back. Nothing a little short
of Hamms' chair by .: ansieht es noch etc. After
das Leben geht weiter goes on .: steps
at 0 by Gib mir die Pfeife

13 no more 7 (rugs)
    cold 3 (Hamm)
    [*erasure*]
    I'll leave you 9
    Clov exit [*erasure*] 15

Clov at Nagg's bin and foll. [following]   27

1. Opens, stoops, straightens, turns holding lid slightly open: Ja [Yes]

2.   ”   ”   ”   ”   ”   ”   : Nur einmal [Once only]

3.   ”   ”   ”   ”   ”   ”   : Er weiss es nicht [He
   doesn't know]

4. On Es wird wohl das zweite gewesen sein[1] [It must have been the second]
   closes and

   Man kann es nicht wissen [We'll never know]

   Silence. Clov starts back. Stopped a little short

of Hamm's chair by Er weint noch [Is he still crying] etc. After

Das Leben geht weiter [Life goes on] goes on till stopped

at o by Gib mir ein Plaid [Give me a rug]

14

Tears 3 (man weint)
grains 3 (time)
Es geht voran 4

14 Tears 3 (Man weint [You weep])
grains 3 (time)
[E]s geht voran [We're getting on] 4

15

Clov entrance ~~##~~ 15
PainKiller 6
no more 8 (painkiller)
mother Pegg 2
no more 9 (coffins)
I'll leave you 10
Clov exit ~~####~~ 16

Entrance 15: will show Clark.

~~Meine Theorieende~~ etc.

H   O   A   Picture

Picture to A backwards observing effect. Stop at
A and turn on *schau dir die Erde an*.
so da sie old sicht forward with exaggerated
solicitude to O a beyond, and stop for
Hast du Halsweh etc., from O to under
wir etwas brummen. Looks up at window.
Turns on Nächtsänger. Moves in toward *Baum*
un tros tohr ich etc. *Exanimum on Hast du* etc.
The first *paradoxical frage ich aci...* *is possible*
to observe *on way* to windows and *rap at*
one on *klar & vernünftig* or the 2 *and*
ich werde on way up.

Down from *ba latter* on ... *falschen Seite*.

Earth latter: 1st *from* on *Clark*! Back on
~~ganz~~ ~~Habsicht~~ ~~and~~ *ich weiss es nicht*, and
... another Treef way to *Turn* on *Baum*
with *faiger writing* for *Als Mitte P.eag* etc.
and *back* to window on *Ja he lachelt* *Oh*,
strapped down as Hot es out in to Baum
for *Es gibt etwas de*
Ich hab unser Geschichten etc. as he begins
to cast *round for telescope*.

Drop telescope on 2nd *Gib mir die Hand*
Give dog & Baum on *Lass uns aufhören*...
Up ... Uhl, without telescope. Back for, eh
and begins inspection. Turns again du
aus der Dunkelheit!

Ich werde ... nachleben ... *latter in*
down telescope to ... on way to dir
or just before ich achene, At ... before
Ich achene - Starts back for weather *and*

15 Clov entrance [*erasure*] 15
   Pain killer 6
   no more 8 (pain killer)
   Mother Pegg 2
   no more 9 (coffins)
   I'll leave you 10
   Clov exit [*erasure*] 16

Entrance 15: with alarm clock.

kleine Ehrenrunde [Winding up] etc.

[sketch] Picture

[From] Picture to A backwards observing effect [of clock]. Stop at
A and turn on Schau dir die Erde an[1] [Look at the earth]
On Da sie dich lockt [Since it's calling you] forward with exaggerated
solicitude to o and beyond and stop for
Hast du Halsweh [Is your throat sore] etc. From o to under
earth window humming.[2] Looks up at window.

Turns on Nicht singen [Don't sing]. Moves in towards Hamm
on Was habe ich [What did I do] etc. to maximum on Hast du [You didn't see]
etc.

The two Manchmal frage ich mich [Sometimes I wonder] if possible
to himself on way to windows and up at
one[3] on klar [lucid] and vernünftig [intelligent] or the 2 und
ich werde [and I'm as . . .] on way up.

Down from sea ladder on . . . falschen Seite [. . . wrong side]

Earth ladder: 1st turn on Clov! Back on
[*erasure*] Ich weiss es nicht[4] [I don't know], and
movement arrested half way to question Hamm
with finger pointing for[5] Als Mutter Pegg [When old Mother Pegg] etc.
and back to window on Ja, du hattest Öl![6] [Yes you had (oil)]
Straight down on Hol[e] es[7] [Go and get it] and in to Hamm
for Es gibt etwas [There's one thing] etc.

Ich habe unsere Geschichten [I am tired of our goings on] etc. as he begins
to cast round for telescope.[8]

Drops telescope on 2nd Gib mir den Hund [!] [Give me the dog!]

Gives dog to Hamm on Lass uns aufhören [Let's stop playing]
up [*erasure*] a step without telescope. Back for [telescope], up
and begins inspection. Turns again on
An der Dunkelheit! [Of darkness!]

Ich werde mal nachsehen[9] [I'll go and see][10] on ladder.

Down[,] telescope discarded on way to door
or just before Ich nehme [I'll take (the gaff)]. At door before
Ich nehme [I'll take (the gaff)] – Starts back for boathook and

Stopped by Lars nur about O . Das trifft
sich gut stare, turn to door, stopped by
Lars mir ku Hause, back pit, gives
it to Hause, goes to door, stopped by
alarm clock, takes sound for ersten glaces
takes it off [illegible] Hugg's bin, starts
pack, thinks Hell's koffer, goes back,
puts alarm on Hell's bin, then back to
door, stops [illegible] puncte
down on I like : ich verlasse dich , goes on
[illegible] stopped about O by say noch etwas ...

Between tödlich verletzten and
ich zage mich manchmal slight turn
toward door, and back
on Vor Glück — more towards door
stopped by . Cut . [illegible] on , on
Nicht's and stopped 2 by der !
[illegible] Half turn + turn self : Das
[illegible] wir ... Round and in on
ich entlasse dich   after wir entlassen
einander back to door and [illegible]
[illegible] back to Hause für [illegible]
no stopped at door by Noch etwas
stick out with back to Hause für
[illegible] aller letzte purde . Then straight
out.

stopped by <u>Lass nur</u>[1] [No! *i.e.* It's not worth it] about O. <u>Dass trifft</u>
<u>sich gut</u>[2] [Lucky for you] there, then to door, stopped by
<u>Lass mir den Haken</u> [Leave me the gaff], back for it, gives
it to Hamm, goes to door, stopped by
alarm clock. Looks round for better place
[for it] & puts it on [*erasure*] Nagg's bin, starts
back, thinks Nell's safer, goes back,
puts alarm on Nell's bin, then back to
door, stops <at O, turns and:> beside
chair on O side: <u>Ich verlasse dich</u> [I'll leave you], goes on
till stopped about O by <u>Sag noch etwas</u> [Say something]
    Between <u>tödlich Verletzten</u>[3] [All these dying of their wounds] and
<u>Ich sage mich</u> [*recte* mir . . .] <u>manchmal</u> [I say to myself – sometimes] slight turn
towards door and back.
On <u>vor Glück</u> [for happiness] – move towards door
stopped by 1. <u>Clov</u> [*erasure*]. On on
<u>Nichts</u> [Nothing] and stopped 2 by <u>Clov!</u>
[*erasure*] Half turn & to himself: <u>Das</u>
<u>nennen wir</u> . . . [This is what . . .]. Round and in on
<u>Ich entlasse dich</u>[4] [I'm obliged to you]. After <u>Wir entlassen</u>
<u>einander</u>[5] [It's we are obliged] back to door and <from>
[*erasure*]
[*erasure*] stopped at door by <u>Noch etwas</u> [One thing more]
Still and with back to Hamm for
<u>Eine allerletzte Gnade</u> [A last favour]. Then straight
out.

16 | clov entrance ~~1916~~ 16

33

Clov entrance 16 while Hamm trying to
move chair. ~~~~~ spill near door watching
Hamm. Turns but aside on first Clov.
Back after gut and motionless till end.

16 Clov entrance [*erasure*] 16

Clov entrance 16 while Hamm trying to
move chair. [*erasure*] Still near door watching
Hamm. Turns head aside on first <u>Clov</u>.
Back after <u>Gut</u> [Good] and motionless till end.

Clov's entrances

1. With ladder
2. Back for ladder
3. On whistle 1 after H's 1st mon.
4. " " 2 " "denken wir ans Fressen"
5. With biscuit
6. On whistle 3 after "für einen Müllkicker"
7. With telescope
8. " ladder
9. " telescope
10. " fleapowder
11. " dog
12. " boathook
13. " clock
14. On whistle 4 after H's HHHH
15. " " 5 " H's 2 mon. ("ich so weit sein") & with clock
16. Dressed for road

3, 4, 14, 15 identical
6 stopped on way by "weg mit diesem Dreck"
5, 7, 8, 10 related through "ich bin wieder da..."
enter ~~with his movements~~ each time with object in left hand
except perhaps ladder

Clov's gänge after opening unveiling:

1. Hast du geblutet?
2. Also lauf! (hin u. her)
3. To ~~Hamm~~ with biscuit
4. Back towards door stopped by "Der ...Die Natur"
5. "Du willst es nicht so zu aus sprechen."
6. To bins on "jns mein damit"
7. Back towards door on "Wir werden die Deckel vernieten" stopped by 1st "es eilt nicht!"
8. [2nd round]
9. To flea window with ladder on "Schau dir den Ozean an"
10. From window to chair for "grau".
11. "Was dein Kopf"
12. "Ein Verrückter...?"
13. Drinking walk
14. Wegräumen
15. Ob ehe ich vergesse...
16. To bins on "Schau nach ob sie tot ist" & 9th round
17. On "fahrs nach unterm Fenster" & ...
17A Es ist zu früh
18. On "das Leben geht weiter" & stopped with "Gib mir den Plaid"

Clov's exits

1.   For ladder.   ⌐ 3. with ladder.
2.   After his 1ˢᵗ mon.
4.   "   "Draussen ist der Tod .. Gut, geh nur"
5.   "   "Gib ihm einen Zwieback"
6.   "   "Seit meiner Geburt"
7.   "   "Ich hole das Fernglas"
8.   "   "Ich brauche die Leiter"
9.   "   "Ich brauche das Fernglas"
10.   "   "ich hole das Pulver"
11.   "   "Hol ihm mal" (204)
12.   "   "Du wirst ~~es nicht~~ "Bald wirst du es nicht mehr
    können" (for boathook)
13.   "   "Ich werde nachsehen" (for clock)
14.   Before H's story on "meines ist es immer gewesen"
15.   "   H's 2ⁿᵈ mon. "Wenn ich diese Ratte ..."
16.   "   after "eine allerletze Gnade"

General principle. When exhale needed Clov stopped as near to
chair as possible. When no stopped at door as c.e.
4 and before so with "Ist mein Hund fertig ?" and
4 before 4 with "Dann muss ich meine Geschichte erzählen"

19.   Ehrenrunde.
20.   In for "Hast du Halbach ?"
21.   Singing - ladder at sea - ladder at earth
22.   Down from ladder for "Es gibt etwas, das ich nicht
       begreifen kann"
23.   Looking for telescope
24.   Down for dog - strikes Hamm
25.   Back up ladder
26.   Down on "Sieht aus wie ein knabe." &c. too stopped
       with "Lass nur"

               stops.

X 1. Ich hole das Tuch   X 12. Hast du nie daran gedacht ?
O 2. "In deiner Küche ?" I   X 13. Ist mein Hund fertig ?
    3. Kein Anruf.   X 14. Hast du deine Erscheinungen gehabt?
X 4. Clov .. Die Natur hat uns vergessen.   O 15. Frag meinen Vater ob er meine Geschichte ...
X 5. In deiner Küche ? II
X 6. Es eilt nicht I (Deckel vernieten)   16. Weck ihn
     "   " II (Laecker)   17. Bonbon
X 7.   18. Praline
   8. Ich werde nachmessen   X 19. Nein ! , "nozum diene ich ?.. gnich die Replik zugeben
   9. Ich hole den Zollstock   X 20. Gib mir ein plaid
X 10. Warte mal ! (after Floss)   O 21. Lass nur (dog)
X   "   II   for Haifische   O 22. Lass mir den Haken
X 11.   "   III   for Augen u. Beinen   X 23. Sag noch Etwas
X   Dann werde ich euch verlassen   O 24. Clov .. nichts
   12. ~~Klage meinen Vater~~   O 25. Clov .. ich entlasse dich
                          O 26. Noch Etwas .

X = turn   O = No need

[*Page 42*]

Clov's entrances

1. With ladder
2. Back for ladder
3. On whistle 1 after H's 1st mon. [monologue]
4.   2   'denken nur ans Fressen' [that's all they think of]
5. With biscuit
6. On whistle 3 after 'für einen Müllkipper' [for a nightman!]
7. With telescope
8. " ladder
9. " telescope
10. " flea powder
11. " dog
12. " boathook
13. " clock
14. On whistle 4 after H's story
15. "   5 " H's 2 mon. [monologue] ('Ah, so weit sein' [Ah, let's get it over!]) & with clock
16. Dressed for road

3, 4, 14, 15 identical
6 stopped on way by 'Weg mit diesem Dreck' [Clear away this muck!]
5, 7, 8, 10 related through 'Ich bien [*i.e.* bin] wieder da . . .' [I'm back again . . .]
enter [*erasure*] each time with object in left hand
except perhaps ladder

Clov's gänge [movements] after opening unveiling

1. Hast du geblutet? [Have you bled?]
2. Also, lauf! [Then move] (hin u. [und] her) [to wall and back]
3. To Nagg with biscuit
4. Back towards door stopped by 'Clov . . Die Natur' [Clov . . . Nature]
5. 'Du solltest nicht so zu mir sprechen' [You shouldn't speak to me like that]
6. To bins on 'Ins Meer damit' [Chuck it in the sea]

7A Es ist zu früh [It's too soon]   7. Back towards door on 'Wir werden die Deckel vernieten' [Screw down the lids] stopped by 1st 'Es eilt nicht' [Time enough]

8. 1st round
9. To sea window with ladder on 'Schau dir den Ozean an[!]' [Look at the ocean[!]]

Transcription continues on p. 166.

[164]

Clov's exits   37

1. For ladder.

2. After his 1st mon. [monologue]   3. With ladder

4< 3>   After 'Draussen ist der Tod . . . Gut, geh nur' [Outside of here it's death . . . All right, be off]

5< 4>   "   'Gib ihm einen Zwieback' [Give him a biscuit]

6< 5>   "   'Seit meiner Geburt' [Ever since I was whelped]

7< 6>   "   'Ich hole das Fernglas' [I'll go and get the glass]

8< 7>   "   'Ich brauche die Leiter' [I need the steps]

9< 8>   "   'Ich brauche das Fernglas' [I need the glass]

10< 9>   "   'Ich hole das Pulver' [I'll go and get the powder]

11<10>   "   'Hol ihn mal!' [Go and get him!] (Dog)

12<11>   "   [erasure] 'Bald wirst du es nicht mehr [. . .] können' [You won't be able to any more . . .'] (for boathook)

13<12>   "   'Ich werde nachsehen' [I'll go and see] (for clock)

14<13> Before H's story on 'Meines ist es immer gewesen' [Mine was always that]

15<14>   "   H's 2nd mon. [monologue] 'Wenn ich diese Ratte . . .' [If I don't kill that rat . . .]

16<15> After 'Eine allerletzte Gnade' [A last favour]

General principle. When space needed Clov stopped as near to
chair as possible. When no [i.e. no space needed] stopped at door as e.g.
4 and before 10 with 'Ist mein Hund fertig?' [Is my dog ready?] and
before 4 [14?] with 'Dann muss ich meine Geschichte erzählen'' [It's time for my
story]

19.[2] Ehrenrunde [Winding up]

20. In for 'Hast du Halsweh?' [Is your throat sore?]

21 Singing – ladder at sea – ladder at earth[3]

22 Down from ladder for 'Es gibt etwas, das ich nicht begreifen kann' [There's one thing I'll never understand]

23 Looking for telescope

24 Down for dog – strikes Hamm

25 Back up ladder

26 Down [erasure] on 'Sieht aus wie ein Knabe' [Looks like a small . . . boy][4] etc. till stopped with 'Lass nur' [No!]

---

10 From window to chair for 'Grau' [Grey]

11 'Und dein Pipi' [What about that pee]

12 'Ein Verrückter?' [A madman?]

13 Thinking walk

14 Wegräumen [clear away]

15 Oh, ehe ich vergesse . . . [Oh by the way . . .]

16 To bins on 'Schau nach, ob sie tot ist' [Go and see is she dead]

17 On 'Fahre mich unters Fenster' [Bring me under the window] & 2nd round

18 On 'Das Leben geht weiter' [Life goes on] & stopped with 'Gib mir ein Plaid'
   [Give me a rug]

X1. Ich hole das Tuch [I'll go and get the sheet]

o2. [*erasure*] 'In deiner Küche?' I [In your kitchen? I]

  3. Kein Anruf [No phone calls]

X4. Clov . . . Die Natur hat uns vergessen [Nature has forgotten us]

X5 In deiner Küche? II [In your kitchen? II]

X6 Es eilt nicht I [Time enough I] (Deckel vernieten [Screw down the lids])

X7   "   "   II [Time enough II] (Catheter)

  8 Ich werde nachmessen [I'll measure it]

X9 Ich hole den Zollstock [I'll go and get the tape]

X10 Warte mal I [Wait I] (after Floss [raft])

X   "   " II [Wait II] for Haifische [sharks]

X   "   " III for Augen u. [und] Beinen [eyes and legs]

X11 Dann werde ich euch verlassen [Then I'll leave you]

<12 Frage meinen Vater> [Ask my father]

X12. Hast du nie daran gedacht? [Did you ever think of one thing?]

X13. Ist mein Hund fertig? [Is my dog ready?]

X14 Hast du deine Erscheinungen gehabt? [Have you had your visions?]

o15 Frage meinen Vater, ob er meine Geschichte [Ask my father if he wants to listen to my story]

 16 Weck ihn [Wake him]

 17 Bonbon

 18 Praline [sugar-plum]

X19 Nein! . . . Wozun diene ich?[5] Mir die Replik zu geben [No! . . . What is there to keep me here? The dialogue.]

X20 Gib mir ein Plaid [Give me a rug]

o21 Lass nur [No! (Don't bother)] (boy)

o22 Lass mir den Haken [Leave me the gaff]

X23 Sag noch Etwas [Say something]

o24 Clov . . . Nichts [Clov . . . Nothing]

o25 Clov . . . ich entlasse dich[6] [I'm obliged to you, Clov]

o26 Noch etwas [one more thing]

X = turn   o = No need

Percival

Son light in bus with holes + drinks?

fixed an Perie for Haemni land & cockpit

faint light from Kitchen?

Null's ~~~~~ limelight colouchen where door opens to

see if she is dead

Clear at bus.

② away on jedem seine Spezialität and stopped
at 0 by kein Arat

④ away on Nebel kondichen + stopped at 0 by
es eilt nicht.

⑧ away on es macht ts and no stop till just
short of door for Glaubst du

⑪ away on falew mich and to shaei.

⑬ "   " das Leben geht weiter and stopped
at 0 by Gib mir ein Maid

General
Dim light in bins \<with holes or chinks\>[1]
Fixation device for Hamm's handkerchief[2]
faint light from kitchen?
Nell's [*erasure*] bin light erloschen [extinguished] when Clov opens to
see if she is dead

Clov at bins.

    2[3] away on <u>Jedem seine Spezialität</u> [Every man his speciality] and stopped
        at O by <u>Kein Anruf</u> [No phone calls]

    4 away on <u>Deckel vernieten</u> [Screw down the lids] and stopped at O by
        <u>Es eilt nicht</u> [Time enough]

    8 away on <u>er macht es</u>[4] [It's a deal] and no stop till just
        short of door for <u>Glaubst du</u> [Do you believe]

   11 away on <u>Fahre mich</u> [Bring me] and to chair.

   13   "   "   <u>Das Leben geht weiter</u> [Life goes on] and stopped
        at O by <u>Gib mir ein Plaid</u> [Give me a rug]

Inside Front Cover

1 – The inside cover of the notebook includes a series of numerical outlines for the play. These outlines reveal that Beckett divided the play into sixteen sections or scenes (compare this with the eight scenes outlined in the *Riverside Nb*), which he then began to group into several possible formal patterns. In addition to listing the page numbers for each section (and here they refer to the 1960 Suhrkamp tri-lingual edition), Beckett also listed the number of pages (roughly) for each section. He first contemplated a two-part structure to the 126 pages of text, the first of 72 pages, the second of 54. But such a structure evidently did not offer enough symmetry, so he treated section eight as a separate entity and divided the material before that roughly in half, into sections of 30 and 28 pages, and the section after eight into sections of 26 and 28 pages. The overall structure of the top outline then was sections of 58, 14 and 54 pages.

But such a structure did not put Hamm's story at the centre, and so Beckett outlined the play again at the bottom of the page, this time dividing the sixteen scenes into sections of 30, 42, 6, 20 and 28 pages, substituting dramatic symmetry for formal symmetry. In this second outline, Beckett included tag lines for the play's sixteen scenes:

1 Clov's first inspection of the world outside the shelter (see also textual notes to line 10)

2 Hamm's opening monologue (see also textual note to line 35), and dialogue with Clov

3 Nagg and Nell's dialogue (see also textual notes to lines 259 and 265)

4 Hamm's first round or tour of the shelter

5 Clov's second inspection of the outside world (see also textual note to line 556)

6 The incident with the flea

7 Hamm's incomplete dog

8 A section of four sub-themes: old Mother Pegg, Hamm's attempts to move the chair with his gaff or boathook, Hamm's story of the mad engraver (see also textual note to line 812), and Clov's plan involving the alarm-clock

9 Hamm's central narrative or story (see also textual note to line 921)

10   Nagg's curse of Hamm

11   A section of three sub-themes: Clov's desire for order (see also textual note to line 1037), Hamm's need to have Clov coax him to go on with his story (see also textual note to line 1065), and Nell's death (see also textual note to line 1117)

12   Hamm's second tour around the shelter

13   A section of two sub-themes dealing with the increasing cold: Hamm's need for a rug or blanket and Clov's refusal to offer any human warmth

14   Hamm's 'self-prophetic' (Beckett's words) monologue

15   Another section of three sub-themes: the rat's escape (which poses a threat to Hamm), Clov's delight in telling Hamm that the supply of pain-killer is exhausted, and Clov's third inspection of the outside when he finds (or imagines) the young boy (see also textual note to line 1399)

16   Hamm's final monologue.

The notebook overall is organized simply, and is itself dominated by outlines. This structural emphasis might surprise the casual reader who thinks of Beckett's texts as disorganized or formless, but such attention to structure and form, evident throughout Beckett's directorial notebooks, is also characteristic of the original creation of numerous texts, and so Beckett's directorial preparations are an extension of the composing process. For so apparently formless a text as *Not I*, for example, Beckett made several outlines in the process of composition, including one in which he divided the work into five 'life scenes', which he then subdivided into sub-themes. Another outline Beckett called 'Analysis', which divided the play into fourteen categories: birth, field, insentience, so far, buzzing, brain, memories, speculation, walking, punishment and suffering, interruptions, beam, speechless and voice (see Gontarski, *The Intent of Undoing in Samuel Beckett's Dramatic Texts* (Bloomington, Indiana University Press, 1985), pp. 142–9).

After the first page of outlines for *Endspiel*, Beckett made a second outline in which he noted the exact starting and ending points of each of the sixteen scenes and also included another series of catchwords slightly different from those of the earlier outline. The remainder of the notebook then contains a section for each of these sixteen scenes. And each section contains another, more detailed outline of the central motifs in that scene (and Beckett carefully noted the sequence and cumulative number of repetitions of each of those themes throughout the play) on the verso, and a description of the revised action for that scene on the facing recto. The notebook ends with yet another series of outlines which chart Clov's entrances and exits, his movements and interrupted movements (called 'stops' by

Beckett), a section of general comments, and a brief outline of Clov's movements at the rubbish bin.

Page 1

1 – The German texts (*Sac(B)*, p. 31, and *Photo*, p. 24) print, 'Was ist denn, mein Dicker.' The notebook wording was apparently a tentative revision which Beckett never made final.

2 – The German text prints 'Bleib nicht da!' Beckett has added in *Sac(B)*, p. 49, the word 'stehen' to each occurrence of this much-used line. The revision appears in *Photo*, p. 34.

3 – 'stehen' again added, *Sac(B)*, p. 55.

4 – The line 'Wären wir bedient', literally 'We'd be served', does not appear in the original German text which stops at *Er lässt die Streudose fallen und ordnet seine Kleider* [*He drops the tin and adjusts his trousers*] (F27, G34, S251), but does appear in the revised *Photo*. (See also *Cuts and Changes* for this addition.) In the English text the section focuses on the linguistic confusion between 'laying' and 'lying', in the French between 'coite' and 'coïte'. For the German, Beckett included a play on the words 'Kuschelt' and 'Kuscht' (*Sac(B)*). This is one of the many changes that bring the German text closer to the French and particularly the English. But, according to Walter Asmus, Beckett did not much like the English 'We'd be bitched' but preferred the French 'Nous serions baisés'. In *Sac(B)*, p. 59, Beckett also alters the line with which Clov would have ended the scene from the printed 'Es sieht so aus' [It looks like it] (F27, G34, S251) to 'Es scheint so' [It appears so] (F27, G34, S251). This change, as Beckett noted, was designed to echo Clov's identical phrasing on *Sac(B)*, p. 29. Both are rendered into English as 'Looks like it' and into French as 'On dirait'. With Beckett's change, the German text also reflects that symmetry.

5 – The German text prints, 'mich weiter so anflehen', which Beckett revised to 'so . . . mich anflehen' in *Sac(B)*, p. 69. That revision was accepted into *Photo*, p. 48.

6 – In order to keep the phrases signifying Clov's threatened departure consistent Beckett altered the printed phrase 'Ich geh jetzt' [I'm going now] to 'Ich verlasse dich' (*Sac(B)*, p. 69) [I'm leaving you]. Again the change increases the number of verbal analogies in the play and draws the German text closer to the English, 'I'll leave you'.

7 – The German text prints, 'Lasset uns beten', which Beckett revised to 'Lasset uns zu Gott beten' in *Sac(B)*, p. 89, and to 'Lass uns zu Gott beten!' in *Schiller Nb. Photo*, p. 58, prints the *Sac(B)* version.

8 – Beckett altered this line in rehearsals to clarify the allusion to Shakespeare's *The Tempest*. Beckett changed the printed line, 'Der Spass ist zu Ende' [The fun is over] to the Schlegel translation of that line, 'Das Fest ist jetzt zu Ende', *Sac(B)*, p. 93, and *Photo*, p. 62. (See also textual note to line 1023.)

9 – German text prints, 'Wir sind es, die einander', which Beckett revised to 'Wir entlassen einander' in *Sac(B)*, p. 133 and *Photo*, p. 86.

Page 2

1 – These numbers in the notebook indicate scene numbers. In the first scene, Beckett simply details Clov's entrances and exits for his opening mime (see also textual note to line 10) and mentions the first appearance of the grains of millet image (see also textual note to line 25).

Page 3

1 – This section begins Beckett's simplification of Clov's opening mime. Beckett eliminated Clov's folding of sheets during the unveiling, questioned his forgetting the ladder between the windows, and changed the place from which Clov delivers his opening monologue. Instead of halting near the door (or kitchen opening), he now delivers the monologue from 'O', his place midway between Hamm's chair and door.

Page 4

1 – Each of these elements marks a recurring motif, the beginning or end of a scene (traditionally marked by an entrance or an exit), or a beat, a change of idea or theme in the developing scene. Beckett notes and counts, for instance, all references to the past, like 'once' or 'formerly'. The deterioration of the characters and their world is outlined with the motifs of depletion or running out of: pain-killer, bicycle wheels, Nagg's pap, nature, etc. Even the discussion of Clov's eyes and legs suggests the slow deterioration that is life. Hamm's mention of Clov's eyes echoes Clov's earlier inspection of Hamm's eyes as he peeped under Hamm's handkerchief near the end of his opening mime. In *Riverside Nb* Beckett writes, 'Peep under H's handkerchief.' 'Something' is indeed 'taking its course' in the world of the shelter. (See also textual note to line 139.)

2 – 'Pardon' refers to Hamm's call for forgiveness, 'Forgive me' (F14, G7, S217). Clov's response is to 'snap' at Hamm (*Gac(A)*).

3 – Occasionally an item gets placed outside its chronological sequence in Beckett's outlines. This line actually comes immediately after Clov's exit 4 in the text, not exit 5 (F18, G9, S227).

Page 5

1 – The double question mark here seems to suggest Beckett's questioning himself about how pervasive to make this change of text. See also *Page 2* note 6 above. Beckett does indeed make this change some ten times but to 'Ich verlasse dich.'

2 – 'O' is the designation for Clov's waiting position, stage left and slightly downstage of Hamm's chair. In the *Riverside Nb*, Beckett calls the spot 'A' and says of it, 'halfway from door to H [Hamm] – where always stops when summoned'.

Page 6

1 – The increasing cold mentioned by Nagg and Nell here and echoed later by Hamm's call for a blanket further suggests a world losing its physical heat and, metaphorically, its humanity. In the *Riverside Nb* Beckett says: 'increasing cold: 2. Nagg–Nell; 7. Clov at SW [i.e., sea window]; Hamm "Give me a rug . . ."'

2 – Beckett was careful to outline the crying motif in *Endgame*. See textual note to line 354.

Page 9

1 – Entrance 6. After Nagg tells the story of the Englishman and the tailor, Hamm whistles Clov to 'Clear away this muck' (F22, G23, S237).

2 – Line cut in the Riverside production but restored for Revised Text.

Page 11

1 – Beckett changed 'Ich bringe die Leiter', which is close to the French 'J'apporte l'escabeau', to 'Ich bin wieder da, mit der Leiter' (*Sac(B)*, p. 49), which is closer to the English 'I'm back again with the steps' and parallel to 'Ich bin wieder da, mit dem Fernglas' (*Sac(B)*, p. 49). Beckett also revised the French to 'Je suis de retour avec l'escabeau' (*Sac(B)*, p. 48).

2 – The telescope scene was simplified considerably both in Berlin and London, as Beckett cut Clov's dropping the telescope on purpose and turning it on the audience to describe 'a multitude . . . in transports . . . of joy . . . That's what I call a magnifier' (F25, G29, S243–5). Moreover, after having Clov look at the sea window, Beckett cut the five subsequent examinations, 'looking' (F26, G30–1, S245–7). In Riverside Clov not only feigned looking, but feigned ascent of the ladder as well. (See also textual note to line 534.)

Page 12

1 – For a discussion of cyclical existence and life forms regenerating themselves, see textual note to line 605.
2 – The erasures here result from Beckett's inclusion into section 6 action that is part of section 7.

Page 13

1 – Beckett decided in favour of the 'elastic waist' that he contemplated here for Clov's trousers presumably so that the trousers could be opened with one hand and for the additional comic effect to be gained from a brisk closing.

Page 14

1 – This note is erased presumably because the action actually opens section 8.

Page 15

1 – These extra lines were apparently never added.

Page 17

1 – The German text prints, 'Ich hab's', as does *Photo*, p. 50.

Page 18

1 – The German text prints, 'Er will deine Geschichte nicht hören', which is not revised in *Sac(B)*, p. 81, nor in *Photo*, p. 54. 'Er will nicht' is very likely simply Beckett's shorthand.

2 – The German text prints, 'Er macht mit', but, as Beckett notes, 'macht's' was 'preferred in rehearsals', and was included in *Photo*, p. 54.

Page 20

1 – Beckett's 'klopt' or 'klopft' from *klopfen*, to knock, is simply an error for 'tropft'.

Page 23

1 – Beckett revised this line in *Sac(B)*, p. 89, from 'Lasset uns beten!' to 'Lasset uns zu Gott beten!' and the change is printed in *Photo*, p. 58. Shortly thereafter, the change is made again; 'Erst beten!' is revised to 'Erst zu Gott beten!' *Sac(B)*, p. 91; *Photo*, p. 58. These revisions also bring the German phrasing in line with the more explicit French, 'Prions Dieu!' and the English, 'Let us pray to God'.
2 – 'Denkste' revised to 'Kein Gedanke' in *Sac(B)*, p. 91, and *Photo*, p. 60, to anticipate Hamm's 'Kein Funke!'
3 – Nagg is cursing Hamm at this point. There is some question, however, as to whether Clov is looking at Hamm or at Nagg. The *Schiller Nb* clearly suggests that Clov is looking at Nagg during the 'I hope' curse. Beckett acknowledged the discrepancy with the following note: 'This seems to contradict earlier note for Clov to look at Hamm at this point the better to relish his discomfiture.' The note in *Sac(B)*, p. 93, at this point apparently reads, 'head a little towards H [Hamm]', but the final letter might as easily be an N for Nagg. See also *Cuts and Changes*.

Page 27

1 – Of Hamm's need of Clov's encouragement to continue his story, Beckett wrote in the margin of his copy 'great writer with disciple', *Sac(B)*, p. 97. The German text prints, 'Oh, ehe ich's vergesse', which is not revised in *Sac(B)*, p. 95, or in *Photo*, p. 66.
2 – The German text prints, 'Och, dann machst du eben eine andere' (S285), which is not revised in *Sac(B)*, p. 99, nor is the line changed in *Photo*, p. 68.
3 – The German text, however, prints, 'Es hat nicht den Anschein'. Beckett did not revise the text in *Sac(B)*, p. 101, nor does the revised version appear in *Photo*, p. 70.

Page 30

1 – Beckett explained to Patrick Magee that the calmness of the sea was due to the fact there were no more navigators left for the sea to try to destroy. See also textual note to line 1182.

Page 31

1 – This path is anti-clockwise so as to balance (or undo) the first round, in section 4, which is clockwise.

2 – What appears to be needed here is more dialogue for the journey between the windows.

3 – This diagram outlines Clov's position in relation to Hamm's chair at each window.

Page 33

1 – The German text prints, 'Es wird wohl das zweite Mal gewesen sein'. Beckett put the 'Mal' in parentheses in *Sac(B)*, p. 107. *Photo*, p. 76, prints the original text.

Page 37

1 – The German text prints, 'Schau nach der Erde', which Beckett revised to 'Schau dir die Erde an' (F46, G72, S297) in *Sac(B)*, p. 115. The revision is included in *Photo*, p. 78.

2 – In the Riverside production and for the Revised Text, Beckett cut all response to Clov's humming. See also textual note to line 1301.

3 – Beckett's explanation here is that Clov is 'up at one', that is, the 'sea ladder', on 'lucid', then at the other window, the 'earth ladder', on 'intelligent'. Beckett also suggested the possibility that Clov might ascend to both windows a bit earlier.

4 – The German text prints, 'Ich, ich weiss es nicht.' Beckett removed one 'Ich' in *Sac(B)*, p. 119, and *Photo*, p. 80.

5 – At Hamm accusingly; that is, Clov is accusing Hamm of responsibility in the death of Mother Pegg.

6 – The German text prints, 'Doch, du hattest Öl!' *Photo*, p. 80, however, prints, 'Doch, du hattest!' But in performance, Clov clearly mentioned the oil, 'Doch, du hattest Öl!'

7 – *Photo*, p. 80, reads, 'Hol' es', but in performance Hamm said, 'Dann hol' es'.

8 – This casting about for the telescope was cut in Riverside.

9 – *Photo*, p. 84, reads, 'Ich werde mal hingehen'. The deviation is part of no detectable revision, however, and in performance Clov said 'nachsehen'.

10 – Both French and German texts contained fuller accounts of Clov's sighting of the small boy than did the English text. Hamm at first expects that Clov has merely seen a leaf, a flower or a tomato. When he learns that Clov has spotted 'someone', Hamm orders him to do his duty and exterminate it. Hamm then grows curious, raises questions about its distance, movement and activity. Hamm believes that the creature is looking at the shelter with the eyes of Moses, but Clov counters with an image of Eastern not Western religion; it is examining its navel, an allusion that might also suggest Belacqua, especially since Hamm then thinks that the child is dead. The cut, which Beckett made in both French and German texts, again brings those two texts closer to the English.

Page 38

1 – *Photo*, p. 84, inexplicably prints, 'Nicht der Mühe wert' three times to replace the 'Lass nur' of the text (*Sac(B)*, p. 127), but in performance Clov and Hamm said 'Lass nur' in this exchange.

2 – The German text prints 'Das kommt gut aus' (S309), which Beckett revised to 'Das trifft sich gut' in *Sac(B)*, p. 129. The revision is printed in *Photo*, p. 86.

3 – Beckett altered the syntax from 'Sieh doch, mit welcher Kunst all diese tödlich Verletzten gepflegt werden' (S311) to 'Sieh doch, mit welcher Kunst sie gepflegt werden, all diese tödlich Verletzten' (*Sac(B)*, p. 131) to follow more closely the English syntax. The revision is printed in *Photo*, p. 86.

4 – The German text prints, 'Ich danke dir, Clov, ich brauche dich nicht mehr', which Beckett revised to 'Ich entlasse dich' in *Sac(B)*, p. 133. The revision is printed in *Photo*, p. 86.

5 – The German text prints, 'Wir sind es, die einander nicht mehr brauchen', which Beckett revised to 'Wir entlassen einander' in *Sac(B)*, p. 133. The revision is printed in *Photo*, p. 86.

Page 43

1 – The German text prints, 'Dann muss ich jetzt meine Geschichte erzählen', which is not revised in *Sac(B)*, p. 79, nor in *Photo*, p. 54.

2 – List of Clov's movements continued from facing page.

3 – Most of this scene was cut in Riverside.

4 – Most of this section from after 'Wenn es nur nicht wieder losgeht' (S305) to 'Er ist vielleicht tot' (S307) is cut. The sighting of the child is reinstated just after the beginning of the cut as follows: Clov's nonsense syllables, 'oh je, oh je, oh je!' are revised to, '*Entsetzt*: Sieht aus wie ein Knabe' and Hamm's, 'Ein Blatt? Eine Blume, Eine Toma? . . . *er gähnt* . . . te?' is revised to '(*sarkastisch*): Ein Knabe!' (S305). (See also *Photo*, p. 84.)

5 – The German text prints, 'Wozu diene ich denn?' (S281).

6 – The German text prints, 'Ich danke dir, Clov, ich brauche dich nicht mehr', which Beckett revised to 'Ich entlasse dich, Clov' in *Sac(B)*, p. 133. The revision is printed in *Photo*, p. 86.

Page 44

1 – Lighting Nagg and Nell from within the bins was tried and subsequently rejected during rehearsals in Berlin. Beckett's designer Matias, for one, did not like the 'ghostly, footlight effect' (*Berlin Diary*).

2 – That is, to prevent its moving once in position.

3 – The numbers in this section refer to Beckett's scene designations.

4 – The German text prints, 'Er macht mit', which Beckett revised to 'Er macht's' in *Sac(B)*, p. 81. The revision is printed in *Photo*, p. 54.

Samuel Beckett's Production Notebook
for *Endgame*
at the Riverside Studios,
Hammersmith, London
May 1980

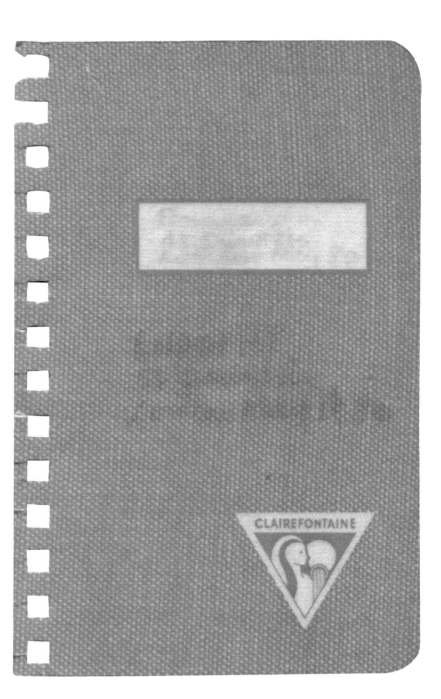

CLAIREFONTAINE

Note on the Manuscript

Reproduced here are the production notes that Beckett prepared for his own production with the San Quentin Drama Workshop at the Riverside Studios in London in May 1980. These notes, catalogued as MS 1975 in the Beckett International Foundation's Archive, are written in a small, green paper covered, originally spiral bound notebook in the 'Clairefontaine' series, measuring 7.5 by 12 cms. The spiral binding was removed before the notes were deposited in the Beckett Archive and the 11 leaves are therefore now separate. Beckett has written on all but three verso pages. Leaves 3 to 10 are numbered by him 1 to 8. On the front inside cover he has written '*Faber Paperback 76* St. Quentin London May 80' and a similar entry has been virtually erased from the laminated front cover.

Minor anomalies are generally omitted from the transcription. Substantive differences are cited in the notes. When a cancelled line is legible it is included between angle brackets, <>.

Beckett directed the San Quentin Drama Workshop in *Endgame* at the Riverside Studios, Hammersmith, in May 1980. This was Beckett's second project with the group. The first was in 1977 when he directed San Quentin Drama Workshop founder, Rick Cluchey, in *Krapp's Last Tape* at Berlin's Akademie der Künste, and in February of 1984, Beckett returned to the Riverside Studios to oversee and adjust a production of *Waiting for Godot* with the San Quentin Drama Workshop.

Faber Paperback 76
St. Quentin
London May 80

Rebecca
Pedrera
588 16 14

22.3 Gregory Gdn 1st
floor whitechapel station

MS 1975

HS 1975

1. 11-12 : C's opening, monologue, exit.
2. 12-18 : H wakes – exit C, H: "we're getting on."
3. 18-22 : Dialogue N-N.
4. 22-26 : H: "Silence" – C's move to chair from Window – H: "you give me the shivers."
5. 26-35 : C: "why this farce." – exit C, H: "Got
   him that time."
6. 35-39 : N: "I'm listening", H's story, N's curse
7. 39-44 : H: "our revels.." – C: "if I don't kill
   that rat.." – exit.
8. 44-53 : H's monologue – end.

Faber paperback 76
St. Quentin
London May 80

[*erasure*]

1.[1] 11–12: C's opening, monologue, exit.
2. 12–18: H wakes – exit C, H: 'We're getting on.'
3. 18–22: Dialogue N–N [Nagg and Nell].
4. 22–26: H: 'Silence' – C's move to chair from win-
          dow & H: 'You give me the shivers.'
5. 26–35: C: 'Why this farce . . .' – exit C, H: 'Got
          him that time.'
6. 35–39: N: 'I'm listening', H's story, N's curse
7. 39–44: H: 'Our revels . . .', – C: 'If I don't kill
          that rat . . .' & exit.
8. 44–53: H's monologue – end.[1]

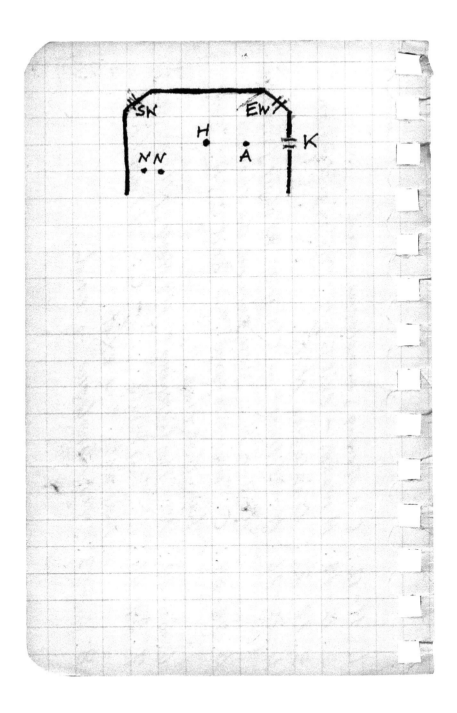

C's walk, posture :
stiff, some at knees?
Waist?
stooped. When still
tries to straighten, re-
stoops

—

moving painful as economical
as possible. When possible
more. Cf. ~~Bosch~~ 2 : "Then
move" & 7 : "Then then
it" : ~~[illegible]~~
~~[illegible]~~

—

sound of footsteps

—

C forgets ~~[illegible]~~ EW,
goes back for it,
starts with it from SW to NN,
brings it back.   Cf. 8

—

MS   1975

[Drawing of set.][1]
[SW = sea window; EW = earth window; NN = Nell and Nagg; A = halfway from K to H; H = Hamm; K = kitchen]

C's walk, posture:
stiff, gone at knees ⎫
           waist ⎭
stooped. When still
tries to straighten, re-
stoops

—

moving painful as economical
as possible. When possible
none. Cf. [*erasure*] 2: 'Then
move' & 7: 'Then open
it.' [*erasure*]
sur place.

—

sound of footsteps

—

C forgets [*erasure*] ladder EW [earth window],
goes back for it,
starts with it from SW [sea window] to NN [Nagg and Nell],
brings it back. Cf. 8

—

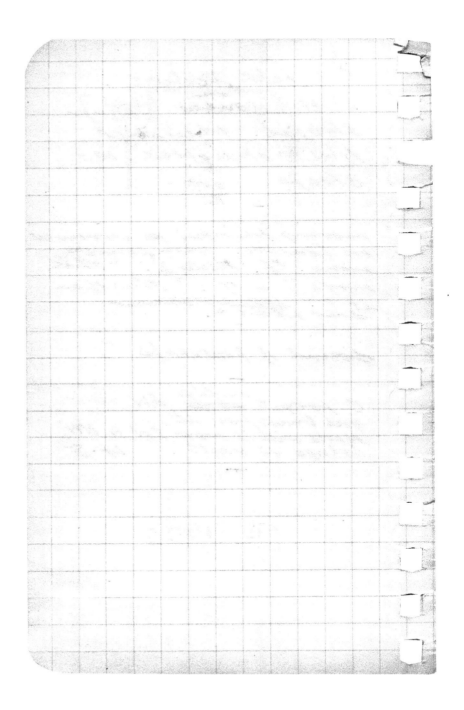

<u>Gate</u>

1. H.

2. NN

3. SW ■

4. EW ■

from (A) =
half way from door
to H — where
always stops
when summoned

Head bowed in perplexity before
going for steps.

<u>Unveiling</u>

1 EW ■ } or looks only if
2 SW ■ } no curtains

3. NN

4. H

cf. general

C perplexed. all seemingly
in order, yet a change.
Fatal grain added to form
impossible heap. <u>Ratio</u>
<u>ruentis acervi</u>. Last straw.

Mirthless chuckle at each
item unveiled.

1.

<u>Gaze</u>
1. H.
2. NN
3. SW [*erasure*]
4. EW [*erasure*]

} from (A) =
halfway from door
to H – where
always stops
when summoned.

—

Head bowed in perplexity before
going for steps.

—

<u>Unveiling</u>[1]
1. EW [*erasure*]
2. SW [*erasure*]
3. NN
4. H

} or looks only if
no curtains

cf. general

—

C perplexed. All seemingly
in order, yet a change.
Fatal grain added to form
impossible heap. <u>Ratio
ruentis acervi</u>. Last straw.[2]

—

Mirthless chuckle[3] at each
item unveiled.

Peep under H's handkerchief.

—

Ladder business simplified
max.

—

At bins: 1st Nell. Deep
stoop. From: behind H.
stet.

Speech: move to door
killed after "I can't be
punished any more." Cf.
8 after "...dying of their
wounds."

—

~~Clov~~ Clov gone most of
ex. trailing sheets

—

H's handkerchief: faint
trace of blood

—

Red faces: cut.

2

C. whistled : ~~the~~ instantaneous
who jinni to aladdin , or
with bag ? If latter exploit
b 99.
—

Dialogue : rahid tac autac,
naeue, re-tac-aa-tac
—

" Then move ." Steps own place.
2 loud : 2 less... " There "
... 2 less : 2 loud ... " Here "

queer strange
—

after H ; "Give him a biscuit "
add C : " I'll go & get a biscuit "
—

Painkiller 1 & 2
I'll leave you 1

no move 1, 2, 3 (bicycle wheels,
pap, nature)
taking its course 1
—

Prepare stauncher for neat
fold in 4 — Cf. 8 : "Since that's
the way ... " No appearance between ?

Peep under H's handkerchief.[1]

—

Ladder business simplified
max. [maximum][2]

—

At bins: 1st Nell. Deep
stoop. From: \<behind\> H.
stet.

—

Speech: move to door
killed after 'I can't be
punished any more.' Cf.
8 after '. . . dying of their
wounds.'[3]

—

[*erasure*] Clov gone most of
ex. trailing sheets[4]

—

H's handkerchief: faint
trace of blood[5]

—

Red faces: cut.[6]

2

C. whistled:[1] [*erasure*] instantaneous
like jinni to Aladdin, or
with lag? If latter exploit
sqq. [subsequently]

—

Dialogue: rapid <u>tac au tac</u>,
pause, <u>re-tac-au-tac</u>[2]

—

'Then move.' Steps sur place.[3]
2 loud: 2 less . . . 'There'
. . . 2 less: 2 loud . . . 'Here'

—

<queer> strange[4]

—

After H: 'Give him a biscuit'
add C: 'I'll go & get a biscuit'

—

Painkiller 1 & 2
I'll leave you 1
no more 1, 2, 3 (bicycle wheels,
pap, nature)
taking its course 1[5]

—

Prepare stauncher for neat
fold in 4 – Cf. 8: 'Since that's
the way . . .' No appearance between?[6]

Fin of staunecher emerging
smart from breast pocket

Mene mene tekel upharsin
~~██████████████████████~~

numbered numbered weighed
divided
Daniel V

3

analogy N's knocks on
lid, H's on wall (4)

Tailor story: analogy
voice + attitude with
H's (6);

MS 1975

Fin of stauncher emerging
smart from breast pocket
—

Mene mene tekel upharsin
[*erasure*]
numbered numbered weighed
divided
Daniel V^{I}
—

3

analogy N's [Nagg's] knocks on
lid, H's [Hamm's] on wall (4)

—

Tailor story: analogy
voice and attitude with
H's [Hamm's] (6).

—

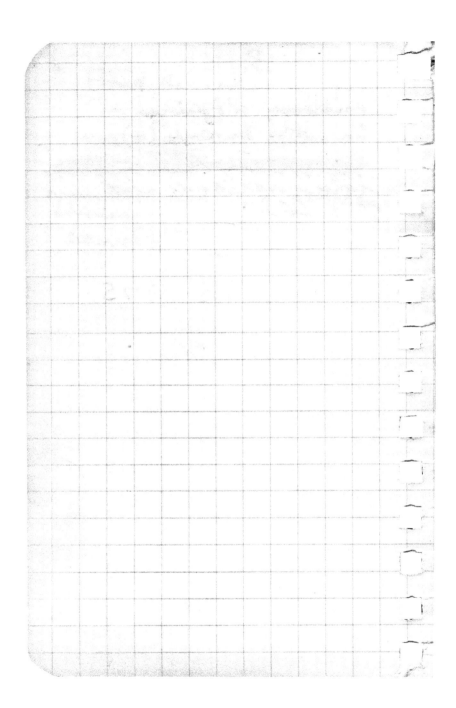

Pain-killer → 3
I'll leave you
No more
Taking its course

"Desert" Hold C holding
wrist, N looking up at him,
before he closes lid & "She
has no further"

C remains at line till "Seven
down ..." Then with "I'll
go & get the driver" (added)
towards door.

Cuts: cf. pp. 23, 24.

after
I'll measure it
I'll go & get the tape } starts to move

after "little more" back in
centre: no moving of chair,
simple 5 thumps crese.,
beginning after "bang
in the centre."

4

Pain killer [*erasure*] 3
I'll leave you [*erasure*]
No more [*erasure*]
Taking its course

—

'Desert' Hold[.] C [Clov] holding
wrist, N [Nell] looking up at him,
before he closes lid & 'She
has no more pulse'[1]

—

C remains at bin till 'Screw
down . . .' Then with 'I'll
go & get the driver' (added)[2]
towards door.

—

Cuts: cf. pp. 23, 24.[3]

—

After
I'll measure it   ⎫
I'll go & get the tape ⎬   starts to move[4]
                    ⎭

—

After 'little turn' back in
centre: no moving of chair,
simple 5 thumps <u>cresc.</u> [crescendo],[5]
beginning after 'Bang
in the centre.'

"Why?" Have you shrunk?
etc." Change or simply
cut.
‑

move from earth to sea.
and push up . after 2
steps back for ladder?
Knock on wall must
sound - Ring? -

prepare back of chair
for thumps - dest
‑

... the shivers.
C to A or break chair? -
‑

windows not high -
low steps - fixed -
justifying - "Have
you shrunk?"

after turn for "what in
God's name ...ing" no
more ......ing

after " Pah you saw yr.
heart " moves forwards
door. Stopped at usual
position for "CN."

—

Painkiller —   4, 5
I'll leave you 2, 3, 4, 5, 6
taking its course 2, 3

—

after each "I'll leave you"
move towards door

—

Parallel between C's reaction
to H's "In my ~~house~~ ..." (cringe)
~~and~~ ~~and~~ H's to N's " It's
natural ... " (6. h: 38)

—

after giving gatt moves away
to A.

—

Pacing for idea:

ah good ↑↓ The pains — leave me ↑
A   ↓   A
What — having an idea A ah!

'Why? Have you shrunk?
etc.' Change or simply
cut.[1]

—

Move from earth to sea:
no business? After, 2
steps back for ladder?[2]

—

Knock on wall must
sound – Ring? –

—

prepare back of chair
for thumps – dust

—

. . . the shivers . . .
C to A or <beside> chair?[3]

—

Windows not high –
low steps – fixed –
justifying – 'Have
you shrunk?'[4]

—

After turn for 'What in
God's name . . .' no
more looking[5]

5

After 'Pah[!] You saw yr. [your]
heart' moves towards
door. Stopped at usual
position on 'Clov!'

—

Painkiller – 4, 5
I'll leave you 2, 3, 4, 5, 6
taking its course 2, 3

—

After each 'I'll leave you'
move towards door

—

Parallel between C's reaction
to H's 'In my house . . .' (cringe)
[*erasure*] and H's to N's 'It's
natural . . .' (6. p. 38)[1]

—

After giving gaff moves away
to A.

—

Pacing for idea:
ah good ↑↓ [2] The pains – leave me ↑
A   A

What – having an idea ↓A ah!

C moves as little as possible
Cf 2. h 14 " Then move ! "

C gives arse not head
of dog into H's hand

after giving gaff back to A
or only after " That means
that bloody awful . . "
                    Barefoot?
Back with alarm on tiptoe & shocks
H with bell .
Schaden grin . so. Later
waking N .

Analogy Clov-dog when
trying to make it stand

C. amused by H's efforts
to move chair with gaff

C's relish of N's curse

—

C's entrance: on flight
from escaped rat?

—

During N's curse eyes
1. On Nagg
2. Forward kitchen (rat)
3. On Hamm (relishing
his distress)

—

4. Witto from "Yes, I
hope I'll live till then ..."
5. Clov's from H's
" yes, one day you'll
know what it is ..."
(5)

—

knocks on lid of bin:
cf. 3 of bin) + 4 (wall)

—

analogy voice + attitude
with N's tailor story (3)

C moves as little as possible
Cf. 2. p. 14 'Then move!'

—

[*erasure*] C gives arse not head
of dog into H's hand[1]

—

After giving gaff[,] back to A
or only after 'That means
that bloody awful . . .'

—

Back with alarm [clock] on tiptoe, Barefoot? shocks
H [Hamm] with bell. [*erasure*]
Schadengrin.[2] Do. [ditto] later
waking N.

—

Analogy Clov–dog when
trying to make it stand

—

C. [Clov] amused by H's efforts
to move chair with gaff

—

6

C's relish of N's curse[1]

—

C's entrance: on flight
from escaped rat?

—

During N's curse [Clov's] eyes
1. on Nagg
2. toward kitchen (rat)
3. On Hamm (relishing
his distress)

—

H. wilts from 'Yes, I
hope I'll live till then . . .'
Cf. Clov's from H's
'Yes, one day you'll
know what it is . . .'[2]
(5)

—

knocks on lid of bin:
Cf. 3 (bin) & 4 (wall)

—

analogy voice & attitude
with N's [Nagg's] tailor story (3)

N's reactions to story:

1. Amused by "Something dripping."

2. Listens till *~~[crossed out]~~* meteo 1 " ... bitter day .. "

3. From which head on hands serum of bei till " ... bread for his br²t " *~~[unclear]~~* listening.

4. Meteo 4 " ... dry day ... " head again on hands till whistle. —

on floor same area (A)

1. ~~Dog~~
2. Tin
3. ~~tin~~ Glass
4. Gaff.

Dirty Crute: 1, 2. Putting ...
away: 3 order · last dust:
4. ~~Dish~~ it

         —

No more : 4, 5, 6 (tide,
navigators, rags)

         —

"Bring me under the window."
difficulty of perch
spoken on the way
Perhaps hold and wait
till "Ah great fun ..."
or try pulling chair

         —

"There you it!" " C :
Clov March - ramp on stage.
Id, after "Close the window ...
with knock on steps for window
opened, after steps & before -
"Give me a rug." stops C
at A on way to door

Entrance Clov; on flights
~~Hope the capped half up~~

N's [Nagg's] reaction to story:

1. amused by 'Something
   dripping'.
2. Listens till [*erasure*] meteo [i.e. weather] 1
   '. . . bitter day . . .'
3. From which head on
   hands on rim of bin
   till '. . . bread for his
   brat' when resumes
[*erasure*] listening.
4. Meteo [i.e. weather] 4 '. . . dry day . . .'[1]
   head again on hands till
   whistle.

—

7

on floor same area (A)
1. Dog
2. Tin
3. [*erasure*] Glass
4. Gaff.
Dirty brute: 1, 2 Putting . . .
away: 3 order . . . last dust:
4. Drop it[1]

———

No more: 4, 5, 6 (tide,
navigators, rugs)

———

'Bring me under the window':
difficulty of text
spoken on the way.
Perhaps hold up start
till 'Ah great fun . . .'
or try pulling chair[2]

———

'Then open it!' C:
brief tramp-tramp on stage
id. [identical] after 'Close the window . . .
with knock on steps for window
opened, after steps and before —[3]

———

'Give me a rug . . .' stops C
at A on way to door.

———

[*erasure*]

" Yes. But now it's empty. "
C goes with alarm to
6 fires, puts it to Nagg's,
moves away, second thoughts,
transfers it to Nell's.
~~words towards door~~
~~stopped~~ "what are you
doing?" " "Winding up . "
moves towards door,
stopped at A by "look
at the earth . " "What'll
I do?" on his way to bins.

—

Consider ending song

—

Painkiller   6
no more   7, 8
(painkiller, "coffins"

*

Words from heart: after
I H vows head, thinking
no more, then raises
head again for 2 .

C forgets ~~ladder~~ at SW.) & I
goes back for it)

[erasure]

8

'Yes. But now it's empty.'
C goes with alarm to
bins, puts it on Nagg's,
moves away, second thoughts,
transfers it to Nell's[1]
<moves towards door.
Stopped> 'What are you
doing?' 'Winding up.'
Moves towards door.
Stopped at A by 'Look
at the earth.' 'What'll
I do?' on his way to bins.

—

Consider cutting song[2]

—

Pain killer   6
no more   7, 8
(painkiller, coffins[)]'

—

Words from heart: after
1 H bows head, thinking
no more, then raises
head again for 2[3]

—

C forgets [*erasure*] ladder at SW. [sea window]   }   cf. 1
goes back for it   }

Creaking lids　　MS 1975

—

increasing cold

2. Nagg — Nell

7. Clov at SW

　Hamm : "Give me a rug …"

—

Knocks 3 : 1 Nagg on lid, ~~once~~ *twice* (3)

　　　　　 2. ~~Hamm~~ ·· wall, twice (4)

　　　　　 3. Nagg " lid, twice (6)

—

C's entrances identical —
same number of steps to A,
same half truth away.

Exceptions : with biscuit (2)

　　　　　　　 " gaff (5)

　　　 "clear away this muck …" = (4)

—

opening looks ⎫ (1) same duration
unveiling   " ⎭
with little extra for 8 (Hamm)
~~and~~ with pick

Creaking lids

—

increasing cold
2. Nagg – Nell
7. Clov at SW [sea window]
    Hamm: 'Give me a rug . . .'

—

Knocks 3: 1. Nagg on lid [*erasure*] twice (3)
          2. Hamm ''   wall, twice (4)
          3. Nagg ''   lid, twice (6)[1]

—

C's entrances identical –
same number of steps to A,
same half turn away.[2]
Exceptions: with biscuit (2)
          ''   gaff (5)
          'clear away this muck . . .' (4)

—

opening looks ⎫
unveiling ''   ⎬ (1) same duration
with little extra for 8 (Hamm)
[*erasure*] with peep.

towards end of speech
- motion - silences -
frozen postures
—

towards end of speech
& motion – silences –
frozen postures

—

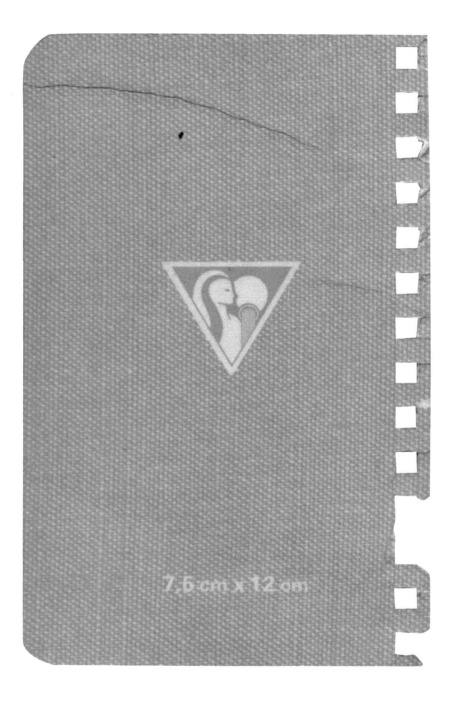

7,5 cm x 12 cm

Page 1

1 – The sixteen scenes of the Schiller *Endspiel* have been trimmed to half that number for the Riverside *Endgame*. The first four scenes remained essentially the same in Berlin and London, but scene 4 in Riverside combined scenes 4 and 5 from the Schiller; scene 5 combined scenes 6, 7 and 8; scene 6 combined 9 and 10; scene 7 combined scenes 11–15; and finally scene 8 in London corresponded to scene 16 in Berlin.

Page 2

1 – Essentially the same drawing exists on p. 11 of *Fac(B)*. (See also textual note to line 7.)

Page 5

1 – Beckett's patterning of action begins early in *Endgame* as Clov's initial gaze at the room and the unveiling of the room's contents are contrapuntal: the gaze is clockwise, the unveiling is anti-clockwise. (See also textual note to line 10.)
2 – Clov's discomfiture at some barely perceptible change in the room is compared here to one of the paradoxes of Zeno the Eleatic and to one of the logical puzzles called *sorites* from the Epistles of Horace (II.I.47). (See textual note to line 25.)
3 – Only the hint of a laugh, said Beckett in Berlin. (See textual note to line 14.)

Page 6

1 – The action was revised so that Clov lifted a corner of Hamm's handkerchief. See textual note to line 21.
2 – One of the many revisions that Beckett made to simplify Clov's opening mime. See textual note to line 10.
3 – Those 'dying of their wounds' is a reference to mercy, one of the 'five dispensers of life's consolations': love, friendship, nature, science and mercy. See textual note to line 1434.

4 – Instead of folding the sheets, Clov drags them off, as he did in the Schiller production. See textual note to line 17.

5 – Beckett used a grey handkerchief in Berlin to replace the bloodstained handkerchief of the printed text. In the Riverside production, however, Beckett moved closer to his original text by reintroducing some blood stains. See textual note to line 19.

6 – The more melodramatic red faces of the printed text were eliminated in both the Schiller and Riverside productions. See textual note to line 8.

Page 7

1 – The whistle Hamm uses to summon Clov, and to which Clov responds immediately, should suggest the aggression between the two. See textual note to line 51.

2 – Beckett is suggesting some of the rapid tempo of this scene's dialogue and the importance of the separating pause. See textual notes to lines 1046 and 1065.

3 – Beckett's translation of *sur place* is 'marks time audibly'. See textual note to line 128.

4 – This change was made at the request of actor Patrick Magee who suggested to Beckett the homosexual overtones of queer. See textual note to line 77.

5 – On the inside cover to *Fac(B)* Beckett also outlined some of the play's major thematic elements as follows:

'I'll leave you': 10 [i.e. ten times, although only nine page numbers are listed here] (15, 17, 29, 30, 31, 34, 39, 44, 50)

Painkiller: 6 (14, 16, 23, 28, 34, 46)

No more . . .

bicycle wheels [p.]	15
pap	"
nature	16
tide	41
navigators	43
rugs	44
painkiller	46
coffins	49

Taking its course: 3 (17, 26, 31)

(See also textual note to lines 118 and 139, and editorial notes to *Schiller Nb*, Inside Front Cover, note 1.)

6 – The answer to this question is clearly, 'No appearance between.' (See also textual notes to lines 19, 1232, 1500 and 1505.)

Page 8

1 – The allusion here is to the biblical Book of Daniel, where Daniel reads the prophecy on the wall. Beckett notes the message first in the transliterated Aramaic and then in English. See textual note to line 219.

Page 11

1 – In this revised death scene, Beckett has added the word 'more' to Clov's observation. See textual notes to lines 417, 418 and 419.

2 – Here Beckett notes the addition of this line. See textual note to line 431.

3 – Reference here is to two pages of the Faber text where excisions had been made. The revisions are detailed in textual notes to lines 450, 451, 463 and 496–502.

4 – Beckett added false starts towards the kitchen for these two lines. See textual notes to lines 482 and 489.

5 – As Beckett revised Clov's moving of Hamm's chair to a series of thumps, he suggested a musical structure to the percussion. See textual note to lines 496–502.

Page 12

1 – Apparently Beckett decided on neither, since the line (520) was retained in Riverside (G28).

2 – This scene was actually cut in Riverside. (See also textual note to line 547.)

3 – 'Beside' here is cancelled in favour of Clov's place called A.

4 – A realistic touch is added here as Beckett suggests using a low, fixed ladder to suggest Clov's shrinking, which is only natural, as Lucky suggests in *Waiting for Godot* since man 'wastes and pines, wastes and pines'.

5 – An important revision which increases the incidence of Clov's disobedience as Clov decreases the number of times he actually examines the without. See textual note to line 556.

Page 13

1 – Both of these are parallel responses to malediction. See textual notes to lines 655 and 1018.
2 – Despite the five dots in each walking sequence outlined here, the pattern in Riverside was a pacing of eight steps. See textual note to line 850.

Page 14

1 – See textual note to lines 751–2.
2 – Instead of the usual *Schadenfreude* ['malicious joy'], Beckett notes.

Page 15

1 – Nagg's curse is here delivered to Hamm. See textual note to line 1018.
2 – Beckett here develops the parallel between Nagg's curse of Hamm, and Hamm's of Clov. See preceding note.

Page 16

1 – Hamm's speech is structured by the weather report. See textual note to line 921.

Page 17

1 – The numbers here are taken from the previous note and refer to the objects that Clov is retrieving in this scene.
2 – Although Clov still pushed the chair in the Schiller production, he pulled it in Riverside, a revision Beckett reaffirmed for the Revised Text. See, for example, textual notes to lines 450–2.
3 – Beckett revised this scene heavily for the Riverside production so that Clov feigns ascent and descent of the ladder. See textual note to lines 1172 and 1186.

Page 19

1 – The revision here shows Clov acknowledging the possibility of Nagg's coming up and knocking over the clock. Since Nell is dead, the clock seems safer on her bin. In the Schiller production, however, Clov removed the picture from the left wall and hung the clock on the exposed nail. See textual note to line 1287.

2 – Beckett not only cut the song in the Riverside production but all reference to it as well. See textual note to line 1301.

3 – Hamm is responding to Clov's outline of the 'five dispensers of life's consolations'. Hamm evidently bows his head on 'love' and raises it on 'friendship'. See textual note to line 1434.

Page 21

1 – In Berlin the pattern varied slightly. Nagg used two sets of two taps on Nell's lid at first. Hamm, likewise, used two sets of two taps on the shelter wall. Nagg then used one set of two taps for his final (and futile) attempt to call Nell.

2 – The emphasis here is on the symmetry of Clov's movements. See textual note to line 51.

Cuts and Changes to the Text
of *Endspiel* (*Endgame*)
for the Production
at the
Schiller-Theater Werkstatt,
Berlin,
September 1967

Page-reference subheadings are to the text Beckett used to prepare for the Berlin Production, *Sac(B)*. *Photo* includes some 90 per cent of dialogue revisions from *Sac(B)*, with the addition of a number of small, sometimes inexplicable anomalies, but it fails to include almost all revisions of action. The following list of revisions then represents a more complete German revised text than that in *Photo*.

Of the following revisions those accepted by *Photo* and printed therein are followed by the page reference to that text. The lack of page reference following the revision indicates its omission from *Photo*. Where pertinent or informative, the *Photo* and *Sac(B)* texts are compared with the record of performance taped for German television, but that text itself contains anomalies, often changes unconsciously introduced by actors after repeated performances. Those variants are usually not noted.

Page 10

In the space between the end of the description of Clov's opening action and his opening monologue, Beckett has drawn a diagram of Clov's movement in the shelter. From the kitchen entrance stage left Clov moves diagonally to sea window right, then, parallel to the upstage wall, to earth window, then diagonally to bins downstage right, then in a semi-circle behind Hamm, just right of the centre line, to Clov's spot midway between Hamm's chair and kitchen opening where he delivers his monologue. Above the drawing Beckett has written:

Sea window, curtains, looks
Earth   „   „   „

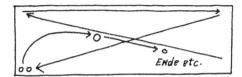

Page 13

After the second *Pause* Beckett added 'Slight move to door immediately checked.'
    Semi-colon after 'drei Meter' revised to comma, *Photo*, p. 14.
    'u. [und] warten' added after 'Wand betrachten', *Photo*, p. 14.
    The italicized 'geht er hinaus' underlined and the figure '1' written in the right margin. These numbers are Beckett's tally of Clov's entrances and exits.
    'Sehr rote Gesichtsfarbe' cut. 'Schwarze' revised to 'Milchig weisse'. *Photo*, p. 14, makes the cut, misses the revision and prints 'Blindenbrille' in place of 'Brille'.
    Hamm's 'Also' revised to 'Ah', *Photo*, p. 16.
    'Ich bin wieder dran' revised to 'Ich bin dran', *Photo*, p. 16.
    Full stop replaces exclamation point after 'Jetzt spiele ich'.
    '*er gähnt*' cut.

Page 14

'Entre Clov aussitôt' is underlined and a figure '1' written in the left margin.

Page 15

'Nein, ich bin allein' revised to 'Clov! (*Pause*) Nein? (*Pause*) Gut.'

The italicized *'Clov kommt sofort herein'* is underlined and a figure '1' written in the right margin.

Clov's 'Ich habe dich gerade geweckt' revised to 'Ich habe dich gerade aufstehen lassen', *Photo*, p. 18.

Clov's 'Ich kann dich nicht alle fünf Minuten wecken . . .' revised to 'Ich kann dich nicht alle fünf Minuten aufstehen lassen . . .', *Photo*, p. 18.

Hamm's 'Sie sollen ganz weiss sein' revised to 'Sie sollen ganz weiss geworden sein', *Photo*, p. 18.

Page 17

Question mark replaces full stop after Clov's 'Du nicht', *Photo*, p. 18.

Clov's 'Immer wieder dieselben Fragen . . .' revised to 'Das ganze Leben dieselben Fragen . . .', *Photo*, p. 18.

'Pause' is cut after Hamm's *'Clov rührt sich nicht.'*

Page 19

'Nicht der Mühe wert' added at top of page then cancelled. Hamm's first 'Nein' cancelled then restored with '*Stet*' in the right margin. *Photo*, p. 18, prints Beckett's original revision, 'Nicht der Mühe wert', but, in performance, Hamm says, 'Nein.'

Hamm's 'Muss ich jetzt nicht meine Pillen einnehmen?' revised to 'Muss ich jetzt nicht mein Beruhigungsmittel einnehmen?', *Photo*, p. 18.

Page 21

Clov's movement, *'bis an die Wand im Hintergrund und lehnt sich mit Stirn und Händen daran'*, was cut, and Beckett wrote in English above the cut, 'To door'.

Clov's 'Da' revised to 'Hier' twice, *Photo*, p. 18.

'Dann taucht der Kopf auf, der mit einer Schlafmütze bedeckt ist' revised to *'Dann*

tauch der [a second 'der' left in] *mit einer Schlafmütze bedeckten Kopf auf*, *Photo*, p. 18, but *Photo* prints 'bedeckte'.

'Ich geh jetzt . . .' revised to 'Ich verlasse dich . . .', *Photo*, p. 18.

Page 23

Clov's entrances and exits are underlined and marked numerically in accordance with the outline in the *Schiller Nb*. On this page entrances 2 and 3 are so noted.

Hamm's 'Wie geht es deinem Rumpf?' revised to, 'Wie geht es deinen Stümpfen?, *Photo*, p. 20.

Nagg's 'Kümmere dich nicht um meinen Rumpf' revised to 'Kümmere dich nicht um meine Stümpfe', *Photo*, p. 20.

Page 25

Clov's 'an seinen Platz neben dem [*recte* den] Sessel zurückgehend' cancelled and replaced by 'standing by bin'.

'*Pause*' after Hamm's 'Jedem seine Spezialität' cancelled and replaced by 'CLOV moves'.

'*Pause*' after Hamm's 'Kein Anruf?' cancelled and replaced by 'Halts'.

Hamm's 'Keiner lacht?' revised to 'Nicht lachen?', *Photo*, p. 22. Hamm retained the 'Keiner lacht?' in performance.

Illegible word in right margin.

'*Pause*' after Hamm's 'Mir auch nicht' revised to 'CLOV moves'.

After Hamm calls 'Clov', '(CLOV *stops at O* [his place midway between chair and kitchen entrance])' added.

Hamm's 'wir ändern uns!' revised to 'wir verändern uns!', *Photo*, p. 22.

Hamm's 'Wir tun, was wir können' revised to 'Man tut, was man kann', *Photo*, p. 22.

Clov's reply, 'Das sollen wir nicht', revised to 'Man hat unrecht', *Photo*, p. 22.

Hamm's 'Hältst du dich für gescheit . . .' revised to 'Du hältst dich für gescheit . . .', *Photo*, p. 22.

'einmalig?' cancelled, replaced by 'nicht', which is then also cancelled. *Photo*, p. 22, prints 'nicht?', which was spoken in production. Illegible sign in right margin here as well.

Clov's 'In tausend Stücken!' cut, *Photo*, p. 22.

Page 27

Hamm's 'Das geht nicht so schnell' revised to 'Es geht nicht schnell', *Photo*, p. 22.

Hamm's 'Muss ich jetzt nicht meine Pillen einnehmen?' revised to 'Muss ich jetzt nicht mein Beruhigungsmittel einnehmen?', *Photo*, p. 22.

Clov's 'Ich gehe jetzt . . .' revised to 'Ich verlasse dich . . .', *Photo*, p. 22.

Hamm's 'Menetekel?' underlined and in the margin Beckett noted 'Balshezar Dan. 5', an allusion to the biblical Book of Daniel.

Hamm's 'Was man nicht alles zu hören bekommt!' at first revised to 'Was man nicht alles zu hören kriegt', but then restored with a note in the right margin, '(stet)'. *Photo*, p. 22, prints 'kriegt!' but 'bekommt' was spoken in performance.

Before Clov's 'Du solltest nicht . . .' Beckett added '(moving in)'. Stage direction missed in *Photo*, p. 22.

Hamm's 'Sind deine Körner aufgegangen?' revised to 'Sind deine Samenkörnchen aufgegangen?'. *Photo*, p. 22, prints 'Samenkörner', but, in performance, Hamm said 'Samenkörnchen'.

Page 29

Hamm's 'Es ist nicht so heiter wie soeben' revised to 'Es ist nicht so heiter wie vorhin', *Photo*, p. 22.

Clov's 'Es scheint so' at first revised to 'Es sieht so aus' in order to conform to same on p. 59, and the page number is noted in the right margin. But Beckett cancelled the revision, and instead revised the line on p. 59 to conform to that on p. 29, *Photo*, p. 22.

Hamm's 'was ist denn eigentlich los?' is unrevised in *Sac(B)* but printed as 'was geschieht eigentlich?' in *Photo*, p. 22. In production Hamm says, 'was ist eigentlich los?'

Clov's movement, '*Er geht zur Tür und bleibt stehen*', cut.

Clov's exit underlined, and the exit number, '4', noted in the left margin.

Page 31

Nell's 'Willst du wieder mit mir schäkern?' revised to 'Willst du wieder mit mir [?]'. *Photo*, p. 24, prints this revision retaining the question mark of the original.

Nagg's 'Schliefst du?' revised to 'Hast du geschlafen?', *Photo*, p. 24.

Nell's 'Warum diese Komödie, immer wieder?' revised to 'Warum diese Komödie, jeden Tag?', *Photo*, p. 24.

Nagg's 'Wie bitte?' revised to 'Was?', *Photo*, p. 24.

Nagg's 'Das sollst du nicht sagen' revised to 'Sag das nicht', *Photo*, p. 24.

Page 33

'an' cut from the end of Nagg's 'Erinnerst du dich an . . .' and added to the opening of his next line so that 'Den Tandemunfall, bei dem wir unsere Haxen verloren' revised to 'An den Tandemunfall, bei dem wir unsere Beinchen verloren', *Photo*, p. 24.

Nagg's 'Haxen' was revised to 'Beinchen'. This revision was missed in *Photo*, p. 24, but delivered in performance.

Nagg's 'Ich friere' revised to 'Mich friert', *Photo*, p. 24.

The exclamation mark after Nell's 'Ja' replaced by a full stop. *Photo*, p. 24, retains the exclamation point.

'*Nagg schaut sie an*', cut.

Nagg's 'Nun ist es Sand, den er vom Strand holt' at first revised to 'er holt ihn vom Strand', then cut to 'Nun ist es Sand'. *Photo*, p. 24, prints 'Nun ist es Sand, er holt ihn vom Strand', which was the line delivered in performance.

Page 35

Nagg's 'Wir müssen maulen' revised to 'Man muss maulen' then to 'Wir müssen das Maul aufmachen'. *Photo*, p. 24, prints 'Man muss maulen', but 'Wir müssen das Maul aufmachen' was delivered in performance.

Hamm's second '*Pause*. Natur!', cut, *Photo*, p. 28.

Nell's '. . . das gebe ich zu' revised to 'zugegeben', *Photo*, p. 28.

Nell's two 'lachten' revised to 'lachen', *Photo*, p. 28.

Page 37

Nell's speech reads '. . . aber man lacht nicht mehr darüber', but *Photo*, p. 28, prints 'aber wir lachen'. The original, however, was delivered in performance.

'würdest' in Nagg's 'Ich dachte, du würdest mich verlassen' revised to 'wolltest', *Photo*, p. 28.

Ellipses inserted twice between Hamm's 'Es ist vielleicht' and 'ein Äderchen', and Nell's repetition of same.

Nagg's 'Ich werde dir die Geschichte vom Schneider erzählen' revised to 'Ich werde dir den Witz vom Schneider erzählen', *Photo*, p. 28.

Page 39

'Er' replaced 'Sie' in Nell's 'Sie ist gar nicht lustig', *Photo*, p. 28.

Nagg's 'Du hast immer darüber lachen müssen' revised to 'Er hat dich immer zum Lachen gebracht . . .', *Photo*, p. 28.

Nagg's 'Wir hätten ertrinken können' revised to 'Wir hätten ertrinken sollen', *Photo*, p. 28.

Nell's 'Ich lachte' revised to 'Es war', *Photo*, p. 28.

Nagg's 'Ach was, ach was, du lachtest über meine Geschichte' revised to 'Ach was, ach was, es war mein Witz', *Photo*, p. 28.

Nell's 'Es war tief, so tief' revised to 'Es war tief, tief', *Photo*, p. 28.

Nell's 'So hell. So klar' revised to 'So weiss. So rein', *Photo*, p. 28.

Nagg's 'Hör sie dir nochmal an' revised to 'Hör ihn dir nochmal an', *Photo*, p. 28.

Page 41

Nagg's 'Ich erzähle sie schlecht' revised to 'Ich erzähle ihn schlecht', *Photo*, p. 28.

Nagg's 'Ich erzähle diese Geschichte immer schlechter' revised to 'Ich erzähle diesen Witz immer schlechter', *Photo*, p. 28.

Nagg's '. . .die Maiglöckchen' revised to '. . .die Osterglocken', *Photo*, p. 28.

Page 42

Hamm's 'Oh pour ça elle est formidable, cette poudre' is bracketed.

Page 43

'Clov kommt herein' underlined.

Nell's 'So klar' revised to 'So weisse', *Photo*, p. 28.

Hamm's 'Wie, bitte? Was erzählt sie da?' revised to 'Was? Was?'. *Photo*, p. 28, picks up only part of this revision, the 'Wie, bitte?' to 'Was?'.

'leise' cancelled in Nell's *'leise, zu Clov'*.

Nell's 'Hau doch ab', at first revised to 'Ich wüsste, was ich täte; ich flöhe' then restored with '(*Stet*)'. *Photo*, p. 30, misses the restoration and prints the revised dialogue. In performance, however, 'Hau doch ab' was delivered.

Clov's *'auf dem Wege zu seinem Platz neben dem Sessel'* revised to 'From bin'.

After Clov's 'Sie hat keinen Puls mehr', Beckett at first added a 'Gut' then cancelled it. *Photo*, p. 30, replaces Clov's original line with 'Gut, dass sie keine Flöhe mehr hat'. And follows that with an expanded version of Hamm's response: 'Oh, das Puder ist prima dagegen. Was hat sie sich in den Bart gebrummt? Heraus damit!' In performance, however, Beckett's original version was delivered:

CLOV: Sie hat keinen Puls mehr.

HAMM: Was hat sie sich in den Bart gebrummt?

'nun' cancelled in Hamm's 'Sind sie nun beide eingesperrt?', *Photo*, p. 30.

Hamm's 'pinkeln' revised to 'pipi machen', *Photo*, p. 30.

Page 45

Hamm's 'Gib mir meine Pillen' revised to 'Gib mir mein Beruhigungsmittel', *Photo*, p. 30.

Clov's 'Es ist zu früh nach deinen Tropfen, sie würden nicht wirken' revised to 'Es ist zu früh nach deinem Stärkungsmittel, es würde nicht wirken', *Photo*, p. 30.

Hamm's 'Er ist natürlich tot, der alte Arzt' revised to 'Er ist natürlich gestorben, der alte Arzt', *Photo*, p. 30.

'tot' again revised to 'gestorben' in Hamm's 'Aber er ist tot', *Photo*, p. 30.

Hamm's 'Eine kleine Runde um die Welt' revised to 'Lass mich machen' and then to 'Eine Runde um die Welt', *Photo*, p 32.

Hamm's 'Es stimmt nicht!' at first revised to 'Es ist nicht wahr', but then Beckett noted 'stet'. In the margin 'ja' in parenthesis is offered as an alternative. The 'ja' was both printed in *Photo*, p. 34, and delivered in performance.

At the foot of the page Beckett drew the path of Hamm's 'turn', from Hamm's place to the upstage right wall, the window stage left and back to Hamm's place. The chair stops at the upstage right wall where Hamm delivers 'Ich stand [doch] genau' etc. On with 'Wir müssten' etc. 'Stop' at left window also noted.

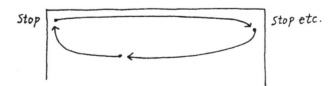

Page 47

In *Photo*, p. 34, '. . . die ANDERE Hölle' is printed 'die andere Hölle'.

Hamm's 'Hohle Steine' revised to 'Hohle Backsteine', *Photo*, p. 34.

Full stop replaces question mark after Clov's 'Ja, dein Platz ist hier?', *Photo*, p. 34.

Page 48

Clov's 'J'apporte l'escabeau' revised to 'Je suis de retour avec l'escabeau'.

Page 49

Hamm's 'Bleib nicht da!' revised to 'Bleib nicht da stehen!', *Photo*, p. 34.

Clov's entrances and exits underlined and their number noted in left margin.

Question mark replaces full stop in Hamm's 'Bist du kleiner geworden', *Photo*, p. 34.

Clov's 'Ich bringe die Leiter' revised to 'Ich bin wieder da, mit der Leiter'. *Photo*, p. 34, prints the revision minus the comma.

Page 50

Substantial cut of telescope scene in French text as follows:

> *Il monte sur l'escabeau, braque la lunette sur le dehors. Elle lui échappe des mains, tombe. Un temps.* J'ai fait exprès. *Il descend de l'escabeau, ramasse la lunette, l'examine, la braque sur la salle.* Je vois . . . une foule en délire. *Un temps.* Ça alors, pour une longue-vue c'est une longue-vue. *Il baisse la lunette, se tourne vers Hamm.* Alors? On ne rit pas?
> HAMM *ayant réfléchi*: Moi non.
> CLOV *ayant réfléchi*: Moi non plus.

Page 51

Clov's entrances and exits again underlined and their number noted in the margin.

Hamm's 'Welch ein Jammer' revised to 'Es ist zum Weinen'. *Photo*, p. 34, prints the revision with an exclamation point.

Beckett thought to introduce Clov's spy glass scene with 'Ich bin wieder da, mit dem Fernglas (?)', but he cancelled the line and trimmed the entire speech to correspond with the cut in the French text made on p. 50. The material cut in the German text is as follows:

> *Er steigt auf die Leiter und richtet das Fernglas nach draussen. Es entgleitet seinen Händen und fällt. Pause.* Ich tat es absichtlich. *Er steigt von der Leiter, hebt das Fernglas auf, prüft es und richtet es auf den Saal.* Ich sehe . . . eine begeisterte Menge. *Pause.* Na so was, dazu kann man wohl Fernrohr sagen. *Er lässt das Fernglas sinken und schaut Hamm an.* Na? Keiner lacht?
>
> HAMM *nachdem er überlegt hat*: Ich nicht.
>
> CLOV *nachdem er überlegt hat*: Ich auch nicht.

Photo, p. 34.

'. . . und' is cut from Clov's '. . . und nichts . . .', *Photo*, p. 34.

Page 53

Clov's 'Das ist es, was du wissen willst?' revised to 'Das möchtest Du wissen?' *Photo*, p. 34, prints the revision with a lower case 'd' in 'du', but precedes this question with a revision of 'In einem Wort?' to 'Mit einem Wort'. No indication of this revision is given in *Sac(B)*, but 'Mit' was delivered in performance.

Clov's 'Kaputt' revised to 'Aus'.

Clov's '. . . *geht ein paar Schritte auf das linke Fenster zu, macht kehrt, um die Leiter zu holen . . .*', cut.

Clov's '*lange*', cut.

Clov's five instances of '*schauend*', cut, the first replaced by 'turning to H. [Hamm]'.

Clov's '*das Fernglas absetzend, sich Hamm zuwendend, voller Ungeduld*', cut.

Page 55

First '*Pause*', cut.

Clov's '*Er setzt das Fernglas an*', cut.

Three more of Clov's '*schauend*', cut.

Clov's '*nachdem er nachgeschaut hat*', cut, and the following 'Denkste' revised to 'Kein Gedanke'. *Photo*, p. 36, prints the dialogue revision only.

Clov's '*Er setzt das Fernglas ab und wendet sich Hamm zu*', cut.

Clov's '*Noch lauter.* GRAU!', cut.

Clov's 'Ein helles Schwarz' revised to 'Hellschwarz', *Photo*, p. 36.

Hamm's 'Bleib nicht da' revised to 'Bleib nicht da stehen', *Photo*, p. 36. In performance, the previous phrase, 'Du übertreibst', was deleted.

Clov's 'Warum diese Komödie, immer wieder?' revised to 'Warum diese Komödie, jeden Tag?', *Photo*, p. 36.

Hamm's 'Darin war eine grosse Wunde' revised first to 'Weh weh [*illegible*]' then retained with *stet*, and finally revised again to 'Darin war eine kleine Wunde', *Photo*, p. 36.

In *Photo*, p. 36, the unrevised 'Was ist eigentlich los?' is revised to 'Was geschieht eigentlich'. In performance, however, the original *Sac(B)* is delivered.

Page 57

Hamm's '*Pause. Ich frage es mich*', cut, *Photo*, p. 36.

After Clov's second '*sich kratzend*', 'Auf mir [*illegible*] ist einer', added, *Photo*, p. 40.

In performance the 'Es sei denn, es ist eine Filzlaus' of *Sac(B)* and *Photo*, p. 40, is delivered as 'Es sei denn das es sich um eine Filzlaus handelt'.

'CLOV: Ich hole das Pulver', underlined.

'*Er geht hinaus*' in parenthesis and underlined, the figure '57' noted in the left margin.

Page 59

Clov's entrance underlined and the figure '8' noted in the left margin.

Clov's '*sein Hemd aus der Hose, die er so aufknöpft und offen hält*', cut, and 'Elastic waist' noted in the right margin.

Clov's 'Die Mistbiene!' revised to 'So ein Biest!', *Photo*, p. 40.

Hamm's 'Hast du sie erwischt?' revised to 'Hast du ihn erwischt?', *Photo*, p. 40.

Clov's 'Es sieht so aus' revised to 'Es scheint so' to conform with same on p. 29, the page number Beckett notes in the right margin, *Photo*, p. 40.

The following dialogue added to end this scene after '*und ordnet seine Kleider*':

Es sei denn, dass er sich kuschelt.

HAMM: Kuschelt! An wen? Kuscht willst du sagen. Es sei denn, dass er sich kuscht.

CLOV: Ah! Man sagt kuscht. Man sagt nicht kuschelt.

HAMM: Stell dir vor, wenn er sich an einen kuschelte, wären wir bedient. *Pause.*

Photo, p. 40, prints this addition with some variation in punctuation. In *Sac(B)*

Hamm's first 'Kuschelt' is followed by an exclamation point, not a question mark. And Clov's 'Man sagt kuscht' and 'Man sagt nicht kuschelt' are followed by full stops in *Sac(B)*, not the question marks of *Photo*.

Clov's 'Ah, das ist gut, das ist gut' revised to 'Ah, das ist schön, das ist schön'. *Photo* missed this revision, but 'schön' was delivered in performance.

Hamm's 'Die Strömungen werden uns forttreiben . . .' revised to 'Die Strömungen treiben uns fort . . .', *Photo*, p. 40.

Hamm's 'Morgen bin ich schon weit weg' revised to 'Morgen werde ich schon weit weg sein!', *Photo*, p. 40.

Page 61

Hamm's 'meine Pillen' revised to 'mein Beruhigungsmittel', *Photo*, p. 40.

Hamm's third 'Warte mal!' is printed 'Warte!' in *Photo*, p. 40, but delivered as 'Warte mal!' in performance.

Hamm's 'Eines Tages sagst du dir' revised to 'Eines Tages wirst du dir sagen', *Photo*, p. 42.

Hamm's 'Dann sagst du dir' revised to 'Dann wirst du dir sagen', *Photo*, p. 42.

Hamm's 'Du sagst dir' revised to 'Du wirst dir sagen', *Photo*, p. 42.

Page 63

Hamm's 'Du betrachtest die Wand ein wenig und dann sagst du dir' revised to 'Du wirst die Wand ein wenig betrachten und dann wirst du dir sagen', *Photo*, p. 42.

Hamm's 'was es ist' revised to 'wie es ist', *Photo*, p. 42.

Hamm's unrevised 'Eines Tages sagst du dir' is printed as 'Eines Tages wirst du dir sagen' in *Photo*, p. 42. In performance, however, the original *Sac(B)* text was delivered.

Hamm's 'Natürlich!' at first revised to 'Freilich!', but then restored with 'stet' in the right margin. *Photo*, p. 42, missed the restoration and printed 'Freilich!'. In performance, however, 'Natürlich' was delivered.

Page 65

Clov's 'Ich geh' jetzt' revised to 'Ich verlasse dich', *Photo*, p. 42.

Hamm's 'Ich bin es, der dir als Vater gedient hat' revised to 'Ich habe dir als Vater gedient' with 'Ich' underlined, *Photo*, p. 44.

Hamm's 'Mein Haus ist es, das dir als Heim gedient hat' revised to 'Mein Haus hat dir als Heim gedient', *Photo*, p. 44.

Clov's 'Ich geh jetzt' revised to 'Ich verlasse dich', *Photo*, p. 44, and '*Moves to door*' added.

Hamm's 'Hast du je daran gedacht, dass . . .' revised to 'Hast du nie daran gedacht . . .', *Photo*, p. 44, and '*Clov halts*' added in right margin.

Page 67

'gar' is circled in Hamm's 'Du brauchst vielleicht gar nicht weit zu gehen', and a delete sign is noted and circled in the left margin.

Clov's 'Ich geh jetzt' revised to 'Ich verlasse dich', *Photo*, p. 46, and '*Moves*' added.

'*Clov stops*' added after Hamm's 'Ist mein Hund fertig?'.

Clov's 'Art Spitz' revised to 'Art Pudel', *Photo*, p. 46.

'*Er zieht sein Taschentuch heraus und ohne es zu entfalten wischt er sich damit übers Gesicht*', cut.

''doch' cut twice in Clov's phrase 'Er ist doch noch nicht fertig'. Question mark in right margin, *Photo*, p. 48. The first 'doch', however, was delivered in performance.

Clov's 'dann legt man sein Halsband an' revised to 'dann legt man ihm sein Halsband an', *Photo*, p. 48.

Page 69

'squatting' added after '*Er reicht den Hund Clov*'.

Hamm's first 'Na und?', unrevised in *Sac(B)*, printed as 'Na?' in *Photo*, p. 48, and so spoken in performance.

Clov's 'Moment!' revised to 'Warte!', *Photo*, p. 48.

'(*Stolz*)' added before Hamm's 'Als ob er mich bäte . . .', *Photo*, p. 48.

'(*Stolz*)' added again before Hamm's 'Oder als ob . . .', *Photo*, p. 48.

Hamm's 'Lass ihn mich weiter so anflehen' revised to 'Lass ihn so . . . mich anflehen', *Photo*, p. 48.

Clov's 'Ich geh jetzt' revised to 'Ich verlasse dich', *Photo*, p. 48, and '(*Moves*)' added.

'(*Stops*)' added after '. . . Erscheinungen gehabt?'

Clov's 'Wie willst du, dass bei irgend jemand Licht wäre?' revised to 'Wie soll bei irgend jemand Licht sein?', *Photo*, p. 48. In performance 'denn' added after 'soll'.

Page 71

Clov's 'Natürlich ist es erloschen!' revised to 'Aber selbstverständlich ist es erloschen'. In *Photo*, p. 48, 'Aber' is omitted, and in performance it is replaced with a 'Ja'.

Clov's 'Aber natürlich ist sie erloschen!' revised to 'Aber selbstverständlich ist sie erloschen!'. *Photo*, p. 48, again omits 'Aber', and performance again replaces it with a 'Ja'.

Clov's 'hübsch' in quotation marks twice.

'Turns' added after Clov's 'Tu dies, tu das, und ich tu's.'

Hamm's 'Du wirst es nicht mehr können' revised to 'Bald wirst du es nicht mehr können'. Revision missed in *Photo*, p. 48, but made in performance.

Page 73

After '(. . . *zu schieben*.)' Beckett added '(Clov standing back & laughing at H's efforts)'.

Clov's 'Ich brauche die Wörter . . .' revised to 'Ich gebrauche die Wörter . . .', *Photo*, p. 50.

Full stop added after Clov's '. . . bring mir dann andere bei', and the 'o' of 'oder' capitalized to begin a new sentence, *Photo*, p. 50.

'(Turns aside)', added. Of this whole section, from Hamm's 'Hol das Kännchen' to the added '(Turns aside)', Beckett noted in the right margin, 'Violent'.

Hamm's 'Ich besuchte ihn oft in der Anstalt' revised to 'Ich besuchte ihn manchmal in der Anstalt', *Photo*, p. 50.

Exclamation mark replaces full stop after '. . . Sardinenboote'.

Hamm's 'Wie schön das alles ist!' revised to 'All diese Herrlichkeit!', *Photo*, p. 50.

'Asche' underlined and in the margin Beckett noted, 'Clov looks at H [Hamm].'

Hamm's 'Der Fall ist anscheinend . . .' revised to 'Anscheinend ist der Fall . . .', *Photo*, p. 50.

Hamm's '. . . der Fall war gar keine . . .' revised to '. . . war der Fall gar keine . . .', *Photo*, p. 50.

'Moving in' added before Clov's 'Ein Verrückter?'

Hamm's 'Welt' underlined and 'Erde' as a possible revision noted in the right margin but cancelled.

Before Clov's 'Die goldene Zeit!' Beckett added 'décrochant'.

Page 75

Clov's 'Lebenslänglich . . .' revised to 'Das ganze Leben . . .', *Photo*, p. 50.

'dann' cut in Clov's '. . . und wenn ich dann nicht gelaufen komme . . .', *Photo*, p. 50.

Page 77

Hamm's 'ob du nur . . .' revised to 'dass du nur . . .', *Photo*, p. 50.

Clov's 'anfangen zu', cut, *Photo*, p. 50.

Clov's 'Das ganze Universum' revised to 'Die ganze Welt', *Photo*, p. 50.

Hamm's 'Ich pfeife auf das Universum!' revised to 'Ich scheiss was auf die Welt!'. *Photo*, p. 50, prints the revision with an apostrophe after 'scheiss'.

'*Nicht sehr überzeugt. Ja. Pause. Überzeugter.* Ja' revised to 'Ah! (With back to H [Hamm]).' Revision missed in *Photo*, but in performance Hamm's 'Na und?' and Clov's 'Warte mal' were cut, as well as the two 'Ja'.

After Clov's 'Ich hab's' Beckett added 'turns to H [Hamm].'

Drawing at the bottom of the page traces Clov's thinking walk in a series of crosses. At right, dialogue is keyed to the walk:

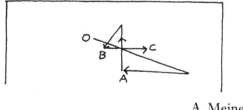

A Meine Beine
B Ich plane
C Ah!

Page 79

Of the exchange from Hamm's 'Ob der Wecker geht?' to his 'Dann, weil er zu wenig gegangen ist!' Beckett has written in the margin, 'Violent'.

'*Spiel mit dem Taschentuch. Kurzes Rappeln des Weckers hinter den Kulissen*', cut.

Hamm's 'meine Pillen' revised to 'mein Beruhigungsmittel', *Photo*, p. 54.

'*Er geht zur Tür und dreht sich um*', cut.

Clov's 'Ich geh jetzt' revised to 'Ich verlasse dich', *Photo*, p. 54.

'(Moves to door)', added after above revision.

After Hamm's '. . . meine Geschichte erzählen', Beckett added, 'Clov stops'.

'Loud' added before Clov's 'Nein'.

After Clov's 'Er schläft', Beckett added, '(moves away tiptoe)'.

Page 81

Before 'bückt sich . . .' Beckett added, 'back to bin'.

'*Unverständliche Worte*', cut and replaced by 'Nagg (Loud) Nein!'

'Moving off', added before Clov's 'Er will deine Geschichte nicht hören'.

'Illegible' added before Clov's 'bückt sich' twice.

After '*Clov richtet sich wieder auf*' Beckett added, 'moves off'.

Clov's 'Er macht mit' revised to 'Er macht's', *Photo*, p. 54.

'. . . öffnet die Tür und', cut with the note 'No door' in the margin.

'und schlägt die Tür hinter sich zu', cut.

'zu' is circled in Nagg's 'Ich höre zu'.

Page 83

Hamm's 'Es ist zerbrochen, wir sind zerbrochen. *Pause*. Es wird zerbrechen' revised to 'Es ist aus, mit uns ist es aus. *Pause*. Bald aus', *Photo*, p. 54.

Hamm's 'Ich stopfte in aller Ruhe mein Pfeifchen . . . aus Magnesit, steckte es mit einem . . .' revised to 'Ich stopfte in aller Ruhe meine Pfeife . . . die aus Meerschaum, steckte sie mit einem . . .', *Photo*, p. 56.

'Grad' cancelled in Hamm's '. . . null Grad auf dem Thermometer', *Photo*, p. 56.

Page 85

Typographical error corrected by Beckett: 'beschädigt' changed to 'beschäftigt', *Photo*, p. 56.

Hamm's 'Warum sind Sie eigentlich hier eingedrungen?' revised to 'Was ist das für eine Aufdringlichkeit?', *Photo*, p. 56.

'Grad' cut in Hamm's 'fünfzig Grad auf dem Heliometer', *Photo*, p. 56.

Beckett began to revise the 'gutes' in Hamm's 'Ja, das ist gutes Deutsch', but after cancelling the word and posing some alternatives he noted 'gutes' again in the right-hand margin.

Hamm's 'als ob das Geschlecht eine Rolle spielte' revised to 'als ob das Geschlecht wichtig wäre', *Photo*, p. 56.

'Grad' cut again in Hamm's 'hundert Grad auf dem Anemometer', *Photo*, p. 56.

Page 87

Hamm's 'doch, überlegen Sie' cancelled. Excision missed in *Photo*, p. 56, but in performance only 'doch' was eliminated.

Hamm's 'Und was dann?' revised to 'Und dann?', *Photo*, p. 56.

Hamm's 'Ich ärgere mich' revised to 'Ich ärgerte mich', *Photo*, p. 56.

Hamm's 'dagegen ist kein Kraut gewachsen!' revised to 'dagegen gibt es kein Mittel!', *Photo*, p. 56.

'Grad' again cut from Hamm's 'null Grad auf dem Hygrometer', *Photo*, p. 56.

Page 89

Hamm's 'Hier können Sie' revised to 'Hier könnten Sie', *Photo*, p. 56.

Hamm's 'mit den Füssen im Trockenen' revised to 'mit den Füssen auf dem Trockenen', *Photo*, p. 56.

Hamm's 'Personen' revised to 'Bettler'. This cut missed in *Photo*, p.56, but 'Bettler' delivered in performance.

Hamm's 'Lasset uns beten!' revised to 'Lasset uns zu Gott beten' twice, *Photo*, p. 58.

Page 91

Hamm's 'Erst beten!' revised to 'Erst zu Gott beten!', *Photo*, p. 58.

'die Hände faltend und', cut. Cut not made in *Photo*, p. 58, and facing photograph shows Nagg with folded hands.

Clov's 'Denkste' revised to 'Kein Gedanke', *Photo*, p. 60.

After Hamm's 'Es gibt keine Pralinen mehr', Beckett added, 'Du wirst nie wieder eine Praline bekommen', *Photo*, p. 60.

Nagg's 'In Ordnung' revised to 'Es ist normal'. *Photo*, p. 60, prints 'Es ist ja normal', and the line is so delivered in performance.

'Wen' is underlined in Nagg's 'Wen riefst du . . .'

Page 93

During Nagg's curse of Hamm, at 'Ja', Beckett notes in the right margin, apparently of Clov, '(head a little towards H [Hamm])'. In the left margin, Beckett notes of the second half of Nagg's curse, 'Violent'. The *Schiller Nb*, however, clearly suggests that Clov is looking towards Nagg at this point and the initial in the right margin might easily be an 'N' for Nagg.

Nagg's 'dass ich dich nach mir rufen höre . . .' revised to 'dass ich dich mich rufen höre . . .', *Photo*, p. 62.

After Nagg's calling of Nell, Beckett notes '(long)' after the *Pause*.

Hamm's 'Der Spass ist zu Ende' is revised to 'Das Fest ist jetzt zu Ende', *Photo*, p. 62, and in the right margin, under the German revision, Beckett noted the English equivalent, 'Our revels etc.' [i.e., 'now are ended'] from *The Tempest*.

After Clov's 'Ich räume alles weg!' Beckett added, '(stoops for glass)'.

'*Er räumt weiter auf*', cut.

At the foot of the page Beckett outlines the clockwise pattern of Clov's clean up, noting the places where objects should be retrieved and lines uttered as follows:

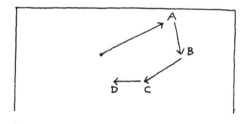

A Dog
B Glass &
   'Ordnung' to
   'letzten Staub'
C Boathook
D Sprinkler.

Page 95

After 'richtet sich auf, leise:' Beckett added, 'Having picked up everything but sprinkler'.

Clov's 'Ich geh jetzt' revised to 'Ich verlasse dich', *Photo*, p. 64.

'(moves)' added after above revision.

After Hamm's 'Nein', Beckett added, '(Cl. [Clov] stops & turns)'.

Before Clov's 'Oh, ehe ich's vergesse', Beckett added, 'moving in'.

In the margin to this section, Beckett noted, 'sehr gespielt'.

Page 97

After Hamm's second 'nur nichts zwingen', *Photo*, p. 66, prints 'das ist verhäng-nisvoll'. In performance, however, the unrevised *Sac(B)* version was delivered, 'dann geht's gar nicht'.

Hamm's *Pause* before 'Gelernt ist gelernt' is underlined and an 'H.' is noted in the left margin.

Hamm's 'wäre' revised to 'bin', *Photo*, p. 66.

Clov's 'Du hast trotz allem ein wenig vorankommen können!' revised to 'Du bist trotz allem ein wenig vorangekommen!', *Photo*, p. 66.

Hamm's 'aber das ist immerhin besser als nichts' revised to 'aber immerhin . . . besser als nichts', *Photo*, p. 66.

Clov's 'Wer denn?' revised to 'Wer?', *Photo*, p. 66.

Hamm's 'Wie bitte?' revised to 'Was?', *Photo*, p. 66.

'both laugh rising' written in right margin for last three lines.

In the right margin, Beckett drew a line from top to bottom of the page and wrote of this whole section, 'Sehr gespielt. Great writer with disciple.'

Page 99

Hamm's 'Sollen wir uns mal halb tot lachen?' revised to 'Sollen wir uns mal totlachen?', *Photo*, p. 68.

Clov's answer is revised to correspond, from '. . . nicht mehr halb tot lachen' to '. . . nicht mehr totlachen', *Photo*, p. 68.

Hamm's 'Wahrscheinlich' revised to 'Vermutlich', *Photo*, p. 68.

Page 101

'*Clov hebt den Deckel von Naggs Mülleimer an und bückt sich*', cut.

The following '*Pause*', cut.

'*Clov klappt den Deckel zu und richtet sich auf*', cut.

Sac(B) and *Photo*, p. 74, print, 'Bei jedem Schritt kipptest du mich beinahe um!' In performance, however, Hamm said, 'Bei jedem Schritt hast du mich beinah umgekippt.'

At the bottom of the page a drawing of Hamm's second tour of the shelter. The path, this time, is anti-clockwise, and Beckett noted the points at which specific lines were to be delivered:

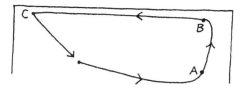

A weiss[t] Du noch etc.
B Schon da etc.
C Das nenne ich Licht etc.

Page 103

Hamm's 'Ist es kein Sonnenstrahl, was ich auf meinem Gesicht spüre?' revised to 'Ist das was ich auf meinem Gesicht spüre kein Sonnenstrahl?', *Photo*, p. 74. In performance, however, Hamm said, 'Ist das ist es kein Sonnenstrahl.'

Page 105

Clov's 'Du wirst es nicht hören' revised to 'Du würdest es nicht hören', *Photo*, p. 74.

Hamm's 'Öffne es also!' revised to 'Also öffne es!', *Photo*, p. 76.

Hamm's 'Alldieweil es keine Schiffer mehr gibt' revised to 'Es gibt eben keine Schiffer mehr', *Photo*, p. 76.

Hamm's 'Fühlst du dich nicht wohl?' revised to 'Ist dir nicht gut?', *Photo*, p. 76.

Page 107

'Mal' in parenthesis in Hamm's 'Es wird wohl das zweite Mal gewesen sein.'

Hamm's 'Er weint noch immer?' revised to 'Weint er noch immer?', *Photo*, p. 78.

Hamm's 'Gib mir ein' circled with the notation, 'i.e., moves towards door, stopped at O by'.

Page 109

'*Clov sucht den Hund*' revised to 'Clov picks up . . .'

Clov's 'Also, ich geh jetzt' revised to 'Also, ich verlasse dich', *Photo*, p. 78, after which '(Drops dog & moves)' is added. *Photo*, p. 78, misses the revised action. But *Photo* revises Hamm's 'Nein, lass nur' to 'Nein, nicht der Mühe wert', which is the version delivered in performance.

Hamm's 'Man weint, man weint . . .' revised to 'Man weint, und weint . . .', *Photo*, p. 78.

Hamm's 'Überlegen Sie doch, überlegen Sie! Sie sind auf der Erde, dagegen ist kein Kraut gewachsen!' revised to 'Überlegt euch doch, überlegt euch! Ihr sind [seid] auf der Erde, dagegen gibt es kein Mittel!' *Photo*, p. 78, prints 'seid'.

Page 111

Hamm's 'Ich werde dann meinen Vater . . .' revised to 'Ich werde meinen Vater . . .', *Photo*, p. 78.

Hamm's 'Er kommt wieder' revised to 'Er wird wiederkommen', *Photo*, p. 78.

Comma added after 'anhält' in Hamm's 'den man anhält . . .', *Photo*, p. 78.

Hamm's '. . . mit einander zu sprechen' revised to '. . . mit einander zu flüstern', *Photo*, p. 78.

Hamm's 'Hirsekörner des . . .' revised to 'Hirsekörnchen des . . .', *Photo*, p. 78.

Page 113

Hamm's '. . . und lebenslänglich wartet' revised to '. . . und das ganze Leben wartet', *Photo*, p. 78.

Hamm's 'meine Pillen' revised to 'mein Beruhigungsmittel', and each 'Pillen' is revised to 'Beruhigungsmittel' throughout this section, *Photo*, p. 78.

Page 115

'drops it' added in right margin during description of Clov's action beginning, '*Clov wird das Gemälde gewahr . . .*'

Hamm's 'Schau nach der Erde' revised to 'Schau (dir die Erde an)'. *Photo*, p. 78, prints the revision without parentheses.

Clov's 'Nicht?' revised to 'Nein?', *Photo*, p. 78.

Clov's 'Hat man nicht mehr das Recht zu singen?' revised to 'Darf man nicht mehr singen?', *Photo*, p. 78.

Page 117

'. . . *und geht ein paar Schritte auf das rechte Fenster zu*', cut, and 'goes straight to earth window' written in right margin.

'*Er geht wieder zurück, um die Leiter zu holen*', cut.

For Clov's 'Manchmal frage ich mich . . .', Beckett noted in the right margin, 'still at E. [earth] window'.

Clov's 'Mal sehen!' revised to 'Moment mal!', *Photo*, p. 80.

Page 119

Clov's 'Du hast Schwein gehabt' revised to 'Da hast du Schwein gehabt'. *Photo*, p. 80, prints, 'Du hast', but in performance Clov said, 'Da hast du . . .'

Hamm's 'Antworte zuerst' revised to 'Erst antworten!', *Photo*, p. 80.

'Fast[,] violent' written in margin for section from 'Erst antworten!' to Clov's 'Das ist doch ganz wurscht!'

One 'Ich' cut from Hamm's 'Ich, ich weiss es nicht', *Photo*, p. 80.

Of Clov's accusation of Hamm about Mother Pegg, 'Als die Mutter Pegg . . .', Beckett notes in the margin, 'soft venom'.

Photo, p. 80, drops the mention of oil (Öl) in Hamm's 'Ich hatte kein Öl' and Clov's 'Doch, du hattest Öl.' In performance, however, the mention of oil was retained as printed in *Sac(B)*.

Photo, p. 80, prints Hamm's 'Hole es' as 'Hol' es'. In performance, Hamm said, 'Dann hol' es.'

Page 121

'[Er] *verliert das Gleichgewicht und klammert sich an die Leiter. Er steigt ein paar Stufen hinab und bleibt stehen*', cut and replaced by 'Straight down & in to H [Hamm]'.

'*Er steigt hinab auf den Boden und bleibt stehen*', cut.

Hamm's 'Lass mich nicht hier stehen!', cut. *Photo*, p. 80, prints the line, but it was not delivered in performance.

Hamm's 'Bin ich genau in der Mitte?' revised to 'Stehe ich genau in der Mitte?'

Page 123

For Hamm's speech beginning, 'Wenn du mich . . .', Beckett notes in the margin, 'Blows'.

'hält an, steigt hinab, sucht das Fernglas, hebt es auf, steigt wieder auf die Leiter', cut, and Beckett notes in the left margin that Clov ascends the ladder with the glass.

Hamm's 'Hat man mir jemals verziehen, mir?' revised to 'Hat man mich je bemitleidet, mich?', *Photo*, p. 82.

Hamm's 'du Klotzkopf!' revised to 'du Trottel!', *Photo*, p. 82.

Hamm's 'Ich setze zum letzten Monolog an' revised to 'Ich rüste mich zum letzten Monolog', *Photo*, p. 84.

Page 124

'Aïeaïeaïe!' circled and 'Roman' noted in the left margin.

'*Clov rapproche l'escabeau de la fenêtre, monte dessus, braque la lunette. Un temps.*', cut.

Clov's second 'Aïeaïeaïe' revised to 'On dirait un môme'.

Hamm's 'C'est une feuille? Une fleur? Une toma– *il bâille* te?' revised to '(*sarcastique*) Un môme!'

Except for the above revised lines, this entire scene was cut:

CLOV *regardant*: Je t'en foutrai des tomates! Quelqu'un! C'est quelqu'un!

HAMM: Eh bien, va l'exterminer. *Clov descend de l'escabeau.* Quelqu'un! *Vibrant.* Fais ton devoir! *Clov se précipite vers la porte.* Non, pas la peine. *Clov s'arrête.* Quelle distance?

CLOV *retourne à l'escabeau, monte dessus, braque la lunette.*

CLOV: Soixante . . . quatorze mètres.

HAMM: Approchant? S'éloignant?

CLOV *regardant toujours*: Immobile.

HAMM: Sexe?

CLOV: Quelle importance? *Il ouvre la fenêtre, se penche dehors. Un temps. Il se redresse, baisse la lunette, se tourne vers Hamm. Avec effroi.* On dirait un môme.

HAMM: Occupation?

CLOV: Quoi?

HAMM *avec violence*: Qu'est-ce qu'il fait?

CLOV *de même*: Je ne sais pas ce qu'il fait! Ce . . .

Page 125

The cuts here follow those of the French text on p. 124.

'*Clov rückt die Leiter näher ans Fenster, steigt hinauf und setzt das Fernglas an. Pause*', cut.

[264]

Clov's second 'Oh je, oh je, oh je, oh je!' revised to '*entsetzt*: Sieht aus wie ein Knabe'. *Photo*, p. 84, however, prints the stage direction here as 'erschrocken'.

Hamm's 'Ein Blatt? Eine Blume? Eine Toma . . . *er gähnt* . . . te?' revised to '(*sarkastisch*) Ein Knabe!'

Again the cutting resumes except for the above revision:

CLOV *schauend*: Du kriegst gleich Tomaten! Jemand! Da ist jemand!

HAMM *hört auf zu gähnen*: Na ja, geh ihn ausrotten. *Clov steigt von der Leiter, Leise*. Jemande! *Mit bebender Stimme*. Tu deine Pflicht! *Clov rennt zur Tür*. Nein, lass nur. *Clov bleibt stehen*. Welche Entfernung?

CLOV *geht wieder zur Leiter, steigt hinauf und setzt das Fernglas an*.

CLOV: Hundert . . . vierzehn Meter.

HAMM: Sich nähernd? Sich entfernend?

CLOV *immer noch schauend*: Regungslos!

HAMM: Geschlecht?

CLOV: Spielt das eine Rolle? *Er öffnet das Fenster und beugt sich hinaus. Pause. Er richtet sich wieder auf, lässt das Fernglas sinken, wendet sich Hamm zu. Erschrocken*. Sieht aus wie ein Knabe.

HAMM: Womit beschäftigt?

CLOV: Wie, bitte?

HAMM *heftig*: Was macht er?

CLOV *ebenso heftig*: Ich weiss nicht, was er macht!

Photo, p. 84.

Page 126

The long cut in the French text continues:

que faisaient les mômes. *Il braque la lunette. Un temps. Il baisse la lunette, se tourne vers Hamm*. Il a l'air assis par terre, adossé à quelque chose.

HAMM: La pierre levée. *Un temps*. Ta vue s'améliore. *Un temps*. Il regarde la maison sans doute, avec les yeux de Moïse mourant.

CLOV: Non.

HAMM: Qu'est-ce qu'il regarde?

CLOV *avec violence*: Je ne sais pas ce qu'il regarde! *Il braque la lunette. Un temps. Il baisse la lunette, se tourne vers Hamm*. Son nombril. Enfin par là. *Un temps*. Pourquoi tout cet interrogatoire?

HAMM: Il est peut-être mort.

Page 127

The parallel cut in the German text continues:

> Was die Knaben eben machen. *Er setzt das Fernglas an. Pause. Er lässt das Fernglas sinken und wendet sich Hamm zu.* Er scheint auf dem Boden zu sitzen, mit dem Rücken an irgend etwas.
>
> HAMM: Am Hünengrab. *Pause.* Deine Sehkraft nimmt zu. *Pause.* Er schaut wahrscheinlich nach dem Haus, mit den Augen des sterbenden Moses.
>
> CLOV: Nein.
>
> HAMM: Wohin schaut er denn?
>
> CLOV *heftig*: Ich weiss nicht, wohin er schaut. *Er setzt das Fernglas an. Pause. Er lässt das Fernglas sinken und wendet sich Hamm zu.* Auf seinen Nabel . . . oder so was. *Pause.* Warum dieses Verhör?
>
> HAMM: Er ist vielleicht tot.

Photo, p. 84.

The text resumes with Clov's 'Ich werde mal nachsehen', and Beckett notes in the right margin at this point, 'knocks over ladder'. *Photo*, p. 84, prints 'Ich werde mal hingehen', but Clov says 'nachsehen' in performance.

Hamm's second 'Lass nur', cut. Of the three 'Lass nur' here, two by Hamm and one by Clov, *Photo*, p. 84, prints them all as 'Nicht der Mühe wert'. In performance, however, the first two are 'Lass nur' as printed in *Sac(B)*, and the third is eliminated as revised.

Page 128

Clov's song cut:

> CLOV *chante*:
>> Joli oiseau quitte ta cage
>> Vole vers ma bien-aimée.

Page 129

Clov's 'Das kommt gut aus' revised to 'Das trifft sich gut', *Photo*, p. 86.

At the top of the page Beckett notes, 'From O [Clov] looks at alarm, then at Hamm (i.e. does not move alarm).'

Beckett revised the following section a number of times before cutting it entirely and replacing it with the English note above. '*Clov gibt ihm den Bootshaken, geht zur Tür, bleibt stehen, schaut nach dem Wecker, hängt ihn ab, schaut sich nach einem besseren Platz um, geht zur Leiter, stellt den Wecker auf die Leiter und kehrt an seinen Platz neben dem Sessel zurück. Pause*', cut. *Photo*, p. 86, prints an earlier revision, '*Clov gibt ihm den Bootshaken und schaut nach dem Wecker.*'

Clov's 'Ich geh jetzt' revised to 'Ich verlasse dich', *Photo*, p. 86, and in the right margin Beckett notes, '(final) & moves'. *Photo*, p. 86, includes a '*Pause*' after Clov's line, which '*Pause*' is not printed in *Sac(B)*.

After Hamm 'Sag noch etwas, vorm Weggehen', Beckett notes, '(stops)'.

Clov's 'In deinem Herzen!' revised to 'Deinem Herzen!', *Photo*, p. 86.

Hamm's 'Aber am Ende, vorm Weggehen, ohne dass ich ihn darum bat, hat er zu mir gesprochen. Er hat mir gesagt . . .' revised to 'Aber am Ende, vorm Weggehen, hat er zu mir gesprochen, ungebeten. Er sagte mir . . .'. *Photo*, p. 86, prints an earlier version of this revision: 'hat er ungebeten zu mir gesprochen. Er sagte mir . . .' In performance the *Photo*, p. 86, version was delivered with the addition of a second 'zu' before the second 'mir'.

Clov's 'Aus meinem Herzen!' revised to 'Meinem Herzen!', *Photo*, p. 86.

Clov's song cut:

> Clov *singt*:
>> Vögelchen, flieg zu meiner Liebsten
>> nist' dich in ihrem Mieder ein.

Photo, p. 86.

Page 130

Clov's song and some following dialogue cut:

>> Niche-toi dans son corsage
>> Dis-lui combien je suis emmerdé
> *Un temps.*
> Assez?
> HAMM *amèrement*: Un crachat!
> *Un temps.*

Hamm's 'Assez!', cut.

Page 131

The German text again follows the cuts made in the French text on page 130.

>> da kannst du ihr dann ja mal piepsen,
>> mir könnte gar nicht mieser sein!
> *Pause.*

Genug?

HAMM *bitter*: Ein Schlag ins Gesicht!

Pause.

Photo, p. 86.

Hamm's interruptions of Clov's speech, 'Artikuliere!' and 'Genug!', have been cut, *Photo*, p. 86.

Clov's 'Man sagte mir immer: Ja, das ist die Liebe, doch, doch, glaub es nur, wie du siehst, [Hamm's first interruption] ist es gar nicht so schwer' revised to 'Man sagte mir: Ja, das ist Liebe, doch, doch, glaub es nur, du siehst schon, wie leicht es ist', *Photo*, p. 86. In performance, however, Clov said 'du wirst schon'.

'die' cut in 'das ist die Freundschaft', *Photo*, p. 86.

'Da, bleib stehn' revised to 'Hier, bleib stehn . . .', *Photo*, p. 86.

Clov's 'Sieh doch mit welcher Kunst all diese tödlich Verletzten gepflegt werden' revised to 'Sieh doch, mit welcher Kunst sie gepflegt werden, all diese tödlich Verletzten', and Beckett added, '(slight move to door immediately checked)'. *Photo*, p. 86, prints the revised dialogue but not the stage directions. *Photo* also adds a '*Pause*' after 'Verletzten' in place of the '*desgleichen*' of *Sac(B)*.

Page 133

Clov's 'oder bin ich es' revised to 'oder ich bin es', *Photo*, p. 86.

'fort', cut in Clov's 'und gehe fort', *Photo*, p. 86.

'obgleich ich sie nie brennen sah' revised to 'obgleich ich sie nie glühen sah', *Photo*, p. 86.

Hamm's 'Ich danke dir, Clov, ich brauche dich nicht mehr' revised to 'Ich entlasse dich, Clov', *Photo*, p. 86.

Clov's 'ich bin es, der dich nicht mehr braucht' revised to 'ich entlasse dich', *Photo*, p. 86.

Hamm's 'Wir sind es, die einander nicht mehr brauchen' revised to 'Wir entlassen einander', *Photo*, p. 86.

Hamm's 'Belebter' underlined and 'ital' noted in the right margin, as it is a stage direction, *Photo*, p. 88.

'hut' added to 'Panama', printed '*Panamahut*' in *Photo*, p. 88.

Page 135

'Nein?' added before Hamm's 'Gut'. *Photo*, p. 88, misses this revision, but 'Nein' was delivered in performance.

'Vorsicht' added between 'Halt' and 'nicht so schnell!', *Photo*, p. 88.

Hamm's 'Noch nicht', cut.

Hamm's 'Und dann?' revised to 'Und nun?', *Photo*, p. 88.

Hamm's 'Rümpfen!' revised to 'Ärschen!', *Photo*, p. 92.

'Er zieht sein Taschentuch heraus und putzt damit, ohne es auseinanderzufalten, seine Brille', cut and [*illegible note in left margin*].

Hamm's 'Sie SINKT' revised to 'Sie NAHT'. *Photo*, p. 92, prints this change with 'naht' in lower case.

'Sie sinkt' again revised to 'sie naht', *Photo*, p. 92.

'Und dann?' again revised to 'Und nun?', *Photo*, p. 92.

'die immer gleich null sind und doch zählen' revised to 'immer gleich null, und die doch zählen', *Photo*, p. 92.

'mitbringen dürfe' revised to 'bei sich behalten dürfe' to conform exactly to the same phrase on p. 99, and Beckett notes in the right margin, '(cf. p. 99)', *Photo*, p. 92.

'Sie wollen, dass er blüht, während Sie, während Sie welken?' revised to 'Sie wollen, dass er blüht, während Sie welken?' Final 'Sie' is underlined. The repetition of 'während Sie' retained in *Photo*, p. 92.

'Viertelstunden' revised to 'Viertelstündchen', *Photo*, p. 92.

Page 137

After '*Er pfeift*' Beckett notes, 'Clov flinches aside'.

Before both instances of 'Gut' Beckett adds, 'Nein?' After the second, Beckett notes, 'Clov back'. *Photo*, p. 92, includes neither of the 'Nein' but they were delivered in performance.

'*Es kommt*' corrected with 'No ital', *Photo*, p. 92.

'Wegwerfen' either underlined or cut; retained in *Photo*, p. 92, and performance.

'Bitte!', cut, but question mark in left margin. Retained in *Photo*, p. 92, and in performance.

After 'Clov. *Lange Pause*' Beckett adds, 'Clov! (*Pause.*)'. *Photo*, p. 92, however, eliminated the 'Lange'.

After 'Nein? Gut' Beckett notes in the right margin, 'Clov flinches aside', and then shortly thereafter in the left margin he notes, 'Clov back'.

'und kein Wort mehr darüber' revised to 'und sprechen wir nicht mehr darüber', *Photo*, p. 92.

'kein Wort mehr' revised to 'sprechen wir nicht mehr'. 'Stet' is at first noted in the right margin and then cancelled, *Photo*, p. 92.

'*Er nähert das Taschentuch seinem Gesicht*' revised to '*Er bedeckt sein Gesicht mit dem Taschentuch u. lässt die Arme auf die Armlehnen sinken*'. *Photo*, p. 92, however, retains the excised material adding Beckett's addendum to it, and further adds, 'und bewegt sich nicht mehr'. Moreover, *Photo*, p. 92, prints 'Hände' instead of 'Arme'.

Note at end: 'Curtain taken without moving. N. [Nagg] and N. [Nell] not to appear. No acknowledgement of app. [applause].'

The following notes appear on the endpapers of the volume and are preliminary revisions with page numbers. Some were finally included in the text. Some were not.

115 Schau dir die Erde an

119 erst antworten

127 lass nur [cancelled]

131 Hamm: genug [cancelled]. Du siehst schon wie leicht es ist

133 gehe fort [fort cancelled] – bin ich es ['bin' and 'ich' transposed]

135 Ob er seinen Kleinen bei sich behalten dürfe (cf. p. 99)

109 *Überlegt euch* doch etc.

111 Hirsekörnchen (cf. p. 11)

91 Du wirst nie wieder eine P. [Praline] bekommen

117 moment bitte

Clov's 2 Denkste

At the bottom of this page is a drawing of the set with a spot [.] marked for 'Clov's place by chair'.

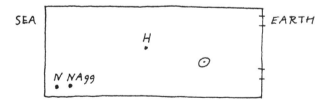

for Tcp. [Telescope?] [These are also page numbers for the major cuts.]

51

125–127

129–131

27 Samen or Körner

Changes consequent on *Witz* for *Geschichte*

37–41

41 blühen schon? [Beckett's original spelling was 'blühten'. Question mark queries the 't'.]

53 Flosse?

29–59 *Scheint so* or sieht so aus [This question Beckett posed to himself is the reason that the 'Scheint so' appeared in the text in parenthesis.]

57 on me there's one

    auf mir gibt es einen (auf mir ist einer)

63 *Wie* es ist

67 doch noch nicht ⎫

  or X „ „ ⎬ bis Pudel [Hence the question mark on page 67]

77 ich scheiss auf die Welt

 „ 1 . 2 dass . . . wärst (?)

81 Ich höre zu ['zu' cancelled, and hence its circle in the text.]

83 Seit den Fontanellen

89 hier *könnten* bei einigem Geschick

91 *nach wem* riefst du / ou bien 93 / dass ich *mich* rufen höre [i.e., the change from 'nach' to 'mich' is made on page 93]

93 Der Spass ist zu Ende (?)

97 aber (das ist) immerhin

105 Du *würdest* . . . ist dir nicht gut

(cf. 35, Nagg to Nell)

107 zweite Mal ['Mal' cancelled here but the text has 'Mal' only in parenthesis.]

BIBLIOGRAPHY

Manuscripts and Annotated Copies of Beckett Consulted

(RUL = Reading University Library)

Endgame A Play in One Act followed by Act Without Words A Mime for One Player. Grove Press, New York, 1958. Annotated copy kept by Walter Asmus, Beckett's directorial assistant, London, 1980. (Referred to throughout this volume as *Gac(A)*)

Endgame A Play in One Act followed by Act Without Words A Mime for One Player. Grove Press, New York, 1970. Acting copy kept by Alan Mandell who played Nagg in the 1980 production. This is a volume from the Collected Works edition, the pagination for which corresponds to the standard Grove Press edition of 1958. (Referred to throughout this volume as *Gac(M)*)

Endgame A Play in One Act followed by Act Without Words A Mime for One Player. Faber and Faber, London, 1958. Annotated copy prepared by Beckett before rehearsals at Riverside Studios, London, 1980. RUL Ms. 1974. (Referred to throughout this volume as *Fac(B)*)

Endspiel Fin de Partie. Suhrkamp Verlag, Frankfurt, 1960. Annotated bi-lingual German edition of *Endgame* which Beckett prepared before arrival in Berlin and modified throughout rehearsals, dated in Beckett's hand 'Berlin. Aug. Sept. 1967.' (Referred to throughout this volume as *Sac(B)*)

Other Editions Consulted

Beckett Dramatische Dichtungen in drei Sprachen. Suhrkamp Verlag, Frankfurt, 1981. (Page references throughout this volume preceded by the abbreviation S are to this Suhrkamp edition)

Endgame A Play in One Act Followed by Act Without Words A Mime for One Player. Grove Press, New York, 1958. (Page references throughout this volume preceded by the abbreviation G are to this Grove Press edition)

Endgame A Play in One Act Followed by Act Without Words A Mime for One Player. Faber and Faber, London, 1958. (Page references throughout this volume preceded by the abbreviation F are to this Faber edition)

Fin de partie suivi de Acte sans paroles. Les Editions de Minuit, Paris, 1957. First edition.

Samuel Beckett inszeniert das 'Endspiel'. Suhrkamp Verlag, Frankfurt, 1967. Photographic edition of the 1967 Schiller-Theater production with revised text. German revised text, however, is seriously marred; see *Cuts and Changes* section of this volume for details. (Referred to throughout this volume as *Photo*)

Beckett as Director

Cohn, Ruby, *Just Play: Beckett's Theater*, Princeton University Press, Princeton, NJ, 1980, chapter 12, 'Beckett Directs Beckett'

Fehsenfeld, Martha, and Dougald McMillan, *Beckett in the Theatre*, John Calder, London and Riverrun Press, New York, 1988, chapter 4, *'Endgame'*.

Haerdter, Michael, *Samuel Beckett inszeniert das 'Endspiel' Bericht von den Proben der Berliner Inszenierung Materialen zu Beckett's 'Endspiel'*, Suhrkamp Verlag, Frankfurt, 1968. Printed in *Photo* (as 'Über die Proben für die Berliner Aufführung') and translated as 'Rehearsal Diary, *Endspiel*, Schiller Theater', in *Beckett in the Theatre*. Translated and reprinted as 'Samuel Beckett répète *Fin de partie*', *Revue d'esthétique*, 'Samuel Beckett' special number, hors-série, 1986, pp. 303–16

Knowlson, James, 'Samuel Beckett metteur en scène: ses carnets de notes de mise en scène et l'interprétation critique de son oeuvre théâtrale', *Revue d'esthétique*, 'Samuel Beckett' special number, hors-série, 1986, pp. 277–89

Schröder, Ernst, 'One Hammer, Three Nails: Experiences of an Actor with Dramatist Samuel Beckett as Director', *Beckett in the Theatre*. Translated and reprinted from *Materialen zu Beckett's 'Endspiel'*

Solov, Sandra, 'Les notes de mise en scène de *Fin de partie*', *Revue d'esthétique*, 'Samuel Beckett' special number, hors-série, 1986, pp. 291–301

Select List of Books on Beckett's plays

Admussen, Richard L., *The Samuel Beckett Manuscripts*, G. K. Hall and Co., Boston, 1979

Brater, Enoch, (ed.), *Beckett at 80 / Beckett in Context*, Oxford University Press, New York and Oxford, 1986

Coe, Richard N., *Samuel Beckett*, Oliver and Boyd, Edinburgh and London, 1964; revised ed., Grove Press, New York, 1970

Cohn, Ruby, *Samuel Beckett: the Comic Gamut*, Rutgers University Press, New Brunswick, NJ, 1962

Cohn, Ruby, (ed.), *Casebook on Waiting for Godot*, Grove Press, New York, 1967

Cohn, Ruby, *Back to Beckett*, Princeton University Press, Princeton, NJ, 1973

Cohn, Ruby, (ed.), *Samuel Beckett, a Collection of Criticism*, McGraw Hill, New York, 1975

Doherty, Francis, *Samuel Beckett*, Hutchinson University Library, London, 1971

Duckworth, Colin, (ed.), *Samuel Beckett, En attendant Godot*, Harraps, London, 1966

Esslin, Martin, *The Theatre of the Absurd*, Doubleday, New York, 1961, and Penguin Books, Harmondsworth, 1968

Esslin, Martin, (ed.), *Samuel Beckett: a Collection of Critical Essays*, Prentice-Hall, Englewood Cliffs, NJ, 1965

Fletcher, Beryl, *et al.*, *A Student's Guide to the Plays of Samuel Beckett*, Faber and Faber, London, 1978

Fletcher, John, and John Spurling, *Beckett: a Study of his Plays*, Eyre Methuen, London, and Hill and Wang, New York, 1972

Gontarski, S. E., *Beckett's 'Happy Days': a Manuscript Study*, Ohio State University Libraries, Columbus, Ohio, 1977

Gontarski, S. E., *The Intent of Undoing in Samuel Beckett's Dramatic Texts*, Indiana University Press, Bloomington, 1985

Gontarski, S. E., *On Beckett, Essays and Criticism*, Grove Press, New York, 1986

Graver, Lawrence, and Raymond Federman, *Samuel Beckett: the Critical Heritage*, Routledge and Kegan Paul, London and Boston, 1979

Guicharnaud, Jacques, *Modern French Theatre from Giraudoux to Genet*, Yale University Press, New Haven, Conn., 1967

Hamilton, Kenneth and Alice, *Condemned to Life: the World of Samuel Beckett*, Eerdmans, Grand Rapids, Michigan, 1976

Hesla, David, *The Shape of Chaos. An Interpretation of the Art of Samuel Beckett*, University of Minnesota Press, Minneapolis, 1971

Janvier, Ludovic, *Pour Samuel Beckett*, Les Editions de Minuit, Paris, 1966

Kennedy, Andrew, *Six Dramatists in Search of a Language*, Cambridge University Press, London, 1975

Kenner, Hugh, *Samuel Beckett. A Critical Study.* New ed., University of California Press, Berkeley and Los Angeles, 1968

Kenner, Hugh, *A Reader's Guide to Samuel Beckett*, Thames and Hudson, London, 1973

Knowlson, James, and John Pilling, *Frescoes of the Skull, the Later Prose and Drama of Samuel Beckett*. John Calder, London, 1979, and Grove Press, New York, 1980

Mercier, Vivian, *Beckett/Beckett*, Oxford University Press, New York, 1978

Pilling, John, *Samuel Beckett*, Routledge and Kegan Paul, London and Boston, 1976

Reid, Alec, *All I Can Manage, More Than I Could*, Dolmen Press, Dublin, 1968, and Grove Press, New York, 1971 (revised edn)

Robinson, Michael, *The Long Sonata of the Dead, a Study of Samuel Beckett*, Rupert Hart-Davis, London, 1969, and Grove Press, New York, 1969

Rojtman, Betty, *Forme et signification dans le théâtre de Samuel Beckett*, Nizet, Paris, 1976

Schoell, Konrad, *Das Theater Samuel Becketts*, Wilhelm Fink, Munich, 1967

States, Bert O., *The Shape of Paradox*, University of California Press, Berkeley, 1978

Ventimiglia, Dario, *Il Teatro di Samuel Beckett*, Liviana, Padua, 1973

Webb, Eugene, *The Plays of Samuel Beckett*, Peter Owen, London, 1972

Worth, Katharine, (ed.), *Beckett the Shape-Changer*, Routledge and Kegan Paul, London and Boston, 1976

Zilliacus, Clas, *Beckett and Broadcasting*, Åbo Akademie, Åbo, 1976